The New
Thought Police

The New Thought Police

Inside the Left's Assault on Free Speech and Free Minds

TAMMY BRUCE

FORUM
An Imprint of Prima Publishing

The author can be contacted at heytammybruce@yahoo.com

Published by Prima Publishing, Roseville, California.
Member of the Crown Publishing Group, a division of Random House, Inc.

Random House, Inc. New York, Toronto, London, Sydney, Auckland

PRIMA PUBLISHING, FORUM, and colophons are trademarks of Random House, Inc., registered with the United States Patent and Trademark Office.

Library of Congress Cataloging-in-Publication Data on File

Bruce, Tammy
    The new thought police : inside the left's assault on free speech and free minds / Tammy Bruce
        p.   cm.
    Includes index.
    ISBN 0-7615-3404-0
    1. Liberalism—United States. 2. Freedom of speech—United States.
    3. Political correctness—United States. I Title.
JC574.2.U6 B78 2001
320.51'3'0973—dc21   2001033069

01 02 03 04 HH 10 9 8 7 6 5 4
Printed in the United States of America

First Edition

Visit us online at www.primaforum.com

For

June Bundy Csida
and
Stephen Densmore

My two best friends, for their patience,
kindness, and support.
June and Stephen showed me what unconditional
friendship and love are all about. Their faith in me
never faded—they remained when others did not.

In memory of Toni Carabillo (1926–1997).
A debt I can never repay, but will spend my life trying.

Contents

Acknowledgments

Many people played different roles in making this book possible. It is truly a project that is a culmination of individuals, with different points of view and certainly of different political persuasions, but all committed to making a difference and improving the quality of life.

Dr. Laura Schlessinger, because of her personal resolve and commitment to the issues, is to be thanked for her example, both professionally and personally. Her standing up for what is right inspired me (even though we disagree much of the time!), and her kindness changed me personally. Thank you, Laura.

June Bundy Csida and Stephen Densmore, to whom this book is dedicated, were invaluable to the work—their ideas, praise, and, most of all, their criticisms kept me on track and focused. I owe them a great deal. Steven Martin, who saw the potential of the project and had the courage to make the original decision to publish. Linda Bridges—an extraordinary woman and brilliant editor—helped me refine my argument, kept me from bludgeoning you with "theory," and made the whole process a joy. You'll enjoy this book and learn more from it because of Linda's work. We all owe her one. Libby Larson, my project editor, as smart and savvy as they come, kept me and the book on track and on time. David Richardson, my acquisitions editor, fought for me and the book, making it all possible. Thank you, David. And to my literary agent, Paul S. Levine, whose confidence and enthusiasm about the project made all the difference in the world. His skill as an agent then made a dream into a reality. Thanks, Paul.

At the University of Southern California, I am in debt to two people in particular—Dr. Ann Crigler, the Director of the Jesse M. Unruh Institute of Politics, provided invaluable advice and direction; and professor of political science, Dr. Richard Hrair Dekmejian, an extraordinary man whose insights into the world of political elites and political psychology were invaluable to the development of my understanding of my own political experiences. And philosophy professor, Christine Holmgren, who, during my time at Santa Monica College, helped me to appreciate the more profound aspects of life, science, and spirituality. Thank you, Christine.

I'd like to thank the people I interviewed, whose advice I solicited, and who made my work possible because of their friendship and support, now and in the past. Forgive me if I have inadvertently not included someone. Lisa Andrew, Christian Arbid, Keven Bellows, Lou Bishop, Denise Brown, Bunz Bruce, Sadie Bruce, Vanessa Coffey, Ward Connerly, David Dismore, Andrea Dworkin, Rabbi David Eliezrie, Brenda Feigen, Dr. Beverly Feinstein, Marc Germain, Bridget Gless, Charles Grodin, Josh Horn, David Horowitz, Dorothy Jonas, Elaine Lafferty, Carol Ann Leif, Sandi Lifson, Shelly Mandell, Susan Carpenter-McMillan, Carol Newman, Gary Oldman, Joanne Parrent, Nicole Perlman, Michelle Phillips, Bill Press, Marie José Ragab, Geraldo Rivera, Janice Rocco, Joel Sachs, Dr. Joyce Sachs, Bonnie Sloane, Jill Stewart, John Stoltenberg, Myra Terry, Douglas Urbanski, and Lynn Wasserman.

Thank you all. Here's to making a difference!

Introduction

I am an openly gay, pro-choice, gun-owning, pro–death penalty, liberal, voted-for-Reagan feminist. Certainly a contradiction in terms. And yet in 1990, I became the president of the Los Angeles chapter of the premier feminist organization in the United States—the National Organization for Women (NOW). Electing me may have been the last risky thing NOW ever did! I'm proud to say, however, that during my tenure (1990–1996) the chapter grew into one of the largest and most productive activist bases in the country.

While working at NOW, and in the years that followed, I watched the development of a disturbing phenomenon that today has gripped almost all of American society: the fear of offending by making a judgment and forming an opinion. Every day, the media, special-interest groups, and the power elite bombard the public with the message that speaking your mind will get you into trouble. Indeed, from the time "political correctness" was first identified in the early 1980s, it has evolved from changing the wording on MEN WORKING and LADIES' ROOM signs into a comprehensive and culturally debilitating pattern of thought and speech control.

Thirty years ago, black, feminist, and gay civil-rights organizations were groups that a classical liberal—someone who values free speech and personal liberty—could be proud to be associated with. Not any longer.

As the organized Left gained cultural power, it turned into a monster that found perpetual victimhood, combined with thought and speech control, the most convenient and efficient way to hold onto that power. Suddenly, it was the Left, the protector of liberty, that was setting rules about what could and could not be said, or even thought. And because we do not give up our freedom willingly, the strategy of the left-wing establishment has become one of intimidation, backed up by legal force.

> Thirty years ago, black, feminist, and gay civil-rights organizations were groups that a classical liberal could be proud to be associated with. Not any longer.

Of course, attempts to manipulate and control what people think have not always been the exclusive purview of the Left. History provides us with a cornucopia of right-wing efforts similarly designed to "improve" society—for example, by imposing gag rules on teachers and health care providers, forming "watchdog" groups to monitor the airwaves, and banning books. Films and novels that someone found shocking or offensive were targets for suppression. In the 1950s, Senator Joseph McCarthy used accusations of "Red!" and "Commie!" as a tool to destroy. Now, the slash-and-burn strategy against freedom of expression is the forte of the Left, its intrusiveness cloaked in concerns about racism, sexism, and homophobia. Don't be fooled by arguments about how different the Right is from the Left. The Left's "outsider" rhetoric is just that—rhetoric; the

Left now wields more cultural and political power than the Right and has been abusing it at our expense.

Most of my friends have as much invested in the success of progressive ideas as do I. When I spoke to them about the content of this book, there was a chorus imploring me not to ignore the transgressions of the Right. I'll say to you what I've said to those closest to me: If we're committed to the principle of expanding personal liberty and ensuring that people are free to live the lives they choose, we must apply the same expectations and critical view across the spectrum—to self-identified progressive social-interest groups as well as to those on the Right who may be convenient scapegoats.

As I told my friends, the attempt to punish someone because of speech or thought is abhorrent whoever applies it. It is even *more* destructive, however, when it is done by the political wing that presents itself as the protector of free speech and personal liberty. It's one thing when the wolf comes to the door; it's quite another when that wolf is disguised as your grandmother. And if you have any doubt about who controls our culture today, consider that Larry Flynt thrives while Dr. Laura Schlessinger struggles.

The Left now wields more cultural and political power than the Right and has been abusing it at our expense.

A View from the Trenches

My years as a feminist activist taught me many things, including the fact that the essential ingredients of social

change—freedom of expression and personal liberty—
have suffered extraordinary damage in the name of "social
equality," "feminism," and "civil rights." Agendas wrap-
ped in these respected labels have turned people away
from what the labels are supposed to stand for and, in
some cases, actually reversed social progress for everyone,
including women, people of color, gays, and others who
have been marginalized in our society.

When I became president of Los Angeles NOW, and
eventually a member of NOW's national board of directors, I knew that there were serious and sometimes dangerous challenges to women's well-being, but I also
believed that everyone, including Republicans of both
sexes and men who enjoyed and honored the women in
their lives, could appreciate the feminist struggle. Not
only did I learn that my belief was not universally shared,
but also I would be floored time and time again watching
the struggle for civil rights being exploited for ideological
power and control.

My conclusions on this issue do not come from work in
a library or think tank. They have arisen over a decade of
being in the trenches with those who formulated the strategy of silencing people whose opinions or attitudes they
considered wrong. I now believe that strategy is backward
and self-defeating. And yet I have not always felt this way.

Although I was aware of the importance of freedom of
expression, my primary concern during my own time as an
activist was improving the quality of women's lives. Success by any means necessary was encouraged within the
feminist establishment, and as the new president of L.A.
NOW, I fully embraced the idea that some kind of censorship was the solution if we were to live in a civil society.

I was young then, 27, and felt that I had found my home in NOW. As someone who does not bow down to pressure or a bureaucratic structure, however, I was bound to become a thorn in the sides of NOW presidents Molly Yard (1987–1992) and Patricia Ireland (1992–2001). Almost from the beginning of my seven-year tenure in the NOW leadership, I learned a great deal about the tactic of attempting to silence those with whom you disagree. I watched as it was applied to others, and I experienced it firsthand as my own colleagues in NOW applied it to me.

It all made me think of George Orwell's book *1984*, a nightmarish view of a totalitarian future written shortly after World War II.[1] The world of *1984* is grim: individualism is suppressed under the reign of terror of the Thought Police. Orwell's novel details the efforts of one man to maintain a personal sense of uniqueness and that man's ultimate failure. From my vantage point on the Left, the political wing in which I was firmly entrenched, I have seen the new version of Orwell's Thought Police emerge under the guise of improving the quality of life.

Opinions Don't Go Away—They Fester

In the chapters that follow, we'll travel down a road that will be both familiar and surprising. I'll explore how and why political correctness devolved into the oppressive speech code that it is today, and I'll share stories with you that explain why the Left has felt so compelled to resort to speech and mind control, thus contributing to a vicious circle of destroying individual liberty. Among the many by-products are a negative impact on Americans' personal community involvement and even on our physical and mental health. In fact, political scientists as well as psychologists are concluding that suppressed opinions, like suppressed emotions, do not go away—they fester. They grow in importance, dig in deeper, and become even more a part of the person who holds them.

At the heart of Thought Police activity is the argument that certain sorts of speech and the expression of certain opinions hurt certain people or groups and as a result should be curtailed. This argument is made both explicitly and implicitly. The explicit message comes in the form of politically correct speech codes. Implicitly, you get the message to keep quiet when you see the virtual assassination of anyone who steps over the line by challenging the Left's status quo by speaking out or making statements that question the Left's cultural orthodoxy.

> From my vantage point on the Left, I have seen the new version of Orwell's Thought Police emerge under the guise of improving the quality of life.

Although I would be comfortable defending the right of extremists to say whatever they please, I'm not talking mainly about extremists. The issue here is the moving of the line of forbidden speech into the territory of *your* thoughts and ideas about the culture. The restriction against yelling "Fire!" in a crowded theater when there is no fire has been extended to a restriction on your free expression of *your opinions* about welfare reform, affirmative action, gay marriage, religion, or any other matter that has societal repercussions. I'm speaking about attempts to stigmatize as outrageous the speech and thoughts of the average person, speech and thoughts whose real offense is straying from the Left's approved range of opinions.

Courtesy of the Thought Police, there is not one segment of American society today that feels entirely comfortable expressing its opinions on the issues, particularly if they're dissenting in nature. One exception might seem to be the few in public life who make a living spouting off, as I do. We pay a price, however. It's difficult to describe what it's like to be called a racist on national television. Sure, you get somewhat used to it, but no matter how thick-skinned you are, you never become immune to the name-calling, accusations, and lies about yourself, your personal life, and your political intentions. It always hurts. In private, I have seen some very famous, very strong men and women cry because of what has been said about them in the media. You may know what it's like to have someone attack you verbally. Imagine that happening in front of tens of millions of people. To survive, you need to develop an emotional vigilance and honesty about what you're doing and what you're feeling. You need to make sure you keep in touch with what really matters.

What Opinions Can Do—and What They Can't

Let's look at an opinion that nearly all of us would agree is in poor taste. In 1977, in a column about John Toland's biography *Hitler*, talking head and future presidential candidate Pat Buchanan described Hitler as "courageous" and a "genius."[2] Now, the twentieth century, the bloodiest century in history, will remain infamous in large part because of Hitler's genocidal acts against Jews, gypsies, and gays.

Any statement of admiration for any of Hitler's attributes could be considered harmful to those groups, particularly Jews. I submit this, however: It's not really the opinion that causes the harm, it's what happened in the past that is hurtful.

The Ku Klux Klan thinks black people are inferior to white people. That's an opinion, a belief. The Klan has also at various times performed actions such as lynching blacks and tarring and feathering whites whom they called "nigger lovers." Those *actions* were undeniably dangerous and hurtful, but is the *opinion*?

Opinions in and of themselves are *not* harmful, regardless of the subject or the conclusion. That's an opinion, but is it dangerous? One of the many good things about the voicing of opinions is that we all get more information with which to come to our own conclusions. I consider people's opinions a window into their soul, reflective of what they have experienced and what makes them tick, a little gift of insight. Most of us learned something extra about Pat Buchanan upon hearing his opinion of Hitler.

One of the more passionate arguments voiced about the harmfulness of expressing opinions is that if people hear a certain thing, it will encourage them to think the same way. I find that concern particularly silly. For it to be valid, you would have to believe that Americans are empty vessels who have been hypnotized into some weird state of suggestibility. You have almost certainly heard, via the news media, the rhetoric of the Klan. Did you become transformed into a white-robed cross burner? As a rhetorician, I have spent hour upon hour spouting off on television, on radio, at campuses, and at street demonstrations. Collectively, I have probably reached tens of millions of people over the course of a decade with some pretty persuasive arguments about the benefits of feminism. If the "conversion" argument held, we'd all be living in an authentic feminist utopia right now.

Shaking Loose

I've written this book because I have had experiences on the inside of a social movement that are unique and must be shared. Despite extraordinary efforts by my colleagues on the Left to stop me, I still think it's important to tell people when the emperor has no clothes.

One of the things about me that should make this book appealing is that I am not a lawyer. Also, I don't represent any group or organization that has an interest in you thinking a certain way or holding certain kinds of opinions. I love you for your mind. And I want that mind to contain whatever *you* want it to—not what someone else thinks should be there. Ah, the danger of that very statement! The left-wing establishment has instilled in us a belief that what lurks in our own minds is to be feared and reviled. We have entered an era in which we have finally, and unfortunately, acquiesced to distrusting, rejecting, and fearing our own intentions.

With this book, I aim to help dispel the myth that we are our own worst enemy, and with it the unwillingness to explore our own opinions and conclusions about significant and, yes, controversial social issues.

You know the impact the Thought Police have had on your life. The fear of offending has effectively paralyzed any willingness we may once have had to engage society. Your commitment to equality, fairness, and individual lib-

> **I aim to help dispel the myth that we are our own worst enemy.**

erty relies on shaking loose from those patterns of fear, isolation, and acquiescence to groups that may have made you feel that unless you heed their warnings and remain silent, the monster of your own racism, sexism, and homophobia will come out from under the bed and get you. It's time to disprove that scary story and begin reclaiming ourselves and our culture.

CHAPTER

1

Beyond 1984

The Rise of the New Thought Police

*"When I use a word," Humpty Dumpty said, in rather a
scornful tone, "it means just what I choose it to mean—
neither more nor less."*

*"The question is," said Alice, "whether you can make
words mean so many different things."*

*"The question is," said Humpty Dumpty,
"which is to be master—that's all."*

—*Lewis Carroll,* Through the Looking Glass

If she can't be controlled, she must be stopped."[1] With that
one chillingly honest sentence, Joan Garry, the executive director of the Gay and Lesbian Alliance Against Defamation
(GLAAD), revealed more than she intended about the
agenda of her organization.

The woman Joan Garry was trying to stop—talk-show host Dr. Laura Schlessinger—had committed the unpardonable sin of expressing an opinion about homosexuality that was not endorsed by GLAAD. Instead of trying to debate the issue, Garry, GLAAD, and their friends in the media unleashed a breathtakingly vitriolic assault on Dr. Laura. She became a symbol of hate, attacked in the press, denounced by the two contenders for the 2000 Democratic presidential nomination, and vilified on television shows ranging from *Frasier* to *The West Wing*.

As I'll explain in more detail in chapter 3, corporations were bullied into pulling their sponsorship of Schlessinger's new television show, and TV stations that had picked up the show were picketed. GLAAD's objective was not only to silence opinions it didn't like but also to destroy, both personally and professionally, the woman who expressed those opinions, thereby sending the clear message that having an unapproved point of view will not be tolerated. On one level, at least, GLAAD won: in March 2001, Dr. Laura's television show was canceled.

> Dr. Laura is only the most visible victim of this new assault on free speech and thought.

Dr. Laura is only the most visible victim of this new assault on free speech and thought. Powerful groups on the Left, groups like GLAAD, the National Organization for Women (NOW), and the National Association for the Advancement of Colored People (NAACP), are waging an all-out war on the free exchange of ideas. The effects of this new intolerance are felt in the media and in the arts, on college campuses, even in offices and factories. The message is clear: Don't speak up. Or else—you'll be fired . . . you'll be sued . . . you'll be called a name.

Name-calling may not sound like much ("Sticks and stones may break my bones . . ."), but it has been a powerful tool throughout history—"Barbarian!" "Heretic!" "Witch!" "Communist!" Today it is one of the hallmarks of the left wing, and it's a pretty clever strategy. Isolating individuals by promoting group identity and the politics of the "other" keeps people from recognizing just how devoid the Left is of actual ideas for progress and the future. Such delineations also undermine the willingness to challenge the status quo; people are afraid of being termed "other" and banished from the group.

Look around you. Labels such as "racist," "sexist," and "homophobe" are routinely used to demonize anyone who utters a word that doesn't support the Left's agenda. Television producers allow their scripts to be edited by groups that purport to represent aggrieved minorities. On college campuses, student newspapers that don't toe the party line are collected and destroyed, and speakers with un-PC views are shouted down.

A Method to the Madness

Despite the risk of being called one of the few names that haven't yet been hurled at me by the Thought Police, namely "red-baiter," it's time to be honest about the real and damaging agenda of today's pseudo-liberal establishment. For the Left, "social justice" has come to mean "protection" for certain groups (such as women, blacks, and gays) from attacks by the "enemy" (principally white heterosexual males, but also women, blacks, and gays who question the authority of the special-interest groups' leadership).

America in the twenty-first century is looking more and more like the world of *1984*. What began so many years ago as a noble cause—ending the scourge of bigotry—has devolved into something far different. It's not bigots that the new Thought Police are after. It's people like Dr. Laura, who dare to speak their mind and contradict the "progressive" point-of-view. More important, it's people like you—people who go to work every day knowing that a careless or opinionated word about a "protected" minority group can ruin their lives.

There is enormous irony in the fact that it is those on the Left—the supposed protectors of all things culturally important—who are imposing severe sanctions on anyone who espouses an idea or expresses an opinion that might be deemed "offensive" to some favored group. There is, however, a method to the madness of those who have chosen to protect us from ourselves.

You see, there is nothing in the theory of feminism or civil rights that requires people to stop thinking their own thoughts. On the contrary, civil rights are reliant on freedom of expression. The spiral down and away from individual liberty can be traced directly to the rejection of the rights of each person in favor of the rights of the many. This group-rights mentality is nothing new; it derives from the "progressive" concept that the individual must submit to what is best for everyone else. This concept, however, stems not from the ideal of civil rights but from the well of socialism, the foundational model of the Far Left. Once we accept group theory, it becomes not only easier to reject individual rights (such as freedom of expression) but also actually essential that we do so.

'You Could Be a Little Nicer'

My friend Richard was a senior vice president at a Fortune 500 company, but he didn't come across like some powerful executive. Although in his fifties, he still had a boyish enthusiasm. He was as good-natured and unassuming as he had been when he first joined the company long ago as an assistant in the accounting department.

Richard had climbed the corporate ladder not by playing politics but by working hard and taking on the projects no one else wanted. Richard also knew how to bring out the best in people. His division regularly outperformed every other division in the company. Several employees actually transferred from other divisions so that they could work for him.

Due to his diplomatic flair, Richard was asked one day to speak with a female junior vice president who had a major attitude problem. She had succeeded in alienating just about everyone with whom she came in contact. She was intelligent, however, and the company thought she had great potential. Richard's assignment was to help her improve her approach and save her career.

In what should have been a situation in which everybody won, Richard was blindsided by a charge that would destroy his career. In an attempt to be gentle, he suggested to the woman that she "could be a little nicer." Thirty minutes later, Richard was summoned by his superior to respond to a sexual-harassment complaint. The woman had charged that when Richard said, "You could be a little nicer," he meant "Give me sex."

There was no dispute regarding what Richard said—the issue became what he was *thinking* when he spoke. Despite his record of personal integrity, the company immediately suspended him and launched an investigation.[2] The incident ended in Richard's departure from the company, leaving him emotionally damaged and in the perilous position of a man in his fifties looking for work.

Out of Proportion

Not everyone caught in the Thought Police's net is as innocent as Richard. Yet, more often than not, the punishment seems way out of proportion to the crime. Take Seth Shaw, a counselor at D. McRae elementary school in Fort Worth, Texas. Shaw made the monumental mistake of saying, "Hello, good-looking!" to a woman standing in the school office. What Seth didn't know was that she was a district employee who was at the school to conduct workshops on sexual harassment. School administrators told Seth that he would be transferred to another school and "allowed" to resign at the end of the school year. That would be after he had served his 20-day unpaid suspension.[3]

> The rules of the new Thought Police have made comments, criticism, dissent, and even compliments nearly impossible.

The rules of the new Thought Police have made comments, criticism, dissent, and even compliments nearly impossible. How did the necessary efforts of yesterday's activists turn into today's repressive environment of speech codes and accusations of racism, sexism, and homophobia?

The PC Devolution

In the early 1980s, we all became aware of "political correctness." Many people were repulsed by the concept and properly considered it a mutant child of the Left. Others found it laughable and dismissed it as a passing fad. In reality, however, it was a harbinger of what was to come: a comprehensive and debilitating program of thought and speech control. Political correctness introduced the idea that only certain things can be said, or considered, or thought (as the necessary precursor to speech), and that some group out there has the authority to decide, for everyone, what is appropriate.

The phrase "politically correct" finally began to take some serious hits in the 1990s. It became the target of appropriate mockery with books such as *Politically Correct Bedtime Stories* and the television show *Politically Incorrect*. You could feel a little like a rebel by not being PC. Unfortunately, by that time the concept had slipped into our subconscious and a sort of conditioning had begun that has been gaining strength ever since. In liberal circles these days, there are rules about what is said or admitted to. You do not talk of finding religion, and you can only whisper to your closest friend that you voted for George W. Bush.

Americans' natural compassion, and the pride we take in not having a rigid class system (some form of which is evident in almost every other country in the world, including the social-democratic regimes of Western Europe), made us easy to manipulate into being afraid of hurting or offending some minority group. Is it any wonder that so many Americans hesitate to engage in some of our more important social debates—debates over such issues as school vouchers, affirmative action, drugs, prison reform, and crime—when almost anything you say might be labeled racist? Our habit of self-censorship has become so automatic that you probably are not even aware of the amount of effort you put into not saying "the wrong thing." Isn't it easier just not to think about certain things at all?

The result is a tremendous isolation. Not only are we isolated in communities along lines of race and ethnicity, but this problem also percolates at the individual level. Some people blame technology for the growing retreat of the individual. But I say the alienation has more to do with the feelings of hopelessness engendered by the tactics of the Thought Police.

Hateful Bunny?

A brief example will show how insane things have become. In 1999, Bugs Bunny, the Wascally Wabbit, came under investigation for violating Canada's Sex Role Portrayal Code. Really. In the past, Mr. Bunny's cleverness had always made up for his occasional arrogance, but not in the era of the new Thought Police.

In a 1954 episode entitled "Bewitched Bunny," Bugs uses magic powder to transform a witch into a sexy lady bunny. As they walk away together, Bugs turns to the viewer, winks, and says, "Aw, sure, I know! But aren't they all witches inside?"

Judith Hansel, a grown woman, saw the episode on a rebroadcast and complained that she was "horrified" by the remark. She demanded an apology, which propelled the Canadian government to investigate whether Bugs was guilty of hate speech. The six-member Canadian Broadcast Standards Council, after a yearlong inquiry, finally acquitted the Wabbit.[4]

My first reaction to this story was probably the same as yours—I laughed. Keep in mind, though, that the American Left considers Canada an island of sanity in an insane world. Government policies that enforce the most rigid, politically correct speech codes in the world serve as the model for our own Thought Police.

The Education of a Feminist

It was through my own feminist work that I first encountered the strategy of enforcing silence. I was dedicated to what I thought was the same agenda as the establishment feminists—achieving legitimate success on the issues. I quickly realized that not only did their strategy not address our core issues, but it also was the antithesis of authentic feminism, which embraces freedom of expression and the acceptance of divergent opinions. These tenets were part of our message, and as activists we relied on them to move our message. In asking myself why speech control had become the preferred strategy for groups that rally in the name of personal liberty, I came to realizations that shed light on the emergence of the Left as the new Thought Police.

Consider this. The "constituency" of feminist and civil-rights organizers are the victimized. One of the organizers' quandaries, then, is: How do you make it appear that you are working for your constituents and making progress, without making too much progress, which would give the impression that you are no longer needed?

Speech codes look like the perfect solution for both the short- and long-term needs of the special-interest group. In the short term, controlling what people are "allowed" to say (i.e., "political correctness") makes it appear as though a certain constituency, be it feminist, gay, or black, has tremendous power. The ensuing silence then also gives the impression that actual progress has been made on the issues. Of course, none has, but the illusion of progress helps the long-term goal of the Left: staying in business.

Meanwhile, the actual underlying problems remain, rearing their ugly heads often enough to restore the power base—a vicious circle of manipulation. The sense of perpetual victimhood precludes even the concept that the members of a victimized minority could actually rise above their assigned position in society and meet that society on their own terms. To do that would mean taking personal responsibility for the conditions of their own lives; instead, today's "progressives" have designed an argument that leads not to the encouragement of personal change and growth but to entitlement, group rights, and the eradication of the individual, all in the name of progress.

I find it ironic that a number of my friends who are active in progressive political circles consider my concern about self-censorship to be a sign of closet conservatism. (Even the suggestion that I would have to be in the closet to be a conservative makes my point!) When accused of this, I remind my friends that an environment of personal freedom, at all levels, is the only hope the members of any minority have of being able to lead their lives without fear. If you are not a straight, white male, your lifestyle depends on a culture that does not impose arbitrary limits on thought or speech. It's imperative that we be comfortable with a variety of ideas, which is exactly what the feminist, black civil-rights, and gay and lesbian communities ask of everyone else.

Yes, everyday protocol and even the law demand that we not deliberately provoke other people, but, as we've seen, what I'm talking about goes much, much further than tolerance and good manners. We are now paralyzed by the fear of offending someone. In fact, so consuming is this fear that the Left itself has been paralyzed politically. Unable to effectively address the enemies of progress and improve the quality of people's lives, the Left has instead ensnared the public in a net of fear and silence.

> **Unable to effectively address the enemies of progress and improve the quality of people's lives, the Left has instead ensnared the public in a net of fear and silence.**

In other words, it has applied the Vietnam War argument that in order to save the village, they have to destroy it. We are now being told that in order to ensure civil rights and liberty, we must be silent and conform.

The Home Fires of Totalitarianism

In commenting on his novel *1984* soon after its publication in 1949, George Orwell wrote that he had sought to emphasize that "totalitarianism, if not fought against, could triumph anywhere."[5] With the fall of the Soviet Union, Americans have been lulled into a sort of political laziness that keeps us from exercising any kind of vigilance over our cultural direction. In fact, the most vigilant should be those who do not think it could happen to them.

I know it may seem odd to hear concerns about totalitarianism in America at the beginning of the twenty-first century. After all, isn't totalitarianism something from long ago and far away, and not to be feared now that the Stalins and Hitlers of the world have been dispatched? Unfortunately, not only is the totalitarianism of socialism not a thing of the past, but it is thriving right here at home as well. Sure, the new Thought Police don't have gulags and death camps, but they do have powerful ways of punishing dissent.

Arthur M. Schlesinger Jr. put it this way: "A totalitarian regime crushes all autonomous institutions in its drive to seize the human soul." It was post-Holocaust thought, coupled with the atrocities committed by the Stalinist state in Russia, that led to the classification of the Nazi and Communist regimes as totalitarian. What made them different from repressive regimes of the past was that they sought not only submission to state power but also complete internal assent. Stalin wanted to create New Soviet Man, molded to the needs of the state. Our new totalitarians have proceeded slowly, but with a similar end: the elimination of individuality, uniqueness, and dissent.

Keep in mind, there are many regimes within a society—cultural, political, social, governmental. What I am talking about here is the cultural regime—including NOW, Jesse Jackson and his Rainbow Coalition, the Urban League, the NAACP, GLAAD, the American Civil Liberties Union (ACLU), Gloria Steinem, and nearly the entire film and television industries (with a few exceptions, such as the Fox News Channel, that challenge the status quo). It is this regime that is carrying the politics of victimhood into the twenty-first century.

When 'Liberal' Meant Liberal

It hasn't always been this way. Between the mid-seventeenth and the mid-nineteenth centuries, liberals fought oppression and abuses of power; they encouraged individuality and personal freedom, along with personal obligation, moral accountability, and respect for the choices of others. They made government the servant of the people, not their master.

The American culture is rooted in this classical liberalism. That is what has made the United States the greatest country on earth. Our commitment to individual liberty is why people from all over the world struggle to immigrate to America. Untold tens of thousands have died for that commitment in our comparatively short history.

> Today's Left doesn't remotely resemble the Lockean ideal of classical liberalism. Instead, it has morphed into a movement obsessed with identity politics, victimhood, and an us-versus-them mentality.

Today's Left doesn't remotely resemble the Lockean ideal of classical liberalism. Instead, it has morphed into a movement obsessed with identity politics, victimhood, and an us-versus-them mentality. How did this happen?

In the beginning, when civil-rights efforts were directed toward achieving equal opportunity, there was no effort to force anyone to think a certain way. But gradually, equality of opportunity gave way to equality of outcome, and personal rights to group rights. After all, personal rights bring personal wealth, personal success, and competition, and, yes, some people are left behind. The socialist ideal is a false equality premised on the lowest common denominator. The only way to achieve that Potemkin village is to drown the uniqueness of the individual in an ocean of group sameness.

In this kind of scheme, still failing in North Korea, China, and Cuba, the individual must submit to what is best for the group. Individual wealth is eliminated so that it can be "redistributed" throughout the group. There are no individual rights, which, by their very nature, conflict with group "rights."

When ideologues entrench themselves in the system, they exploit and ruin those on whose backs they rode to power. Just ask the minorities of the former Soviet Union how their socialist dream turned into a nightmare, one in which tens of millions who were different, or who spoke and wrote differently, or who were suspected of thinking differently from the ideologues, went to their death.

In this country, the radical Left's activists took center stage during the 1960s, working for laudable causes such as an end to discrimination, increased workplace protections, and reproductive choice. As these activists enjoyed success on their foundational issues, they went from the streets to the suites. Tom Hayden moved from street thug outside the 1968 Democratic Convention to California state senator. Jesse Jackson, a hanger-on of Martin Luther King Jr., heads one of the country's largest special-interest groups, and his son has become a congressman. No, these sixties radicals and most of their peers did not move to Woodstock to sip green tea and watch pot grow. They became media moguls, journalists, lawyers, and politicians. They became, in the words of Drs. Robert and Linda Lichter and Stanley Rothman, "America's new powerbrokers," entrenched in a culture they've always hated and continue to try to destroy.

The famous speech Martin Luther King Jr. delivered on the steps of the Lincoln Memorial on August 28, 1963, included the sentence: "I have a dream that my four children will one day live in a nation where they will not be judged by the color of their skin but by the content of their character." Today's left wing, through identity politics, affirmative-action policies, and hiring quotas, has shattered that dream.

Not What They Seemed

In order to attract as wide a base as possible, the sixties Leftists hid their socialist sympathies and, in some cases, actual Communist Party membership. Betty Friedan is a classic case. In the book that launched the modern feminist movement—*The Feminine Mystique*, published in 1963—she portrayed herself as a politically inactive housewife who simply had had enough of sexism.

Forty years later, Friedan told the real story. In *Life So Far*, published in 2000, she recounts, "I would come into New York on my days off from the hospital [and] would go to Communist Front meetings and rallies . . . I looked up the address of the Communist Party headquarters in New York and . . . went into their dark and dingy building on 13th Street and announced I wanted to become a member." This was in 1942, a quarter-century before she and a few others founded NOW. Friedan's revelation that, while she may have been a bored and frustrated housewife, she had also been a member of the Communist Party, shed some much-needed light on how left-wing politics has been masquerading as authentic feminism.

Martin Luther King Jr. awakened hopes for justice in millions of American blacks. King himself, however, was not motivated purely by a desire for justice and equality. He identified himself, euphemistically, as an "anticapitalist." He linked the African American civil-rights struggle to anticolonial struggles throughout the world and frequently situated the Montgomery movement in the context of the "great struggle of the Twentieth Century" between "exploited masses questing for freedom and the colonial powers seeking to maintain their domination."[6]

> Friedan's revelation that, while she may have been a bored and frustrated housewife, she had also been a member of the Communist Party, shed some much-needed light on how left-wing politics has been masquerading as authentic feminism.

King's advisors included Hunter Pitts (Jack) O'Dell, a longtime Communist Party organizer in New Orleans, and Stanley Levison, a financier for the Communist Party.[7] His most trusted advisor and strategist was Bayard Rustin, a black pacifist affiliated with the War Resisters League, who had begun his activism with the Young Communist League. Rustin served as chief organizer of the event that brought King his greatest fame, the 1963 March on Washington.

In fact, as with Friedan, it is revealing to look at King's premovement political attitude. Here is the opinion of capitalism he expressed in the form of notes to himself in 1951:

. . . I am conviced [sic] that capitalism has seen its best days in American [sic], and not only in America, but in the entire world. It is a well known fact that no social institut [sic] can survive when it has out-lived its usefullness [sic]. This, capitalism has done. It has failed to meet the needs of the masses.

We need only to look at the underlying developements [sic] of our society. There is a definite revolt by, what Marx calls, "the preletarian", [sic] against the bourgeoise [sic]. . . . What will eventually happen is this, labor will become so power [sic] (this was certainly evidenced in the recent election) that she will be able to place a president in the White House. This will inevitably bring about a nationalization of industry. That will be the end of capitalism . . . there is a definite move away from capitalism, whether we conceive of it as conscious or unconscious Capital-ism finds herself like a losing football team in the last quarter trying all types of tactics to survive.[8]

Planning Serendipity

Most Americans believe that the civil-rights struggle was full of serendipity, that it was a spontaneous grassroots move-ment of average people who wanted to make a difference and improve their lives. Rosa Parks, for example, has been portrayed as an Everywoman who happened to take the bus one day in 1955 and somehow crashed through the barriers of her ordinary, run-of-the-mill life by deciding not to relin-quish her seat to a white man.

In truth, the Montgomery, Alabama, chapter of the NAACP had been looking for months for a test case to challenge bus segregation. For this, they needed a bus rider to be arrested so their challenge could move through the courts— but it had to be the right sort of bus rider. In fact, Parks wasn't the first black to refuse to relinquish a seat to a white person. The first to personally challenge bus segregation earlier in 1955 had been 15-year-old Claudette Colvin, followed by another teenager named Mary Louise Smith. The NAACP leaders, however, didn't think that either of the girls would cut the right kind of figure in court.

Parks was a veteran activist and an officer of the Montgomery NAACP. In actuality, she wielded great power in the chapter; she was the one who had noticed Martin Luther King Jr. and asked him to join the executive committee. She was at the meeting where the Montgomery NAACP leaders considered the possibility of using Colvin or Smith as the test case.

In December of 1955, six weeks after the NAACP's rejection of the teenagers, Parks was arrested for refusing to give up her seat. Parks told *Time* magazine, "I did not get on the bus to get arrested. I got on the bus to go home."[9] That may have been true for Colvin and Smith but certainly not for Parks. Rosa Parks was a "bus rider" the way Betty Friedan was a "housewife."

Deceit in the Pursuit of Power

These early relationships and associations are important because they help explain the direction and attitude of the current establishment Left. While I wouldn't say that these people are the villains of the current Left vacuum, their politics did push us away from true liberalism, which prizes individual liberty, equality, and accountability, and into the maze of Thought Police totalitarianism we face today.

The preference for deceit in the pursuit of power is one of my biggest disappointments with the Left. Ranging from the extraordinary and reprehensible behavior of both Bill and Hillary Clinton as leaders of the Democratic Party to the music industry's lionizing of the vile rapper Eminem, the Left has given us the legacy of a disintegrating culture. Certainly, lip service has been paid to the idea of values—the Clintons attending church every Sunday, Jesse Jackson always putting the word "Reverend" before his name, and so forth. In fact, these things are nothing more than cynical window dressing when your role-modeling tells society you can lie about your life, cheat on your wife, and compromise principles for the sake of power.

I Am a Jelly Doughnut!

Let's look at some cases that illustrate what has happened to the classical liberal beliefs of openness, tolerance, and freedom of speech. In a normal world, the following example would belong alongside John F. Kennedy's classic declaration, "Ich bin ein Berliner!" President Kennedy obviously wanted to say, "I am a Berliner," but instead, because of a mistaken word, he proclaimed his jelly doughnutness.

His German audience may have had a moment of bewilderment, but they quickly accepted and applauded what Kennedy meant to say. In our speech-code universe, however, a slip of the tongue can be devastating. In what the *Los Angeles Times* termed a potential career-ender,[10] the lieutenant governor of California, Cruz Bustamante—a Democrat and the first Latino elected to statewide office in California in 128 years—was addressing the Coalition of Black Trade Unionists (CBTU) at their Black History Month dinner. Then it happened. While reciting the name of an organization with the word "Negro" in it, he slipped and said "nigger."

The 48-year-old Bustamante, known as a champion of civil rights, is not a man who should easily be suspected of racism, but more than 40 of the 400 people in attendance at the dinner got up and left. After finishing his speech, Bustamante apologized. That was on February 9, 2001, and he's been apologizing ever since, making the rounds of California's black leadership in a desperate attempt to make reparations for his mistake. In what can only be characterized as begging, Bustamante has repeatedly said that he was "humiliated" by his error; he has been described as "shell-shocked" about the episode.[11] The poor man was right to be worried, but he should also contemplate the absurdity of his situation.

According to Bustamante, many of California's black leaders, including San Francisco Mayor Willie Brown, Los Angeles County Supervisor Yvonne Brathwaite Burke, and U.S. Representative Maxine Waters, have expressed their support for him. "Others," he added, "are trying to find some theory—that it's some latent thing. I've agonized over it. I've prayed over it. Is there really something back there?"[12]

One of the most pathetic and confused statements about Bustamante's obvious slip and swift apology came from Lawana Preston, staff director of one of the CBTU's member unions: "I think you accept the apology, but . . . I think there has to be a dialogue about why it happened and where do we go from here."[13] Right: a dialogue about educating women like herself to get over it and move on.

Two weeks after the incident, Bustamante canceled an appearance at a banquet of Latino business leaders in Santa Barbara, where he was to be the keynote speaker, citing "exhaustion." Now his position as a leading contender for California's governorship in 2006 seems in doubt. Steve Chawkins of the *Los Angeles Times* had this to say about the larger impact: "But [the controversy] sends a chill through all who are scared that they'll blurt out something lousy, stupid, and insensitive while speaking to a Scout troop on 'How to Tie Amazing Knots' . . . in other words it sends a chill through everyone who is scared of public speaking, which is to say, nearly everyone."[14]

When the N Word Isn't Really the N Word

Cut to the angry mother of a black high school senior in Clovis, California, who found out how the speech code and victimhood can backfire. Rosemari Martin still can't understand why her son was suspended for two days for addressing a friend as "nigger." Nathan Martin's suspension came after a white student, who had apparently been properly educated about what words one may and may not use, overheard the greeting and told school officials. Nathan, 17, defended his use of the term because, gosh, he and his black friends use it "in a fun, friendly, affectionate way."[15]

Eventually, Jim Fugman, deputy superintendent for the Clovis Unified School District, agreed, which confirms that it's not really the use of a term, it's what you're thinking when you use it. "We-can-say-it-because-we're-black" reveals an undeniable double standard, one for protected groups and another for everybody else. Could a white person say the word "nigger" in a fun, friendly, and affectionate way? Oh

Lord, no! Fugman told the press, "If a white student said it to another white student, it would be a racial slur."[16]

This kind of confused, hypocritical doublespeak is inevitable because our speech-code culture has effectively determined that words mean different things for different people—depending on your color, depending on what you're thinking, depending on your past work, depending on whether you're Republican or Democrat, depending . . . depending . . . depending. The Thought Police Rule Book is one that the IRS would be proud of: no one can figure it out, and it gets more complicated every day.

No Water Buffalo Allowed

In fact, the rules are so vague that even words without a tainted history can ensnare their unsuspecting users. Eden Jacobowitz, who was born in Israel, lived in a mostly Jewish suburb in New York. He wanted to attend the University of Pennsylvania specifically because it offered him a diversity he couldn't get at home. Jacobowitz found out the hard way how modern "diversity" works. At three o'clock one morning during his freshman year, he was awakened by a group of black sorority sisters partying outside his window. He called out, "Shut up, you water buffalo. If you're looking for a party, there's a zoo a mile from here."[17]

In the Kafkaesque episode that followed, Jacobowitz was charged with racial harassment and hauled before a collegiate board to answer the charge. Penn had a policy prohibiting "racial epithets" meant to "inflict direct injury," and the authorities decided "water buffalo" fit that definition. Jacobowitz insisted that he had simply translated the Hebrew word *bahema*, which literally means "water buf-

falo," but is slang for "rude person" and has no racial over-
tones. Charges were eventually dropped, but the young
man's first year in college was a disaster, and the press bom-
barded his family in the United States and Israel. In the end,
Jacobowitz commented on the seriousness of the episode: "I
hope people really understand that this was a miscarriage of
justice. It could have ruined my future."[18] He ultimately decided to transfer out of Penn.

The Sounds of Silence

The damage to a Richard or an Eden is obvious. But what of
the growing number of people like my friend Paul? Paul
complains of his general discomfort in office meetings. He is
afraid he may say the wrong thing, and he isn't even sure
what that wrong thing is. His solution is to say as little as possible.

This is not a man who doesn't trust himself. He is religious, thoughtful, and intelligent. He's a regular guy, with a wife and two kids, who cares
about doing the right thing. He's not someone who's going to ask for sex in exchange
for a pay raise. But he knows how much he has to lose.

> The end result is that classical liberals and other thoughtful people who try to act consciously and respectfully are retreating from public participation.

I trust that you, especially if you're a white male, can
personally relate to Paul's choice. I submit that this enforced
silence, although more difficult to document than actions
like the ones against Richard and Eden, is one of the most
insidious effects of the new Thought Police.

The ironic thing is that those who are inclined to sexually harass, and those who really are bigoted, are the last people to care about how they're perceived in an office or academic situation. They act regardless of what the environment or the law requires of them. Having legal recourse against those who discriminate in hiring or promotion, or those who use their power to exact sexual favors, is essential, but speech codes affect the innocent at least as much as the guilty.

The end result is that classical liberals and other thoughtful people who try to act consciously and respectfully are retreating from public participation. Resentment generated by the political correctness code spills over onto genuine efforts for civil rights and tolerance.

'You're Not One of Those Anti-Abortion Nuts, Are You?'

Although we may read about someone like Eden Jacobowitz or Cruz Bustamante, the private experiences average people have with the Thought Police don't make the newspapers. The woman who heads up one of my favorite charities can testify to the prudence of saying nothing.

I've known Betty (a pseudonym) for many years. She runs a nonprofit animal rescue shelter that helps hundreds of dogs and cats find new homes every year. One afternoon, when I was delivering a donation of dog and cat food for the critters, Betty took me aside and asked if I had a problem with her pro-life position. Betty, you see, is a practicing Roman Catholic and lives her life according to her beliefs.

I thought it an odd question but told her that, for me, encouraging women to find their own voices means whatever those voices might be, including a pro-life voice. No, I told her, I had never had a "problem" with her pro-life stance and had always admired her convictions on the issues and the way she applied her principles. She explained that she had broached the question because not all her donors felt the same way.

Earlier that week, a woman who had never been to the shelter but was a regular writer of checks finally visited the facility. She had brought some toys and food and was starting to write a check as well, when Betty, in her naiveté, said the simplest thing. The donor, referring to the number of abandoned kittens and puppies, said it was too bad dogs and cats didn't have access to abortion. Betty replied that the real tragedy was that women did. As soon as the words left her mouth, Betty realized that she had made a major mistake. The donor asked, "You're not one of those anti-abortion nuts, are you?" Betty answered—no doubt in a defensive, shell-shocked kind of way, like Cruz Bustamante—"Well, no, I don't sit in front of abortion clinics or anything, but I do work to help women and girls think of adoption as an alternative to abortion. . . ."

Nothing else was said as the donor closed her checkbook and walked out (she left the food and toys, at least). Betty subsequently received calls from two other donors who had heard from the offended woman. They, too, felt the need to punish Betty for her beliefs by withdrawing their support. Of course, in the end, it's the animals that were punished, but that didn't occur to those bullies.

Betty confided to me that she had always felt guilty about not talking about her church work. She wanted to feel proud, but a part of her just didn't feel safe. Unfortunately, her first foray into speaking her mind confirmed her worst

fears. Now, when I arrive at the shelter, she doesn't feel comfortable talking about the issues of the day until others have
left. I'm lucky—I can still enjoy conversation with her. The
tragedy is that a vibrant woman with an opinion, the kind of
woman feminism has tried to encourage, has been silenced,
probably by feminists.

Rocker's Reeducation

When I say average people should be able to speak their
mind, I mean John Rocker, too. In a *Sports Illustrated* story
titled "Rocker Shoots from the Lip," Rocker, a relief pitcher
for the Atlanta Braves, made some choice comments about
New York City, and especially about the riders of the ele-
vated train to Shea Stadium.[19] Mr. Rocker spared no one,
ranging from single mothers to his fellow baseball players,
and he didn't sound like someone you or I would invite to
dinner. His punishment for the misdeed of speaking his mind,
however, included physical attacks, death threats, a call by
baseball fans to assault him during his appearances in New
York, suspension from his team, fines, and a demotion to the
minor leagues. An awful lot for a guy with an opinion (regardless of how boorish). But, oh, what a message to you!

Enter the mayor of New York, Rudolph Giuliani. It
might be thought that His Honor, as a Republican, would
have been less inclined to fall into the Thought Police pattern. In fact, the mayor's comment exemplifies how deep-
seated the acceptance of thought control has become:
"Something should be done about this so that Mr. Rocker is
held accountable for his vicious and bigoted remarks, and
maybe he should go into some kind of training where he be-

comes more educated, or, uh, and reflects a little better on the sport that he's actually engaged in."[20]

Think about the implications of the mayor's remarks. In suggesting that Rocker undergo "some kind of training," the mayor seems to be implying that a little brainwashing might just do the ballplayer some good. The presumption is that Mr. Rocker's *process of thinking* needs to be changed. And the instrument that will get the job done is the favorite tool of the Thought Police: sensitivity training, which is a euphemism for directly applied thought control—a kind of modern-day nonsurgical lobotomy.

In case you're not familiar with sensitivity training—also sometimes called encounter groups, human relations training, or group dynamics training—the sessions can last anywhere from two hours to several days. A leader "guides" the preferably small group into areas of discussion during which, inevitably, something is said or an attitude exhibited that requires "examination" of internal racism, sexism, or whatever. From my own experiences and from interviews I've engaged in with business and academic leaders, the drumbeat in a training session is that the participants are racist or sexist, and this fact needs to be "exposed" to them in the group. Participants are alternately cajoled, bullied, and pressured to accept that thinking certain ways or saying certain things is "insensitive," "bigoted," or otherwise "wrong." I'll discuss in chapter 2 the similarity of this approach to cult mind-control efforts, but it is worth noting here that the only purpose sensitivity training serves is to indoctrinate people into a way of thinking that they currently do not hold. It is one of the most obvious devices of the Left, and one of the most dangerous.

'Some Kid with Purple Hair'

Now let's take a closer look at the comments that got Mr. Rocker into so much trouble. The *Sports Illustrated* interviewer asked him whether he would ever play for a New York baseball team, and he replied: "I would retire first. It's the most hectic, nerve-racking city. Imagine having to take the [Number] 7 train to the ballpark, looking like you're [riding through] Beirut, next to some kid with purple hair next to some queer with AIDS right next to some dude who just got out of jail for the fourth time right next to some 20-year-old mom with four kids. It's depressing."[21]

Let's start with the "queer with AIDS" comment. Considering that the gay community itself has embraced the word "queer," it's difficult to see how that word is offensive or homophobic. Is the real problem perhaps Mr. Rocker's *feeling* that he does not want to sit next to a gay guy with AIDS? If so, then we've slipped into judging the thoughts and feelings associated with words. "[S]ome 20-year-old mom with four kids." Since when did uttering those words become offensive? Again, it seems that Rocker's critics were reacting to what they imagined he was thinking, not to what he said. "[S]ome kid with purple hair." I know—you can't believe I had the guts to repeat that one!

The Chicken Little Syndrome

When I bring up the idea of people speaking their minds, many of my liberal friends panic and talk as if encouraging people to say what they think will destroy civilization. My friends, and perhaps you, too, feel that if individuals arrived at their own opinions and were honest about them, all hell would break loose.

When faced with this cynical outlook, I ask my Chicken Little friends to think about what they are saying. Why are they so convinced that the only way civilization will remain intact is if we all lie to each other about our true feelings concerning the state of our lives, the culture, and the world? The sky-will-fall belief is another by-product of the never-ending conditioning by special-interest groups. Do we really believe that deep down inside every one of us is a little Hitler that needs to be controlled? That the desire to enslave blacks, kill Jews, and throw women back into the Dark Ages will once again consume society, and all will be lost forever?

While I acknowledge that there are those who would prefer that we return to the nineteenth century (Pat Buchanan comes to mind), they are few and far between. And who really believes that anyone with an already formed opinion is going to change that opinion simply because he or she is not allowed to speak about it? I believe it is even more dangerous not to know what your neighbor is thinking.

It's fair to say that most people who hold prejudiced feelings about one segment of society or another have little, if any, social contact with the group they have judged. If we draw our conclusions from Jerry Springer or even the nightly news, then everyone is sleeping with his sister-in-law or murdering his neighbor. The more we allow the media to shape our views and create our world, the more we become a co-cooned, isolated society, and the more we will condemn each other with opinions based on stereotypes and fear. The more we interact, however, the more we will promote and enjoy the classic American values of the exchange of ideas, mutual respect, and participation in shaping our society.

Pursued by a Grand Dragon

There has always been the danger of abusing a principle, and the danger is particularly great in a society that is fumbling around for its moral compass. Someday I suspect we're going to hear a batterer claim that he has a right to beat his wife because, after all, he's merely expressing his hate for her.

Embracing the principle of freedom of expression comes with the responsibility for knowing where the lines are truly drawn. This is not brain surgery, and yet now that free speech has become a casualty of political correctness, it's not surprising that the standards have become blurred. A perfect example is the recent harassment of Bonnie Jouhari, a fair-housing activist in Philadelphia, and her daughter Danielle. Almost every day, Roy Frankhouser, a former Grand Dragon of the Ku Klux Klan, sat menacingly on a bench outside Jouhari's office window. Sometimes he would photograph her as she worked and then display her picture on his cable-television show. He made a threatening video labeling her a "race traitor," referring to the fact that she is white, and her daughter's father is black. Frankhouser's threats and intimidation continued for more than 15 months, during which the family moved four times, attempting to escape the harassment.[22]

> Now that free speech has become a casualty of political correctness, it's not surprising that the standards have become blurred.

Jouhari finally filed a claim with the U.S. Department of Housing and Urban Development, accusing the self-described "chaplain" of the Ku Klux Klan of violating a federal law that prohibits the intimidation of fair-housing advocates. In the settlement of the claim, Frankhouser agreed to stay 100 feet away from Jouhari and her daughter and to pay Jouhari five percent of his salary for 10 years.

But HUD forced Frankhouser to do much more than this. He also had to apologize on his cable show, to display a fair-housing poster in front of his house, and to attend HUD-approved "sensitivity" sessions. This man, who has a history of criminal convictions in connection with a school-bus bombing and synagogue vandalism, agreed to the terms, but he vowed to stand by his views nevertheless. "If they think they're going to brainwash me, they're in for a big surprise," he declared.[23]

For her part, Jouhari complained that Justice Department officials "have failed us miserably," both by declining to bring criminal charges against Frankhouser and by not offering her and her daughter any assistance in establishing new identities and a safe home.

The officials in this case rightly understood that freedom of expression does not translate into a license to stalk someone (any more than it excuses rape, domestic violence, or sexual harassment). They then illustrated, however, how far our confusion about expression has gone by attempting to compel Frankhouser not only to stop his harmful behavior, but also to make statements contrary to his beliefs and even to undergo schooling in the wrongness of his beliefs.

Do you see what has happened here? First, we are indoctrinated into silence. And then, once we have become accustomed to having others decide for us what we are not to say and not to think, it's only natural that the authorities start demanding that we say and think certain prescribed things.

This is a warning that is screaming to be noticed—because the next person who is forced to say something contrary to what he or she believes can easily be you.

The Goodness of Not Getting It

You may think that it couldn't hurt for people who are prejudiced to be "reeducated." After all, it's for their own good, and it will be better for everyone else. But before you accept the effort to "improve" or "sensitize" people as a good idea, consider how you would react if the same tactic were used on you. I'll use myself as an example. As a gay feminist, I embody and act on beliefs that certain sectors of society think are dangerous and offensive. I would not want to be forced into "training" designed to change how I think or feel. To have the mayor of the Imperial Capital of the World (and I love New York) casually suggest "training" for John Rocker shows how deeply we have accepted attempts at brainwashing.

I've heard many people express self-doubt regarding their own "commitment to diversity" or even their own compassion when they find themselves confronted by the uproar someone else's comments have caused. Some smart, educated, and experienced people struggled with such doubts even when faced with something as overblown as the reaction to John Rocker. Instead of feeling that the outrage toward Rocker was grossly exaggerated, they feared that they themselves didn't "get it." They believed that their own reaction must have been wrong in some way if they weren't outraged at what it is politically correct to be outraged at.

In fact, not "getting it" is the first sign that you may actually have a different opinion on a controversial social issue. That is the time to stop and recognize that your individual critical mind has something to say. That critical mind deserves respect and attention and will lead you toward your understanding of the truth.

Once that step is taken—the walk away from an orthodoxy demanded by the collective—your awareness of how your opinions differ from the group's should lead you to even more critical thinking, more debate about the issues, more discussion about controversial subjects, and, above all, more trust in yourself.

2

Groupthink

The Politics of "Hate"

"The Party is not interested in the overt act: the thought is all we care about."

—*George Orwell*, 1984

In 1998, two grisly murders made the news in Laramie, Wyoming. One of them instantaneously became a national story; the other never made it past the local news. The reason for the unequal attention given to the two cases lies in the way the Left and its foot soldiers in the press value people on the basis of the groups to which they belong.

A Tale of Two Murders

On October 6, 1998, two high school dropouts, Aaron McKinney, 22 years old, and Russell Henderson, 21, encountered Matthew Shepard, also 21 and a student at the University of Wyoming, at the Fireside Bar in Laramie. Accounts differ as to what was said, but eventually the three young men left the bar together, got into a pickup truck, and drove away. Henderson later told the court that he was driving and that McKinney began beating Shepard almost immediately.

When they reached an out-of-the-way spot, Henderson and McKinney hauled Shepard out of the truck, tied his hands behind him, and hooked him to a fence post so that his feet dangled four inches off the ground. They took his money and then began the final beating. Shepard endured 18 blows with a Smith & Wesson .357 magnum, and yet he was still alive when Deputy Reggie Fluty of the Albany County Sheriff's Department found him 18 hours later.[1] It was another six days before Shepard died.

A few weeks later, 38-year-old Kevin Robinson went on trial for murdering 15-year-old Daphne Sulk. Less than a year before the Shepard murder, Daphne's butchered, frozen body was found in the Laramie foothills. As the story came out at the trial, Robinson had followed Daphne to a teen support group one afternoon and struck up a conversation. They began to date clandestinely, and Robinson got Daphne pregnant. When she refused to have an abortion, he stabbed her 17 times and dumped her body in the snow-covered hills, leaving her to bleed to death.[2]

Almost every media outlet in the country picked up Matthew Shepard's murder. The networks played it up on their evening newscasts, and *Time* magazine made it a cover story. There was an off-Broadway play about it, and a made-for-TV movie is in the works. Almost overnight, the Shepard murder became a symbol of what the Left believes is the undercurrent of hate that permeates this country. You see, Shepard was homosexual, and his murderers were heterosexual. The case fit perfectly into the Left's worldview, in which there are groups of victims who require special protection from our culture's victimizers. The murder of Matthew Shepard was a made-to-order example of why America needed "hate crimes" legislation.

For Daphne Sulk, on the other hand, there were no magazine cover stories, no TV movies, no candlelight marches. In the first place, Daphne was killed because she refused to have an abortion—not exactly the kind of person the Left wants to immortalize. Second, and far more important, her murder did not rise to the level of a hate crime. Women are a victim group, but not for hate crimes. The Hate Crimes Statistics Act of 1990 defines a hate crime as one motivated by bias against a particular race, religion, ethnicity/national origin, disability, or sexual orientation.[3] Because Daphne did not belong to any of the protected categories, her murderer did not have the requisite type of hatred when he stabbed her 17 times and then dragged her body over rocks and gravel, logs and branches, and down a hill path before dumping it in a clump of trees.[4]

Of course, Daphne Sulk and Matthew Shepard are equally dead. They both died in brutal ways, their killers striking out with an abandon that was, in every normal sense of the word, hateful. Kevin Robinson, Daphne's killer, was convicted of *voluntary manslaughter* and was sentenced to the Wyoming State Penitentiary for 22 to 29 years. Parole hearings will allow him the constant hope of being released far earlier. Russell Henderson and Aaron McKinney, however, will be spending the rest of their lives in prison without possibility of parole. In fact, the only reason they avoided the death penalty was the intercession of Shepard's mother.

My beef is not that Matthew Shepard's murderers deserved any less—it's that Daphne Sulk's killer deserved at least as much. The dirty little secret is that hate-crime legislation has nothing to do with stamping out hate or with reducing the number of murders and rapes in this country. This legislation does not criminalize for the first time actions that were previously legal. Murder, vandalism, rape, assault—all have been crimes for a long time, and all are, or should be, punished accordingly. No, hate-crime legislation was enacted to give special protections to select constituencies, and, as practiced, it makes certain people more valuable than others in the eyes of the law—exactly the kind of thinking that civil-rights, feminist, and gay-rights groups wanted to combat.

> **The dirty little secret is that hate-crime legislation has nothing to do with stamping out hate or with reducing the number of murders and rapes in this country.**

Be Careful Whom You Hate

If we're going to embrace the concept of "hate crimes," we have to ask ourselves why hate for a group is worse than hate for a person. Any line we draw to make a distinction between personal hate and group hate is going to be arbitrary and rife with identity politics. Consider this scenario: One woman is killed during a carjacking. Another woman, a gay woman, is killed by a grocery-store clerk because he hates gay people. The action was the same in both cases, and the two women are equally dead. The carjacker, however, is not guilty of a hate crime, whereas the grocery clerk is.

But why? Why is the random killing of an individual less serious than the killing of a member of a group?

As with everything else we're discussing, my own position on this issue has developed over time. I'm not proud of this, but I, too, passively accepted the idea of "hate crimes." Frankly, I never really delved into it, in part because it benefited me. It wasn't until the last few years that I even felt comfortable looking at issues such as this one with a critical eye.

As a gay woman, it's kind of flattering to have the government say that if someone who has the wrong kind of hate kills me, it's a special killing. But flattery should go only so far. My selfish side likes to be viewed as "special" by the FBI, but my honest side knows that this is both unfair and treacherous. As a gay woman, I refuse to be part of a system that tells me that I count more than any other woman who gets raped or murdered.

Here is the most compelling argument that the proponents of hate-crime prosecutions have to offer. They maintain that the murder of Matthew Shepard (or the murder of James Byrd Jr., the black man dragged behind a pickup truck in Texas, or the beating of three Jewish students in Brooklyn by a group of kids from the largely Italian neighborhood of Bensonhurst) actually harms the entire gay (or black, or Jewish) community. The FBI signs onto this explanation in the foreword to its *Hate Crimes Statistics Report:* "The diversity of its people makes the United States a unique nation. However, when crimes are committed because of our differences, the effects can reverberate beyond a single person or group into an entire community, city, or society as a whole."[5] Because hate crimes have this larger impact, proponents say, punishment must be more severe.

But really, give me a break.

All crimes have an impact on the communities in which they are committed, and with television, that impact now stretches even further. I guarantee that when Daphne Sulk was murdered, all those who learned of the event—no matter how far away, and no matter their color, economic background, sexual orientation, sex, or age—suddenly became worried about the safety of the teenaged girls in their family or neighborhood.

> If we accept the arguments by supporters of hate-crime legislation, we must accept that somehow gays and Jews and blacks are unusually neurotic, to the point that crime affects them much more than it does everyone else.

If there is a burglary at your neighbor's house, you empathize and simultaneously worry that you might be next. Your neighbor may not be the same sex or color or ethnicity as you, but you worry anyway, for a simple reason: crime does not discriminate.

Reports of rape frighten not only all women, but men, too. Reports of murder alarm everyone, everywhere. Home-security systems, German shepherds, the .38 on the night table, the double- and triple-locked doors defending houses and apartments—these are employed everywhere.

If we accept the arguments by supporters of hate-crime legislation, we must accept that somehow gays and Jews and blacks are unusually neurotic, to the point that crime affects them much more than it does everyone else. Not only is that absurd, but it is also an insult to individuals within those groups. It is especially an insult to those gays and Jews and blacks who have been working to not be thought of as separate and different. People have died fighting for the principles of desegregation and equal opportunity. If we buy into the notion of "hate crimes," we accept that stereotype.

The Truth About 'Hate Crimes'

With overwhelming national media coverage and federal legislation aimed at stomping out hate crimes, our society has been left with the impression that crimes such as the murder of Matthew Shepard are plaguing this nation. Have you actually stopped to think about it though? For the sake of argument let's accept the concept of hate crimes for a minute and ask, How many people *are* killed each year because they're gay? Or because they're black, or Jewish? I wondered, and what I found will probably surprise you as much as it did me.

The FBI's *Hate Crimes Statistics Report for 1999* (the most recent one available) shows that hate crimes are far from being an epidemic—in fact, they're extraordinarily rare. In 1999, there were *17* murders among the reported "hate-motivated incidents," as the FBI terms them. Compare that to the total number of murders in the United

States in 1999: *12,658*.[6] Of the 17 "hate crime" murders, 3 were attributed to "sexual orientation bias," 9 to "racial bias," 3 to "ethnicity/national origin bias," and the remaining 2 to "religious bias."[7] Keep in mind, this is not to belittle the awfulness of the 17 murders but is simply a reality check about the rarity of what has been falsely presented as a plague.

The reality is that hate-crimes legislation makes about as much sense as legislation banning the Ebola virus. Yes, it would be horrible if it were here, but it's not. My point is that the obsession with hate crimes furthers the victimization of certain groups anointed by the Left—especially blacks and gays—which, of course, furthers the need for special protections for these groups. It also bludgeons our society with the lie that we're so racist and homophobic that we're killing the objects of our disdain, which reinforces general paranoia and distrust.

I found especially interesting the FBI's *Training Guide for Hate Crime Data Collection* for local law-enforcement officials. This booklet notes, "There are, of course, many kinds of bias. Some of the more common kinds are those against race, religion, disability, sexual orientation, or ethnicity/national origin. But, there are also biases against rich people, poor people, men who wear long hair and/or beards, people who dress oddly, smokers, drinkers, people with diseases such as AIDS, motorcycle gangs, rock musicians, etc. *The types of bias to be reported . . . are limited to those mandated by the enabling Act* [emphasis mine] and its subsequent amendments, i.e., bias based on 'race, religion, disability, sexual orientation.'"[8]

The Act referred to is the Hate Crimes Statistics Act of 1990, which requires local law-enforcement officials to report to the FBI the hate crimes committed in their area, but only, as the FBI notes, the "limited" variety mentioned in the Act. As we've seen from our small sample of murders in Laramie, young girls—along with smokers, drinkers, and people who dress oddly—are also not included in the list made special by the label of "hate crimes." This is one demonstration of the absurdity of "hate-crime" legislation.

What Is Hate?

In all this talk of hate, the concept itself sits on the thinnest of ice. Have you ever thought about what hate really is? Hate is even more amorphous than a thought— it's actually a feeling. But what is the genesis of that feeling? It would be difficult to find a five-year-old who says that when he grows up he wants to hate the world and become a rapist or serial killer. There's a period in a child's life when hope and expectations prevail. Somewhere down the road the hope and expectations are likely to be eradicated by experience, and the result will be, in various degrees, resentment, distrust, and, yes, hate.

Most of the time, when the news media have presented us with an awful crime that involves the hate du jour, the portrayal of the perpetrator is quite one-dimensional. That person is a "hater" who did a "hateful" thing, a sort of monster that has no individual identity. There is nothing to know about the perpetrator except that he or she hated a protected group.

Ironically, FBI and Prison Bureau statistics indicate that the vast majority of those who commit crimes have experienced abuse in their own lives (personal hate directed at them) and disfranchisement (society's larger hate). It is possible that, by targeting those who act out in tangible hate against a protected group, the hate-crime theory actually revictimizes those who were initially the victims of hate.

Consider the Columbine tragedy. Eric Harris and Dylan Klebold committed one of the deadliest school massacres in American history. Their 1999 rampage at Columbine High School in Littleton, Colorado, left 1 teacher and 12 students dead (14 students, if you count Harris and Klebold, who finished by committing suicide). This was not a "hate crime" because none of the targets were chosen because of any protected group status—but they *were* targets. Harris and Klebold *hated* athletes and preps. As the investigation proceeded, it was reported that the two young men had been part of a group, known as "the Trench Coat Mafia," and described as "geeks" and "techies" who had endured hazing and actual physical attacks by the school's jocks because they were "different." One student who was part of that group remarked, "We were just all these people who routinely got made fun of, all through elementary school and junior high."[9]

> Hate will never be abolished, and we may never even completely understand it, but at least we can keep it from becoming a slogan used by the Thought Police in their attempts to carry out their special plans for a lobotomized society.

Kids can be extremely cruel when someone is different. The jocks and preps saw the Harris and Klebold clique as "losers" and "ragtag outcasts," regularly taunting them with calls of "Faggot!"

in the hallways, and even pelting them with rocks and bottles. One student, Kevin Koeniger, who was a 17-year-old junior at the time and a member of the Columbine Rebels football team, acknowledged that some athletes had "teased" Harris and Klebold but added, "If they're different, why wouldn't we look at them as weird?"[10]

There is never any excuse for violence, but there is usually a reason. Like the vast majority of men in prison who grew up with sexual abuse or domestic violence, Harris and Klebold ended up hating their tormentors. My point is not that anyone at Columbine deserved what happened that day, but that it is the projection of hate, the striking back by those who have been damaged, that is at the foundation of violence.

Hate will never be abolished, and we may never even completely understand it, but at least we can keep it from becoming a slogan used by the Thought Police in their attempts to carry out their special plans for a lobotomized society. We can work at overcoming hate and facing it down, just as we should anyone who suggests that one kind of hate is more serious than any other kind.

Thought Crime

The line between wanting to change society for the better and enforcing submission to a particular way of thinking can be a fine one. After all, if you want to change society, you have to decide what part of society needs fixing. Both sides of the political spectrum have come to their own conclusions in this regard, but the Left's efforts to eradicate injustice and discrimination have led it down an extraordinary road: the actual criminalization of the most private, personal, and subjective part of our lives—what we *think*. If you believe that I'm being an alarmist and it couldn't happen here, I hate to be the bearer of bad news—it already *has* happened. That's what hate-crime legislation is all about. Although a shocking turn of events, it is not entirely inexplicable.

Group dynamics and the decision to sacrifice the individual for the group are the first steps in a march down the road to Thought Crimes (euphemistically termed Hate Crimes) and totalitarianism in its purest form. I know these are stark terms, but bear with me; what I'm trying to do is throw the curtain back on a series of events that the Left has spun as something they're not. Hiding behind the terms "progressive" and "liberal," the Left insists that certain steps (including hate-crime legislation) are necessary to stop racism, homophobia, and sexism. What we fail to recognize is that today's "progressives" are not actually interested in dealing with those issues; they're simply exploiting them to further their much more complex and menacing agenda, which is all about power and control.

Let's go back to our carjacker/grocery-clerk scenario. This time, let's say both of the victims are gay. The grocery-store clerk, as before, kills his victim because he hates gay people. In the case of the carjacking, the guy wants the woman's car, she's in the way and represents everything he hates (he's poor and disfranchised, she is not), so he hates her in that moment and kills her. Whereas the grocery clerk is still guilty of a hate crime, the carjacker still is not, despite the fact that they both killed a gay woman. The actions were the same. The only difference is what the person was *thinking* when he committed the crime.

This is very different from the traditional legal concept of "intent." That concept is as objective as possible. It doesn't involve asking what the individual was thinking; it involves only asking whether a reasonable person would have expected a particular action (such as hitting someone in the head with a tire iron) to have a particular result (the death of the person who was hit). This concept opens the door for self-defense pleas and the insanity defense, which operate as a protection for the accused. What makes this acceptable is that it applies to everyone and is an extremely narrow window. Our society, through the courts and legislatures, has decided that this is a fair way to address issues of intent.

But that is not the way hate-crime legislation addresses intent. Make no mistake—"hate crime" is a euphemism for Thought Crime, allowing the government to gain the public's assent to prosecute people for what they *think* in addition to what they *do*.

My guess is that most murders include some element of hate. Yet a man can murder his wife, whom he hates at the moment (perhaps he's always hated her), and that's not a hate crime. An office worker who has

> **How is it that we have accepted the idea that hate adds to the severity of a crime when it is identified as homophobic or racist but not when it is personal?**

been fired hates his colleagues for betraying him and comes back to the office and kills them all with a sawed-off shotgun, but that's not a hate crime. How is it that we have accepted the idea that hate adds to the severity of a crime when it is identified as homophobic or racist but not when it is personal?

Isn't the next logical step to try to *prevent* any Thought Crime from even occurring? Society has already made a pact to try to prevent crime; we have neighborhood watches, drug-free zones, hotline numbers. With a little imagination, we can begin to see how our zeal for prevention could come to apply to potentially criminal thoughts. Sound impossible? If someone had told you in 1970 that we were eventually going to piggyback a Thought Crime on top of an actual crime, that would have sounded impossible, too.

I'm not suggesting that Jesse Jackson, Patricia Ireland, Al Sharpton, and Ellen DeGeneres are sitting somewhere in a smoke-filled room beneath a looming portrait of Stalin trying to figure out how to send us back to the Dark Ages. Although there are individual leaders in the forefront of perceived civil-rights efforts, the desire for control and power—coupled with group dynamics—takes on a life of its own. Those perceived leaders have, in a way, become victims of their own false conviction that their way must be forced onto society for its own good.

Of course, there has to be a "spin" to make punishment of "wrong thinking" palatable to the average American. That spin was provided by the development of "hate crimes." For those who can succeed only when the rest of us have been lobotomized, the final and actual criminalization of thought itself has become their measure of success.

Where is the debate on this issue? Who needs debate, the Left rationalizes, when those who disagree are bigoted, homophobic, sexist pigs? Dealing with their arguments is just a waste of time. In this model, dissenters begin to look less and less like members of society with a right to their own opinions and more and more like speed bumps on the road to social change.

Groupthink

A powerful force driving the organized Left along this path, and implemented on society at-large, has been what Irving Janis, one of the world's leading authorities on decision making, identified as "groupthink." In his seminal work, *Victims of Groupthink: A Psychological Study of Foreign-Policy Decisions and Fiascoes* (1972), Janis describes the eight "symptoms" of groupthink that help propel groups into failed policy and "irrational and dehumanizing actions directed at out-groups." These symptoms are:[11]

1. The illusion of invulnerability

2. Belief in the inherent morality of the group

3. Collective rationalization

4. Out-group stereotypes

5. Self-censorship

6. The illusion of unanimity

7. Direct pressure on dissenters

8. Self-appointed mindguards

Sound familiar? In all my work with NOW and other progressive organizations at both the local and the national levels, every one of those symptoms was present. Groupthink is the termite of the Left; it has burrowed in and effectively destroyed the foundation of what appears to still be a sturdy building. And outside the building, society's submissive acceptance of the concepts of hate crimes and group rights shows how deeply groupthink has affected us.

Let's take a closer look at the eight symptoms of groupthink. Understanding these elements will give us insight into some of the more bizarre behaviors of the special-interest groups that are feeding off our personal liberty.

1. *The illusion of invulnerability.* People act differently in a group; you see it all the time. At its worst it becomes mob action; but even in more benign settings, you know that when you get together with your buddies to watch a football game or are in the middle of a gang celebrating a major sports victory, there is a sense of strength in numbers that makes the group feel invulnerable. Think about it: Who on his or her own goes out and sets fire to a police car? Now apply that to any close-knit activist group. Get the picture?

2. *Belief in the inherent morality of the group.* "If all these people feel the same way, it must be right." This is how the sense of "the good guys against the bad guys" develops, as well as the myth that "our decisions are in everyone's best interests."

3. *Collective rationalization.* Groups are seduced by the false impression that they are right no matter what the evidence may actually say. Members of the group then reassure each other, using the morality of the group to reinforce their "rightness."

4. *Out-group stereotypes.* "Racist!" "Sexist!" "Homophobe!" "Religious radical!" "Right-wing nut!" Need I go on? Outsiders, or "the enemy," are stereotyped as either weak or stupid or both and unable to counter the decisions made by the group. Members of the group can be stereotyped, too, particularly those who are considered renegades, or even just those who "slow down" the decision-making process by asking questions and making objections.

5. *Self-censorship.* We all know that it can be incredibly uncomfortable to be the only person making an objection in what seems to be a unanimous group. While I was in the NOW leadership, I was told by feminist activist colleagues that voicing objections to the direction of NOW or to the way policy was made inside the group carried too high a price to be worth it. If belonging to the group is important, we are inclined to remain silent on issues where there is perceived consensus (*perceived* being the operative word here), rather than risk humiliation and rejection.

6. *The illusion of unanimity.* Self-censorship relies on the perception of consensus. When it appears that a majority opinion is taking shape, or as leaders make their own position clear, there is a tendency to overlook quiet dissent and to presume that everyone supports the position.

7. *Direct pressure on dissenters.* A group member who disagrees with the direction or policy of a

group will be pressured to conform. If that doesn't work, there may even be efforts to discredit the dissenting member. This eliminates dissent by the targeted member and also sends a message to other members that challenging the "consensus" will be punished. I'll go into more detail in chapter 5, but I'll say here that some inside NOW feel that I was used as an example of what would happen to them if they challenged the internal status quo. Of course, this was also utilized against Dr. Laura by GLAAD in the larger societal arena.

8. *Self-appointed mindguards.* Janis suggests that certain members of the group will work to keep dissenting opinions away from the leaders. Then, as word gets passed along to other members that the leadership is unwilling to hear criticism, those other members apply self-censorship, which strengthens the illusion of unanimity. Mindguards also work to shield the group from adverse information that might crack their shared complacency.

For someone like me, who has worked within the sickrooms of establishment feminism, I can tell you that groupthink is a cancer that is destroying its body. Furthermore, society at large has come to exhibit some of the same symptoms. We see it in the self-censorship and out-group stereotyping that are the basis of hate-crimes legislation and speech codes, while the symptoms are played out publicly by the Left in its attacks on the well-known who step out of line.

The Cult of Mind Control

At the heart of any theory of policing thought is mind control. The public humiliation of those who challenge the Left is intended to intimidate both the target and society into a different way of thinking.

Probably the most comprehensive analyses of mind control and its prerequisite circumstances are offered in the *Cultic Studies Journal* (*CSJ*). This is a semiannual, peer-reviewed, multidisciplinary journal that seeks to advance understanding of cultic processes and their relation to society. Its contributors examine the broad social and cultural implications of cultism, as well as its effects on individuals and families.[12] The *CSJ* is the only scholarly journal devoted to this field of inquiry, and its editorial board is composed of academicians from major universities and nationally recognized experts in the field of the psychology of social influence.[13]

Here is how the *CSJ* describes mind control: "Mind Control (also known as "brainwashing," "coercive persuasion," and "thought reform,") refers to a process in which a group or individual systematically uses unethically manipulative methods to persuade others to conform to the wishes of the manipulator(s)."[14]

If you think there's nothing here of any real consequence—that this is just the theorizing of eggheads—do I have news for you! When analyzed, what may appear to be random activities of the Thought Police actually come together in a very methodical, organized fashion. Although I hesitate to suggest that the special-interest groups on the Left are cults per se, in the course of my research I was surprised to find direct correlation between cultic methods of mind control and the strategies employed by the Left. After all, if thought reform is your goal, it should not be surprising that the method you adopt is the one that has the strongest record of success, ranging from North Korean brainwashing of American soldiers in the early 1950s to the "Reverend" Jim Jones leading his followers into death by Kool-Aid to the nonviolent but still frightening methods of the Moonies.

If there is one thing that stands out for me from all of this, it's that if the Left has any real "vision" amid its frenzy to control what people think and say, it is simply to keep conservatives from any kind of power. An absolute essential of collectivism is that everyone must think the same way—otherwise it won't work.

> **What does the Left need more than anything else to maintain its empty form? It needs you not to notice, not to ask, not to question. It needs you to agree that the emperor has, indeed, the most beautiful clothes in the world.**

The problem is, socialism does not work because people do not think the same way. Therefore, the thought reformers end up putting their creative energy into manipulating people and wielding power instead of into solving social problems—such as intolerance, social division, violence, and a culture devoid of values—which, ironically, they themselves have facilitated. The Left now exists for the perpetuation of itself. Its political theory does not stand as a container for bright and constructive ideas. The political attitude itself—collectivism—is the goal.

In the following chapters we'll explore how this works in practice by looking at various areas of American society and culture—specifically the gay, feminist, and black civil-rights organizations, multiculturalism, the academy, and the media. In each case, the same question arises: What does the Left need more than anything else to maintain its empty form? It needs you not to notice, not to ask, not to question. It needs you to agree that the emperor has, indeed, the most beautiful clothes in the world.

3

Pot. Kettle. Black.

The Hypocrisy of the Gay Establishment

"All animals are equal,
but some animals are more equal than others."

—*George Orwell,* Animal Farm

When I was growing up, *Animal Farm* was one of my favorite books, and it still is today. A classic of twentieth-century literature, it has a political message that transcends age and party lines. Orwell was a man of the old Left, but he was fully aware of the pitfalls of power. In this allegory reflecting his bleak view of communism, he tells of animals who, after mistreatment and abuse by a drunken farmer, take over Manor Farm and rename it Animal Farm. With revolutionary zeal, they declare their Seven Commandments. Creatures that move about on four legs or wings are friends; the two-legged (humans) are, by definition, the enemy. No animal shall drink alcohol, wear clothes, sleep in a bed, or kill a fellow animal. Most important is the Seventh Commandment: All animals are equal.

Everything goes well until the pigs, who because of their intelligence have become the leaders at Animal Farm, fall into the trap of power and rewrite the Seventh Commandment: "All animals are equal, but some animals are more equal than others."

The narrator describes the rest of the animals watching through a window as the pigs meet with some neighboring farmers: "No question, now, what had happened to the faces of the pigs. The creatures outside looked from pig to man, and from man to pig, and from pig to man again; but already it was impossible to say which was which."

Once in power, the oppressed will become the oppressor. That is the theme of *Animal Farm*. It is odd and disturbing how effortlessly the previously marginalized in our society (gays, women, blacks), now in the warm seats of power, are taking up the oppressor's tools and marginalizing the Left's opponents (the religious and conservative). Indeed, it is already becoming impossible to say which is which.

We all know Lord Acton's maxim that power corrupts and absolute power corrupts absolutely. Remembering that saying is more important than ever. No matter how noble the original intentions, the seductions of power—combined with groupthink and a lack of moral grounding—can turn any movement from one seeking equal rights into one that would deny them to others.

GLAAD's original mission was certainly admirable. Gays and lesbians, who had long endured the cold shoulder of a disapproving society, finally had an organization that would speak out on their behalf and fight injustice. But,

like so many well-meaning organizations, GLAAD fell victim to the process described by Lord Acton. Seemingly
overnight, it went from character building to character assassination. Fattened up
with newfound power,
it chose not to debate
those with differing
opinions but to try to
destroy them. For polit-
ical scientists, this is not
a revelation. But for
those of us who have
emotional capital in-
vested in the ideal of

> No matter how noble the
> original intentions, the
> seductions of power can
> turn any movement from
> one seeking equal rights
> into one that would deny
> them to others.

progressive thought and action, the attack on Dr. Laura
Schlessinger should be a serious wake-up call.

The War on Dr. Laura

"[We want] to help them recognize that they didn't buy
controversy when they bought this show, they bought
trouble."[1]

This is not a comment by Southern Baptists about
Ellen, or by the American Family Association about
NYPD Blue. It comes from a speech that GLAAD's executive director, Joan Garry, delivered during a rally protesting production of the *Dr. Laura* television show.

I should say up front that I like Laura Schlessinger. I
got to know her when we were hosting radio programs at
the same station in Los Angeles, and I have seen her go
out of her way to give support to someone she not only
barely knew but also actually considered an ideological

opponent. That person was me. Ironically, in all my work with the feminist establishment, I seldom encountered the level of encouragement and support that Dr. Laura, the supposed anti-feminist, showed me.

The values she espouses are genuine and are reflected in the way she lives her life. She is an Orthodox Jew whose comments about life are based on the Torah. Although she and I are at opposite poles when it comes to certain social issues, I have tremendous respect for the woman and admire her conviction, consistency, and honesty in applying her principles. It was my own knowledge of Laura Schlessinger, coupled with my experience within the Left, that first made me question the sincerity of the gay establishment's assault on her.

What She Really Said

GLAAD's attacks on Dr. Laura began in May 1997, when, in a newspaper column, she termed homosexuality a "biological faux pas" and described lesbian and gay parenting as "inferior" to heterosexual parenting.[2] Additional GLAAD complaints centered on her use, in her columns and on her radio programs, of such terms as "biological error," "dysfunction," and "disorder" to describe homosexuality.

The press reprinted GLAAD's accusations with wild abandon. Activists described Dr. Laura as representing the epitome of "intolerance" and "double standards,"[3] and some went so far as to suggest that her opinions were a contributing factor in the deaths of people such as Matthew Shepard and Brandon Teena, the girl whose story was the subject of the Academy Award–winning film *Boys Don't Cry*.

One thing you probably haven't heard or seen in all this uproar is an actual verbatim quote of the statements Dr. Laura made—and bear in mind that she isn't just a talking head; she's a certified family and marriage therapist. Let's take a look at one of her opponents' favorite sources for out-of-context phrases, her radio program of December 8, 1998:

> I'm sorry, hear it one more time perfectly clearly: if you're gay or a lesbian, it's a biological error that inhibits you from relating normally to the opposite sex. The fact that you are intelligent, creative, and valuable is all true. The error is in your inability to relate sexually, intimately, in a loving way to a member of the opposite sex. *It* [emphasis mine] is a biological error. People who are gay or lesbian are not to be hated or attacked. I spent most of my career supporting groups like Parents and Friends of Lesbians and Gays because I didn't want families to throw out their children simply because they were gay or lesbian. They are still decent and functional human beings—or maybe they're not, because that indecency goes everywhere. A bunch of guys having sex after leaving bars with each other is indecent. Likewise, a bunch of heterosexuals leaving bars with each other and having sex with each other is indecent. I don't care which way it flies.[4]

Here in context, it is clear that what Dr. Laura was referring to as a biological error was homosexuals' sexual orientation and not homosexuals themselves. In fact, as you can see here, she makes some of the more balanced statements about gays heard on talk radio. If your tactics include lifting single words and short phrases out of sentences, however, you can twist someone's comments into just about anything you like.

Much has also been made of Dr. Laura's supposedly referring to gays and lesbians as "deviants" on her radio program of September 8, 1998. Let's take a look at the actual comments she made that day. She starts by reading aloud a letter printed in the *Los Angeles Times*. The letter says:

> What hypocrisy! The Catholic Church holds that homosexual orientation is objectively disordered, and that homosexual acts are intrinsically evil. Yet it claims to condemn bigotry in any form, as well as violent malice in speech or in action. I wonder what portion of all that jargon gay-bashers listen to.

Dr. Laura then comments on the letter:

> I read the entire report from the Catholic Church, and that's exactly what it said: that people with a homosexual orientation are to be loved, nurtured, helped, protected, not hurt in thought, word, or deed. I'm paraphrasing, but they say that it is quite possible to believe that a sexual behavior is *deviant and disordered* [emphasis mine] and not wish to have any harm come to that person; moreover, to have spiritual and psychiatric help come to that person. But the radical activists do not allow that; they just jump on the bigotry word. And that is so offensive.[5]

Where, exactly, does Dr. Laura call homosexuals deviants? I don't see it, do you? The word comes up in a discussion of the position of the Catholic Church, and even then it is used in relation to behavior, not individuals.

If you think that I must be mistaken and that she must have used those words in another, actually inflammatory context on some other program—nope. The above text came directly from the GLAAD Web site, which indicated September 8's as *the* offending program.

In a *Time* magazine interview, Dr. Laura responded to the complaints: "I never called homosexual human beings deviants. I have pointed out that homosexual behavior deviates from the norm of heterosexuality and is forbidden by scriptures . . . I stand behind basic civil rights—where someone is able to live, and work at his job—and always have."[6]

Letting Dr. Laura be heard without the din of the Thought Police, however, was too fair for *Time*. In what seems to be an unprecedented move, *Time* then ran an essay by Joan Garry in the next issue specifically to refute Dr. Laura's comments.

Not the Rose Parade

What's interesting is that GLAAD and others have directed the bulk of their outrage at Dr. Laura's comments that imply or state that homosexuality is not normal. What is normal, anyway? Let's consult *Webster's New World Dictionary* (Pocket Books, 1995), just so we're all on the same page:

Deviant: deviating, esp. from what is considered normal.

Normal: conforming with an accepted standard or norm . . . the usual state.

Certainly, the average person considers heterosexuality to be "the usual state." In fact, if you accept estimates that somewhere between 4 and 12 percent of the populace is gay, then homosexuality is *not* the normal state of affairs. Actually, that is fine with me. I *like* being different; I *like* deviating from the norm.

The sensitivity to terms strikes me as particularly silly and rife with hypocrisy considering that we're dealing with a community that has embraced the word "queer" to describe itself. Just two examples are the aggressive gay-activist group Queer Nation (known for the slogan "We're here. We're queer. Get used to it.") and the Web site for Stanford University's gay and lesbian support organization,

> **Homosexuality is not the normal state of affairs. Actually, that is fine with me. I like being different; I like deviating from the norm.**

Stanford Queer Resources.[7] In any event, if there is suddenly such a concern within the gay community about appearing "normal," perhaps men in suits should replace men in G-strings at gay-pride parades.

I was at an organizing meeting for a gay-pride group that shall remain nameless. One of the bigger arguments at the meeting involved whether or not to have a giant penis on a float, à la the Rose Parade. After a contentious debate, the Giant Penis Float lost out, but just barely. The women in the room were not amused, and a discussion ensued about how negatively the gay community appears to the rest of the country when our ambassadors are men dressed as female high school cheerleaders.

From Education to Terrorism

"Consumer education" has always been an important weapon in the arsenal of civil-rights activists. We live in a free-market economy where the choices we make as consumers send messages about what is and is not acceptable, and there is more than enough room for activists to "educate" the public about a company and its practices. Essentially, the strategy is to remind people they do indeed have the power to influence media outlets and other corporate structures by being selective in what they purchase.

As a feminist activist, I've employed some creative tactics (described in chapter 9) to protest the publishing of a book that sexualized violence against women, the airing of television shows that objectified women, and a cozy television interview with a certain wife batterer/killer. I've done so, however, without calling for pulling or canceling the book or show at issue, and certainly without attempting to destroy those responsible, no matter how much I despised them.

It's a fine line, but one that can, and must, be walked. Calling attention to, challenging, and educating the public about objectionable ideas or people is a fundamental necessity in our society. When we begin, however, to demand the silencing of someone because we're offended by his or her opinion, we've crossed the line. The campaign against Laura Schlessinger was presented by its organizers as a traditional "consumer education" project, but in fact it took on a much more sinister tone.

Almost daily, the stopdrlaura.com Web site and GLAAD online reported, gleefully, how sponsor after sponsor of Dr. Laura's new television show was dropping out. Even I, as a veteran of successful consumer actions, was quite surprised by how swiftly sponsors abandoned her, considering that they had signed up to support a woman who was a known commodity and has never been bashful about her opinions.

Was this response due to simple phone calls from an overwhelming number of angry gay people? Not exactly. Ms. Keven Bellows, the general manager of the *Dr. Laura* radio show and the senior vice president of Premiere Radio Networks, which syndicates the show, told me that the FBI has been Premiere Radio's and Laura Schlessinger's constant companion since the "education" campaign began. Why? Laura shared with me how, at the beginning of the campaign, sponsors began to receive bomb threats. Sponsors reported to her and her team that retail outlets were also being threatened with vandalism if they carried the sponsors' product (so much for letting the consumer decide!). Dealing with consumers and their opinions is one thing; having to face bomb threats is quite another.

The FBI is also investigating the numerous death threats against Dr. Laura herself, which began with the initiation of the gay campaign and ended with its success in the cancellation of her television show. References to her opinion about gays and lesbians, and to the campaign against her, accompanied the death threats. Isn't that ironic? Individuals threatening to kill someone because they don't think *she's* tolerant enough?

Ethics and Bombs

The episodes that hurt Schlessinger most, she told me, were when some in the Jewish community abandoned her or in some instances, directly joined in the attack, instead of standing up to the cowards and bullies running the campaign against her.

For instance, she had been booked for two years to speak to the International Conference on Jewish Medical Ethics, scheduled to take place in San Francisco from February 16 to 19, 2001. In August of 2000, during the height of the campaign against her, she was informed by Rabbi Sholom Fine, the son-in-law of Pinchas Lipner, dean of the Institute for Jewish Medical Ethics of the Hebrew Academy, which sponsored the conference, that she was being removed from the program. She received a fax from Rabbi Fine, expressing his and his wife's regret that Dr. Laura had been canceled as a speaker. His letter to her made it clear to Dr. Laura that both he and his wife were fans of hers, and were indeed upset by what had transpired. Then the fax alluded to the reason why she was removed as a speaker—threats of violence had been conveyed to Rabbi Lipner. Once again, this campaign of terror reached beyond Dr. Laura—to those who would dare support her, and who share the same religious convictions.

Laura told me that this letter led to a conversation with Rabbi Fine, in which he filled in the details: If she appeared at the San Francisco conference, Rabbi Lipner had been warned, the conference would be bombed. Not only would the conference attendees be in danger, he was told, but so would his students at the Academy itself.

Dr. Laura, who eventually spoke with Rabbi Lipner, was angry at his decision, not only to surrender to threats, but also his refusal to contact the FBI, the police, or even speak to the press about the extraordinary coercion to which he was subjected. Wounded by the entire incident, it was especially sad for her (and should be for everyone) to see Jews, who know so well and so personally the importance of standing up to threats and intimidation, submit to a threat so regularly used by bigots and anti-Semites. She greatly appreciated Rabbi Fine's support, but she felt abandoned by many she had thought would stand by her.

Rabbi David and Goliath

It didn't end there, however. It's one thing to bow down to a threat of violence and quite another to condemn someone simply because it has become the thing to do. It became clear that no organization is immune from the impact of groupthink and the tactics of the Thought Police.

The Anti-Defamation League (ADL), founded in 1913, was one of the more respected Jewish hate-monitoring groups. Its task, according to its original mission statement, is "to stop the defamation of the Jewish people and to secure justice and fair treatment to all citizens alike." On March 24, 2000, in a letter addressed to Laura Schlessinger, the ADL condemned her. The letter read in part: "We believe that a tone of demonization and needless hostility characterizes your remarks on these issues . . . we are concerned that others might use such statements to justify acts of violence or discriminate against gays and lesbians." A curious statement considering that the only person in this whole episode who was receiving death threats, whose scheduled appearance had evoked bomb threats, and who needed to use 24-hour armed security was the Jewish woman under attack.

Of course, the ADL didn't send the letter only to Dr. Laura. No, that wouldn't have served the purpose. WABC in New York somehow received it, and it was also posted on the stopdrlaura.com Web site. And at one public event, one of the organizers of the anti–Dr. Laura campaign pulled out the letter and waved it in the air, declaring in triumph, "Your own Jewish people have condemned you!"

Enter Rabbi David Eliezrie. It takes heroic individuality to confront a Goliath of the special-interest Left, but that is just what Rabbi Eliezrie did. He believed the injustice of the ADL's attack should be confronted and its hypocrisy exposed. He telephoned and spoke to Elizabeth Coleman, the director of the Civil Rights Division of the ADL, and on May 31, 2000, he followed up that conversation with a letter. He wrote in part:

> You write that you find "these accusations unfair." Did you seek a clarification from a spokesman of Dr. Laura about her views? Did you investigate the context of the statement . . . ? If she used the exact words of the Torah that Homosexual acts are "an abomination" would you also decide that those words are unfair . . . ?
>
> . . . as you said yesterday in our conversation, "it is the question of the venue." . . . Is the ADL now going to challenge free speech rights of religious Jews who dare to express their views outside the confines of Boro Park or Crown Heights? . . .
>
> The ADL has allowed itself to be used by the Homosexual groups as a tool to condemn a Jew who articulated opinions reflective of Torah principles. . . . Instead of sending a letter to Dr. Laura challenging her articulation of Jewish values in a public forum, with pride the ADL should honor her for having the moral conviction and strength of character to share Jewish morality with the broader society.[8]

Rabbi Eliezrie is the hero of this story because he recognized an injustice and stood up to it. Did the ADL hear him? Probably not. Groupthink apparently precluded their being able to hear anything but their own drumbeat or to recognize how awful it really sounds.

> I believe the fact that Laura Schlessinger is a woman and a Jew contributed to the ease with which her attackers gained support.

I believe the fact that Laura Schlessinger is a woman and a Jew contributed to the ease with which her attackers gained support. Historically, neither women nor Jews are supposed to speak out, be strong, *or* challenge the status quo. Shame on Elizabeth Coleman, the ADL, and every other progressive person (and Jew in particular) who decided that it was okay to trample on this particular woman's rights. The Jewish community especially should know the dangers of Mob Rule. It has cost millions of them their lives.

Hitting Home

Unidentified supporters of the GLAAD campaign embraced the decision that harassment and terrorism would be much more effective than the drudgery of a traditional education campaign. Using a tactic designed by anti-abortion extremists to frighten and harass doctors who perform abortions, someone mailed fliers to everyone in the neighborhood where Laura Schlessinger and her family live. Quoting scripture, the anonymous (of course) letter reveals to its recipients that Dr. Laura is their neighbor, informs them when she is likely to be walking in the neighborhood and to be physically accessible, and encourages them to confront her personally about her "destructiveness" to the lives of gays and lesbians, equating the potential results of her comments with the Holocaust and the genocides in Rwanda and the former Yugoslavia.

The flier begins:

> Dear Friend, As you may know, Dr. Laura Schlessinger, the nationally syndicated talk-show host who daily attracts more than 18 million listeners, lives near you. . . .
>
> Again and again on her show, hour after hour, she has told her many listeners that gay men and women are "deviant" and "biological mistakes" . . .
>
> *The physical and economic harm Dr. Schlessinger's words cause to innocent men and women is incalculable and very real* [emphasis theirs].

After comparing her with Hitler and Milosevic, the flier then suggests that "there are a few things you can do . . . when she's walking to and from synagogue on Friday evenings and Saturday mornings, stop her. . . ." At the end of this extraordinary document, the writers exhort: "If you believe in G-d and believe that He, in His mercy intervenes in human affairs, *please pray.* . . . [emphasis theirs]"

Pro-choice activists have for years decried anti-abortion extremists' tactic of "fliering" the neighborhood of a doctor because it exposes the target to a dangerous level of personal vulnerability. This tactic has in fact sometimes preceded the murder of that doctor. Any activist in the pro-choice or gay community knows the origin of this method and the results. So does the FBI, which is still investigating the fliering of Dr. Laura's neighborhood as a threat to her and her family's personal safety.

Do we know specifically who is behind the terrorist tactics used against Dr. Laura, her family, her co-workers, and her sponsors? No. The threats and the neighborhood flier are all anonymous. But what is important for you to know is that the "success" of this "consumer education" project was achieved in part by people who felt comfortable resorting to terrorism and threats of death to get their way.

No Death Threats Here

In case you are still convinced that the attacks on Laura Schlessinger, however out of control, were motivated by genuine concern, let me tell you about one person who is not on the gay establishment's list of people to destroy: the rapper Eminem.

In the song "Kill You," Eminem rants, "Kill you, you faggots keep egging me on/Till I have you at knife point then you beg me to stop . . ."

In "Criminal," he declares, "My words are like a dagger with a jagged edge/And I'll stab you in the head, whether you're a fag or a les. . . ."

These lyrics are on Eminem's CD, *The Marshall Mathers LP*, released in May 2000, at the same time that GLAAD was stepping up its assault against Dr. Laura and demanding that Paramount peremptorily cancel her television program. No, GLAAD didn't entirely ignore Eminem. It issued a news release criticizing his label, Interscope Records, a division of Universal Entertainment. The release stated: "The hatred and hostility conveyed on this CD have a real effect on real people's lives as they encourage violence against gay men and lesbians." So what action did GLAAD urge? It concluded its release by suggesting, rather reservedly, that Interscope, Eminem, and retailers of the record "have a responsibility . . . to consider its impact on an impressionable audience."[9]

GLAAD also called for a telephone campaign because "Eminem's lyrics are soaked with violence" and "the market for this music has been shown to be adolescent males, the very group that statistically commits the most hate crimes."[10] Oddly, though, activists weren't told to call Universal or Interscope or MTV, or their sponsors. They were told to call Eminem's *manager*.

Apparently, the word "deviant" warrants an organized, national campaign to force the person who utters it off the air, yet the words "kill you, you faggots" and "hate fags" and vile and graphic descriptions of violence against gays and lesbians merit only a phone call to staff.

In early September 2000, GLAAD did manage to arrange for a picket outside the MTV Music Awards, where Eminem performed. In February 2001, GLAAD organized another picket outside the Grammys, where Eminem was receiving three awards. Sure, they're complaining about him, but with such *reserve*. The harshest word GLAAD could come up with in response to gay icon Elton John's decision to perform a duet with Eminem at the 2001 Grammys was "misguided." Whew! That must have put the fear of God into both of them.

As of this writing, the gay establishment has yet to suggest any concerted anti-Eminem campaign against Interscope, Universal, or MTV even remotely comparable to the one directed against Laura Schlessinger and her producers.

As an activist, what strikes me as exceptionally bizarre is that Universal, which would seem to be particularly vulnerable to a consumer-education effort, is effectively being ignored, as are Universal's parent corporations, Seagram and the French water company Vivendi. And MTV's sponsors could easily receive the same kind of attention the gay establishment afforded Dr. Laura's advertisers.

What's wrong with this picture? Plenty.

Show Me the Money

Dr. Laura is being attacked and Eminem is not, I believe, for specific reasons. First, her audience is mainstream America—exactly the people upon whom the speech code needs to be enforced. Second, because Laura "Go-Do-The-Right-Thing" Schlessinger and her audience care, there is the possibility that complaints of discrimination and intolerance, regardless of their merit, may have some impact, giving GLAAD's constituency the impression that they are achieving success on an issue. One could bet that Eminem, his manager, and his audience don't give a hoot's patooty what GLAAD thinks. Third, Dr. Laura is doubly a member of the newly marginalized—she's conservative and she's religious. Eminem, it's safe to say, is neither.

We can still ask: Why not campaign against both? Here's something to consider. One of Universal's parent companies, as I've mentioned, is Seagram. Seagram distributes Absolut vodka in the United States and in major international markets. Well, Absolut is *the* major corporate sponsor of GLAAD, and it contributes significantly to many other gay and lesbian organizations as well. Is it possible that a financial relationship has hobbled GLAAD's response to Eminem? MTV has also been a regular donor to GLAAD. Now guess what Joan Garry did for a living before she took the reins at GLAAD. She was an executive at—surprise!—MTV.

The Intolerance of Gay Tolerance

As a gay woman, I am greatly concerned when people come to conclusions about homosexuality that I feel are wrong. Not only is some of what is said personally hurtful, but also I find some opinions about gays downright juvenile or simply mean. It is even more troubling, therefore, when actual supporters of gays and lesbians, such as Laura Schlessinger, are used as scapegoats because the real problems can't be addressed.

Furthermore, I've heard too many times, publicly and privately, that gay people who don't agree with silencing our critics are "self-hating" and "traitors." Demeaning characterizations of group members who dissent from the "consensus" is an obvious groupthink symptom. Everyone should be concerned when those entrusted with social activism conclude that intimidating people into silence is somehow going to improve communication between diverse groups and help solve our most critical social problems.

> Everyone should be concerned when those entrusted with social activism conclude that intimidating people into silence is somehow going to improve communication between diverse groups.

A number of people, for example, have expressed to me their concern about the content of this book. They worry about the "other side" using it for their own purposes. In the words of a letter writer who responded to a pro-Schlessinger op-ed piece of mine published in the *Los Angeles Times*:

> Tammy Bruce's "Nothing Is Gained In Silencing Dr. Laura" commentary sounds very much like the "Uncle Tom" faxes Schlessinger receives from self-loathing gay people and reads so gleefully on her radio show. No doubt Dr. Laura will read all or part of it in support of her anti-gay crusade. Thanks, Tammy, for giving the nation's No. 1 gaybasher more ammunition.

This stereotyping (with a racial pejorative thrown in) presumes that because I and other gay people see the anti–Dr. Laura campaign for what it really is, somehow we're stupid, self-loathing, and ignorant. This symptom of groupthink is especially dangerous within a community that purports to fight stereotyping and ignorance. For far too long, the argument has been that any criticisms we make of one another will be used against "us" by "them" (read: the religious and conservative). The principal danger I see right now is the perplexing self-righteousness of those on the Left as they revel in their perceived omnipotence.

When Freedom of Expression 'Doesn't Apply'

At least the Left is consistent in its inconsistency. With all this talk about freedom of expression, one might ask, "Where is the American Civil Liberties Union when it comes to Laura Schlessinger?" After all, here is a group so committed to principle that it will even support neo-Nazis in their efforts to march in a Jewish neighborhood. In Dr. Laura's case, though, it seems that a Jewish woman with an opinion doesn't merit the same risk-taking.

Comments made by ACLU staff attorney Peter Eliasberg during an appearance on ABC's *World News Tonight* (May 20, 2000) shed some light on the organization's position. "When Paramount decides that it wants to put on Dr. Laura, or doesn't want to put on Dr. Laura," Eliasberg said, "the government's not involved. And therefore the First Amendment and the freedom of speech, the legal freedom of speech protections, don't apply." So much for the ACLU's legendary commitment to freedom of expression.

Furthermore, this statement doesn't seem to square with some other recent activities by the guardians of our personal liberty. For example, also in 2000, the ACLU and the ubiquitous Peter Eliasberg rushed to the aid of an artist who had a "constitutional right" to use Barbie dolls in a way that Mattel, Barbie's manufacturer and trademark owner, was challenging in court. According to the ACLU, "artist Tom Forsythe, of Kanab, Utah, has used Barbie dolls to parody Barbie's embodiment of America's culture of consumption and conformism," through a series of Barbie photographs. "My Barbie series of photos critiques the Barbie doll and the shallow, consumerist values fostered and perpetuated by it," said Forsythe.

Last time I checked, Mattel wasn't the government, but here's a segment of the press release the ACLU issued after prevailing in court:

"The ACLU of Southern California . . . stepped in to stop Mattel's use of litigation as a method of bullying artists into abandoning their First Amendment rights. . . . 'Today's statement from the court should give Mattel and its attorneys pause,' said Peter Eliasberg, Staff Attorney at the ACLU of Southern California. 'Their strategy of trying to bury Tom Forsythe's First Amendment rights in an avalanche of legal documents will not work.'"[11]

And here is my favorite part of the release:

"'There are a few things money and power can't buy in America,' said Annette Hurst, of San Francisco's Howard, Rice, Nemerovski, Canady, Falk & Rabkin, pro bono co-counsel in the [Forsythe] case, 'and one of them is the silence of someone determined to express a viewpoint. That's what the First Amendment is all about.'"[12]

Really? That's what I thought, too, but for everyone. The ACLU and the pro bono counsel were determined to keep Mattel, not the government, from impinging on the artist's freedom of expression. The ACLU may argue that court involvement makes a difference, but who's kidding whom? It was Mattel, not the government, that initiated this action. This is particularly important if you support the ACLU because you truly believe that the First Amendment is more than just a legal codification—that the spirit of the law and the principles behind it are what really matter.

Did GLAAD have secret telephone calls in the night with the ACLU about Laura Schlessinger? As far as we know, no, but the left-wing power elite is small and interconnected. Different groups have overlapping constituencies and share a similar history and tactics, allowing for tacit agreements about attitude and approach. In the case of Dr. Laura, the ACLU sees where GLAAD is going and takes its cues from its left-wing cousin. Am I just being cynical? No—the behavior of the ACLU speaks for itself, and I've seen it operate far too may times from the inside.

Five Friends

Despite the news media's assumption that the gay community exists within the equivalent of a Vulcan mind-meld, we don't. The chorus you hear about "the gay community" implies that every gay and lesbian person on the planet feels the same way about the strategy against Laura Schlessinger. I can tell you, however, that I am not the only gay person—or the only liberal person—who recognizes the attack on Dr. Laura for what it is: a heavy-handed assault on freedom. I have a number of gay friends who are just as appalled at the tactics being used against her as are my conservative friends.

The news media, of course, do not bring you that other point of view. It serves their agenda to present the entire gay community as a single-minded entity. What would have happened if CNN had reported, "Five people who hate Dr. Laura want her show canceled"? That doesn't exactly lend itself to nationwide coverage. But that was in fact the situation. The campaign against Dr. Laura was designed and controlled by as few as half a dozen people. They admitted this themselves:

> As you know, five friends got together to launch stopdrlaura.com on March 1, 2000, out of concern that there was no national voice calling on Paramount to drop Dr. Laura's TV show.
>
> . . . we were the first national voice to unequivocally demand that Paramount drop the show, and that

is why we launched and ran the nationwide—no, worldwide—campaign to stop Dr. Laura.[13]

National voice? No, more like five friends on the Internet. It's amazing what impressions the Internet can give to both the public and corporate America. In its desire not to be outshone by a project that the media wanted to assist, GLAAD tagged along, giving this Internet band of Laura-haters a legitimacy they did not deserve.

The Web site has since shut down. It did not morph into stopeminem.com or stopjessehelms.com or stophomophobes.com. Instead, we're assured that stopdrlaura.com "has so exposed Dr. Laura's anti-gay rhetoric to the world that she now cannot even sneeze without the major national media, and thousands of individual activists like yourselves, watching, recording her every word, and pouncing when action is needed."[14] And right now Eminem is probably trying to figure out where to put all his Grammy awards.

Meanwhile, many of those in the gay community who disagree with the Web site's slash-and-burn tactic remain afraid to speak up because they don't want to be targeted themselves. Let's be honest: most people don't want to face a fraction of the hate that Laura Schlessinger has faced for bucking the speech code.

Anything You Can Do I Can Do Better

A terrific example of the gay establishment's we-can-do-it-but-you-can't approach to stifling dissent comes from Gainesville, Georgia. In 1998, the Gainesville newspaper that had been printing Atlanta's lesbian and gay newspaper, *Southern Voice,* announced that it would no longer do so. The *Gainesville Times* issued a two-paragraph statement announcing its decision, a portion of which reads: "Southland Publishing remains committed to be non-discriminatory in our business practices and printing operations. We will continue to work with any group . . . regardless of its religious, racial or lifestyle affiliations, provided the organization and its needs are legal and within the bounds of accepted business and printing practices. Recent operational and press scheduling conflicts have made it necessary for us to reevaluate our commercial printing commitments. . . ."[15]

A "disturbed" GLAAD jumped into action, with a prophetic comment by none other than Joan Garry. "The very wording of this statement," she said, "causes us great concern. It is a vague and indirect response to a very serious and potentially precedent-setting matter."[16] It *was* precedent setting—for GLAAD itself.

According to Garry's press release, almost immediately after the *Gainesville Times* first began to print *Southern Voice,* it was targeted by "religious political extremists who urged readers and sponsors to cancel their subscription and advertisements."[17] The release concluded with Garry proclaiming, "GLAAD hopes that all businesses will stand firm in the face of fear and intolerance. This was a perfect opportunity for the *Times* to demonstrate such resolve."[18]

Shouldn't that exhortation also apply to Procter & Gamble, Sears, and the scores of other sponsors that fled Dr. Laura two years later in the face of GLAAD's campaign of "fear and intolerance"? No, because the Left doesn't want you tolerating anything they won't tolerate.

For the gay establishment to exhibit concern about intolerance only when its interests are at stake is both short-sighted and unfair. Pressure that *eliminates* a point of view should be resisted, even if the point of view is offensive, mean, or even dangerous—everything the Religious Right has claimed about gay speech and activity.

The root of any problem is never addressed by silencing unpleasant or disagreeable opinions. Dr. Laura, after all, was merely restating what certain organized religions have been preaching for more than two thousand years—that homosexual practices are sinful and not what God wanted. "Love the sinner, hate the sin." Dr. Laura's is an opinion held by millions of people around the world—but not because of the power of a slight, Jewish woman with a radio and television show. And it's not going to go away if she is silenced.

The Amazing Invisible Homosexual

The rhetoric of those trying to silence Laura Schlessinger includes the claim that she personally contributes to the suicide rate of gay teens by what she says on her program. There might be something to this charge if Dr. Laura were in fact a "gay basher" who encouraged gay teens' families to reject them—but quite the opposite is true. In fact, as noted earlier in the chapter, she has been personally involved for years with Parents and Friends of Lesbians and Gays (PFLAG), one of the more respected gay and lesbian organizations. PFLAG Los Angeles became a favorite charity of Schlessinger's, and she got involved with the organization specifically because she recognized the importance of its mission of providing support to the families of gays and lesbians.

No, Laura Schlessinger cannot be held responsible for the social isolation gay teens feel, or for their alcohol and drug abuse, which intensifies the feelings of loneliness and hopelessness. It's not because of anything she has said that too many gay teens believe they cannot be both gay and successful in the world.[19] That responsibility lies elsewhere—squarely with the gay and lesbian community itself. There's plenty the gay community can do about the primary factors of gay teen suicide, if it takes responsibility and stops trying to deflect the problem onto someone else.

> Laura Schlessinger cannot be held responsible for the social isolation gay teens feel, or for their alcohol and drug abuse, which intensifies the feelings of loneliness and hopelessness.

First, prominent gay organizations should get out of their very public bed with the alcohol companies. Alcoholism rates are sky high in the gay community. In fact, most studies, confirmed by the experiences of clinicians who work with gay men and lesbians, estimate an incidence of substance abuse of all types in the range of 28 to 35 percent; this estimate contrasts with an incidence of 10 to 12 percent in the general population.[20]

We've already seen how financial relationships with some corporate sponsors can be perceived as weakening activist efforts. The glamorization of alcohol, through the "bar" lifestyle and corporate sponsorship of gay and lesbian events, convinces many children and adults alike that drinking is an important social rite.

But perhaps the largest contributor to suicidal young gays' inability to see a future for themselves is the perceived nonexistence of prominent homosexuals, which is why the Department of Health and Human Services emphasizes the need for role models in the effort to curb gay teen depression and suicide.[21] Of course, they're out there—just closeted. The coming out of gay and lesbian Oscar-winning actors, talk-show hosts, soap-opera stars, pop-music heartthrobs, and politicians—people in various walks of life who are respected, loved, and admired—would make a world of difference in the way our society views gays and the way gay teens feel about themselves.

While a guest on *Larry King Live*, Liz Smith, the famed gossip columnist, made a telling observation about closeted celebrities. In a discussion of "blind items"(the items a columnist prints without revealing names, as in, "What dancer is dating what famous movie director?"), Smith said she had written only one blind item in her career, and she regretted it. It was an item about the pending coming-out of a "talk-show host," which she said she had gotten virtually from the horse's mouth. She ran it as a blind item and received *nine* telephone calls, all from different talk-show hosts. They all believed the item was about them and insisted they were *not* coming out.[22]

The gay community gives a free pass of silence to those who, by their very existence, could counter the most ugly of the homophobic rhetoric that contributes to the isolation gay teens feel. This in turn leads the gay establishment to try to impose silence on anyone who dissents with its view about homosexuality *because those words can't be countered by people who have chosen to remain hidden.*

If the gay establishment truly feels harmed by someone uttering the word "deviant," wouldn't the impact of the word be lessened if one of America's sweethearts—someone loved by people on both coasts and in Middle America—came out and said, "Hey, I'm gay. You make the call whether or not I'm deviant." If, as GLAAD claims, one comment by a talk-show host can "dehumanize" gay people, then perhaps it should redirect the energy it spends trying to stifle such comments into convincing our closeted cultural heroes to come out and actually speak up.

Would coming out of the closet jeopardize careers or alter personal life paths? Absolutely. If we truly believe what we say, however, it should be a price worth paying—certainly a lower price than erasing the First Amendment. My career has certainly been different because I'm out—just as my position with the establishment Left and the gay community is different because I "came out" in disagreement with their efforts and tactics. But I prefer to live the truth, speak my mind, and operate with honesty.

The Misery Merchants

How the Black Civil-Rights Establishment Has Betrayed the Dream

"Since [the totalitarians] do not actually believe in the factual existence of a world conspiracy against them, but use it only as an organizational device, they fail to understand that their own conspiracy may eventually provoke the whole world into uniting against them."

—*Hannah Arendt*, The Origins of Totalitarianism

On November 28, 1987, a 15-year-old girl named Tawana Brawley, who had been missing for four days, was found not far from her home in Dutchess County, New York, by residents of her family's former apartment complex. She was lying in a fetal position in a plastic trash bag, and her body was covered with dog feces and racial slurs written in charcoal. Brawley, who is black, claimed to have been abducted and raped by six white law-enforcement officers, including Dutchess County Assistant District Attorney Steven Pagones.

Three black agitators based in New York City— C. Vernon Mason, Alton Maddox, and the Reverend Al Sharpton—quickly offered their services as advisors to the Brawley family. In the months that followed, they appeared on television show after television show calling the six officers racist rapists.[1] Tawana Brawley herself became the poster child for the victims of racism. Convicted rapist Mike Tyson visited her and gave her his expensive watch. She rubbed shoulders with fight promoter and convicted killer Don King.

What the people in the black community didn't seem to question was the plausibility of a claim that six law-enforcement officers, including police and an assistant district attorney, were capable of doing this. But, of course, in a community that has been conditioned to believe the worst of white people and of their own hopeless situation, anything is possible.

Well, perhaps not quite anything. Less than a year later, in a 170-page report, a grand jury declared Tawana Brawley's story a hoax and specifically exonerated Pagones.[2] Apparently, Tawana had been out late and was afraid to return home, so she concocted the story of being raped by white law-enforcement racists.

Even after the grand-jury report came out, though, Al Sharpton gave another interview, this time to *Spin* magazine, in which he said: "I know Steven Pagones raped Tawana."[3] This was too much for Pagones, who sued all three "advisors" for defamation. He eventually won a judgment of $345,000, but it took another nine years, during which his name was repeatedly dragged through the mud. In fact, the three advisors made increasingly out-rageous statements, not only about Pagones but also about others who were involved in the Brawley investigation. Maddox accused state Attorney General Robert Adams, a special prosecutor in the case, of masturbating over photos of Brawley; Sharpton compared Adams, a Jew, with Adolf Hitler; and the three linked then-governor Mario Cuomo to organized crime and the Ku Klux Klan.[4]

Aside from the damaged reputations, the real tragedy of this sordid episode is that no one in the black community questioned the veracity of Tawana Brawley's story or the claims by Sharpton et al. that her "rape" was one battle in a larger race war. No one stood up to disavow the ugly slanders against whites in general and the six officers in particular. Brawley's family and supporters instead bought into the groupthink mentality and sank further into the swamp of victimhood.

The Victim Industry

What started as a struggle for equal rights and a more color-blind society has turned into a major industry—the victim industry. Like the rest of the Left establishment, today's black civil-rights establishment—the Misery Merchants, as I call them—work to propagate divisions and hopelessness, with the single goal of holding onto the money, power, and prestige that come from leading the supposedly downtrodden.

As in every other power elite, relatively few individuals are running the show. The Misery Merchant vanguard consists of Jesse Jackson of the Rainbow/PUSH Coalition, Julian Bond and Kweisi Mfume of the NAACP,

Congresswoman Maxine Waters of the Congressional Black Caucus, Louis Farrakhan of the Nation of Islam, and, of course, the ever resourceful Al Sharpton.

Their positions rely on a series of myths that relegate those they lead to perpetual victimhood: the myth of rampant racism, the myth of hate crimes, the myth of a conspiracy among whites to keep blacks down. The Misery Merchants tell us, for example, that most blacks are poor. In fact, only one in four black families is poor, and only one in five lives in an inner city.[5] They tell us that there has been an "epidemic" of racist arson against black churches. In fact, there are seven times as many white churches burned *every year* as there were black churches burned during the seven years from 1990 through 1996. By spreading myths such as these, the Misery Merchants do not encourage success among their constituents; they only deepen the sense of misery. They are working 24/7 to make sure that their version of life, one of divisions and hatred, becomes your reality.

> **What started as a struggle for equal rights and a more color-blind society has turned into a major industry—the victim industry.**

John H. McWhorter, the black author of *Losing the Race: Self-Sabotage in Black America*, observes that the perpetuation of these myths is doing more today than racism is to obstruct black achievement in this country. As McWhorter puts it, the America of the Misery Merchants "remains a racist purgatory in which all black effort is a Sisyphean affair that renders even just keeping one's head above water a victory."

Ironically, those whom the Misery Merchants say they represent see a different America. According to most polls, the primary concerns of the average black person are the concerns of all of us: poor schools, unaffordable health care, crime, and the unsettled economy. In fact, in one poll, when blacks were asked, "What do you think is the single most important problem facing the country today?" "racism" came in eleventh of 12 issues named, behind the nation's "moral crisis" and "gun control" and surpassing only "world affairs."[6]

Lessons of the Past

Hannah Arendt (1906–1975), the German-born American political scientist and philosopher, is best known for her critical writing on Jewish affairs and for her study of totalitarianism. In her legendary book *The Origins of Totalitarianism* (which provided the epigraph to this chapter), Arendt traces the rise of totalitarianism in both Hitler's Germany and Stalin's Russia and points out its application as a distinctive pursuit of raw political power, to the neglect of material or utilitarian considerations. Arendt's analysis of totalitarianism is useful not only in looking back at the Hitler and Stalin eras but also, unfortunately, in looking at the efforts of Thought Control in the United States today.

An understanding of Arendt's caution about the use of victimization as an organizational tool would greatly benefit today's black "civil rights" power elite. The "power of organization," she writes, can do only so much for so long; oppressing people into retreat, enslaving thoughts and minds, and repressing the individual ultimately cannot cover up the emptiness—the lack of the "power of substance"—at the core of efforts toward raw power.

> Today's Misery Merchants do an incredible injustice to the thousands of community activists who are working through their church and community organizations to improve the quality of life in their families and neighborhoods.

Ironically, it is the legacy of the genuine civil-rights movement in the sixties—the monumental work to end segregation and enfranchise millions of black voters—that now works to lead American blacks into a pit of desolation and victimhood. Today's Misery Merchants, the heirs to the original civil-rights movement, do an incredible injustice to the thousands of community activists who are working through their church and community organizations to improve the quality of life in their families and neighborhoods.

Doublespeak

During the annual NAACP meeting in February 2001, Kweisi Mfume, the president of the NAACP, said of the Republican Party, "Our desire is not to embarrass them but rather to open doors." Funny, because at the same meeting, Julian Bond, the chair of the NAACP's board of directors, gave a description of the new administration's personnel choices that could only lead President Bush, if he is wise, to keep the door closed tight:

They selected nominees from the Taliban wing of American politics, appeased the wretched appetites of the extreme right wing, and chose cabinet officials whose devotion to the Confederacy is nearly canine in its uncritical affection.[7]

Enter House Majority Leader Dick Armey. There is not much Mr. Armey and I would agree on when it comes to social issues, but I must tip my hat to him for his response to Bond's bombastic statement. After hearing about the comments, Armey wrote to Mfume: "I believe there is a phenomenon in American politics today that would justly be called 'racial McCarthyism' or 'reverse race-baiting' . . . In my opinion it has become an all-too-common practice to spread unfounded, racially charged falsehoods against Republicans for political advantage."[8] Armey then wrote that he would be glad to meet with Mfume to discuss real issues.

Mfume's response? An NAACP spokesman explained, "Mr. Mfume objects to the mention in the letter about racial McCarthyism. We just haven't done that. . . . The NAACP has never been divisive. . . . We have members of all races . . . we have a Jewish rabbi board member."[9]

"Wretched appetites" . . . "extreme right wing" . . . "devotion to the Confederacy" . . . "nearly canine" . . . But my favorite is "the Taliban wing of American politics." Associating someone with the Taliban is not a nice thing to do. The Taliban is the fundamentalist Islamic sect in Afghanistan that has condemned women, girls, and non-Muslims to lives of isolation, oppression, and violence. The Taliban has ordered Hindus and Sikhs to wear yellow as a mark of religious identity (sound familiar?), and women and girls are not allowed to attend school or even emerge from the home unless they are accompanied by a male relative and are covered in the *burqa*, a stifling full-body and face shroud. Women who remove the head covering of the *burqa* for a moment to breathe have been beaten in the streets by the Taliban Morality Police.[10]

As of this writing, a meeting has yet to be set between the "never-been-divisive" NAACP and Representative Armey's office.

The Exclusion Illusion

Remarkably omnipresent, Jesse Jackson manages to appear at every black disfranchisement-of-the-month event, spouting his rhymed incitements to racial tensions where none originally existed. In 1999, harrumphing about the "inclusion illusion," Jackson was attempting to bully his way into Silicon Valley. As he and his cohorts tried to intimidate companies there into race-conscious hiring practices,[11] T. J. Rodgers, the CEO of Cypress Semiconductor, Jackson's main target, refreshingly pointed out that the emperor had no clothes. Speaking to a local television station, Rodgers said, "To me, Jackson makes a living on dividing people."

John Templeton of the Coalition for Fair Employment, an ally of Jackson's, responded in classic Thought Police fashion: "We can now officially describe Cypress Semiconductor as a white supremacist hate group."[12]

The irony is that Cypress is actually one of Silicon Valley's more diverse companies. The *San Jose Mercury*

News reported that more than one-third of Cypress employees in the United States are minorities, including 42 percent of the company's senior vice presidents. In this case, Jackson's attempt to paint the reality of inclusion as an illusion failed, but only because of the courage of both Rodgers and the *Mercury News*.

Show Me the Money: Part II

The betrayal of the black community by self-appointed "leaders" who depict it as inept and perpetually helpless has excited the wrath of some genuine civil-rights leaders. Steve Taylor, the publisher of a regional black newspaper, the *Kankakee City News* in Illinois, recently wrote an editorial accusing Jackson of playing the race card to make himself one of the wealthiest black ministers in the nation.[13] And in Los Angeles, a protest demonstration was held *against* the veteran protestor. On the lawn of the Federal Building on Wilshire Boulevard, protestors waved signs that included "Show Me the $$"—a shot at Jackson's practice of hiring himself out to causes that need the media attention celebrities can command.[14] What? You thought that Jackson appeared at hot spots because it was simply the right thing to do?

The *New Times*, a progressive newsweekly in Los Angeles, reported on the demonstration:

> "We are here to show the contrast between Jesse Jackson and Martin Luther King," said [Reverend Jesse Lee] Peterson. "Martin Luther King wanted to bring people together. Jesse Jackson's message is to divide

and conquer. Martin Luther King said it was a man's character, not color, that mattered. Jesse Jackson's message is that color, not character, matters."[15]

Real activists, like Reverend Peterson, president and CEO of the Los Angeles–based B.O.N.D. (Brotherhood Organization of a New Destiny), are mostly local community activists addressing the problems that need to be addressed. In touch with the real lives of their constituents, they work in relative obscurity because they're actually trying to make a difference, not to become famous or make a buck on the real or imagined misery in people's lives. Jesse Jackson, however, has no qualms about making a buck (or, indeed, hundreds of thousands of them) in his tireless efforts to bring "justice" to our society.

For decades, Jackson—the man who portrays himself, and is widely accepted, as carrying on the work of Martin Luther King Jr.—has picketed and prayed and negotiated on behalf of bus drivers, coal miners, and steelworkers tangled in disputes with their corporate bosses. According to Gary Massoni, the development director for Jackson's Rainbow/ PUSH Coalition, this is how it works: "When Rev. Jackson meets with union leaders he says, 'I've been involved in labor rights. I've got three things I want you to do.'" The three things, according to Massoni, are to put "someone on the staff payroll," to take part in Jackson's conferences and events, and to make a "cash contribution."[16]

According to an investigative report published by the *Chicago Tribune*, the extent of union donations to Jackson's organizations goes way beyond "someone on the staff payroll." According to the *Tribune*, the unions wind up paying for the salary and benefit packages for some of

Jackson's employees. The *Tribune* reported that among the Jackson staffers who benefited from this sort of arrangement with a union of hotel and restaurant workers was Karin Stanford, Jackson's former employee recently revealed as his mistress and the mother of his out-of-wedlock child.[17]

Consider Jesse Jackson's appearance in Los Angeles in 2000, playing the role of "mediator" in the strike by the United Transportation Union (UTU) against the Metropolitan Transit Authority (MTA). Both the *Los Angeles Daily News* and the *New Times* reported that the UTU paid Jackson $100,000 for his help in negotiating an end to the strike.[18] One of Jackson's lawyers immediately shot off a letter demanding a retraction. "Jesse Jackson was not paid one cent by the United Transportation Union," the attorney wrote. The *New Times* quoted this statement in a subsequent retraction of the story. The retraction story also included a statement by Tracy K. Rice, Los Angeles bureau chief for Jackson's organization: "Reverend Jackson was never offered, nor would he have accepted, any money for his role as mediator of the Los Angeles bus strike negotiations."[19]

Could these categorical denials consist of nothing more than semantics? Here is what is on the record. While the bus strike was still going on, Los Angeles County Supervisor Michael D. Antonovich stated to the *Los Angeles Daily News*, "Right now, the union is spending about $30,000 to bring Rev. Jesse Jackson to give a speech."[20] The *Los Angeles Times* reported, "With union leaders agreeing to cover the expenses of Jackson and his staff, his intervention began in earnest."[21] The $100,000 figure in the *New Times* and *Daily News* may have been exaggerated, but it seems that the union paid quite a lot more than the cost of a round-trip ticket.

Meanwhile, Jackson continues to decline to state how much he collects from all unions each year. "It's none of your business," Jackson told a reporter. He also declined to describe how he solicits union funds. "I'm not getting into that," he said. "I just ask them to help us."[22]

Show Me the Financial Disclosure

Jackson is not shy about his infatuation with money. He recently co-authored with his son an aptly titled financial advice book, *It's About the Money!: How to Build Wealth, Get Access to Capital and Achieve Your Financial Dreams.* Jesse Sr. should know. After all, where does a 59-year-old activist get the money to pay for three homes, first-class travel, and $3,000 a month in child-support payments to a former mistress?[23] But Jackson has never been too concerned about the source of his income; the most striking example is him allowing PUSH to accept $10,000 from Libyan dictator Muammar Gadhafi in 1979.[24]

The serious money, though, comes not from foreign dictators but from good American capitalists who are not willing to stand up to Jackson the way Cypress Semiconductor was. According to the *Washington Times*, Jackson's Citizenship Education Fund (CEF), a tax-exempt nonprofit, has received over the last few years nearly $44 million in pledges from SBC-Ameritech, AT&T, Viacom, GTE, and Bell Atlantic.

The activities of the CEF have drawn the attention of the National Legal and Policy Center (NLPC), which has filed a formal complaint with the IRS asking for an investigation of the nonprofit for alleged violations of tax law. The complaint also suggests that Jackson has used the CEF for "private inurement, or personal enrichment."[25] *National Review* reports that Jackson "has lobbied for Viacom to sell UPN [United Paramount Network] to Inner City Broadcasting, whose board includes Jackson's wife and whose head sits on CEF's board."[26]

Rubbing Salt into the Wound

During my feminist activist days, one of the most appalling statements that I heard uttered by respected feminists was that we "must rub salt into the wound" if we are to make any progress. "Rubbing salt into the wound" means maintaining the pain of your constituency. It can take many forms, but primarily the strategy involves twisting any and every event under the rubric of human relations into an assault on women, blacks, gays, or whatever group is your bread and butter. If the events of the day provide a real example of bias, they must be exploited—and if they don't, then an appropriate incident must be invented to remind your constituents of their victimhood.

No one rubs salt into the wound better than Jesse Jackson. On September 17, 1999, during a football game at a high school in Decatur, Illinois, a fight broke out among some fans in the bleachers. School officials expelled several students for taking part in the fighting.

Jesse Jackson immediately rushed to Decatur, a blue-collar town that boasts about its agriculture, its Fortune 500 companies, and the fact that Lincoln once practiced law there. Recognizing that it would be difficult for even him to paint the school's action as racist—even though all the students expelled were black—Jackson admitted that it wasn't about race but, in his words, about "fairness."[27] Nonetheless, his protests involved marches with thousands of people singing "We Shall Overcome," reminiscent of the civil-rights marches of the sixties. During Jackson's stay in Decatur, racial tensions grew to such a degree that school officials, fearing violence, closed three high schools for several days.[28]

> If the events of the day provide a real example of bias, they must be exploited—and if they don't, then an appropriate incident must be invented to remind your constituents of their victimhood.

This was the ultimate display of cynicism by a "civil-rights" leader so desperate to rub salt into the wound that he embraced a group of young men who cracked skulls at a football game. Jackson did not deny that the fight occurred or that the young men he was supporting were involved. Why, then, did he elevate the incident into an issue worthy of a civil-rights march? "It is an ugly fight at a ball game with no blood, no guns, no gunshots, no stabbings," Jackson explained. "Not as brutal as a hockey fight or NBA fight."[29] That, apparently, is the new standard for a civil-rights project.

Is this really how black Americans perceive their struggle—championing young men who represent what *not* to become? I certainly don't think so. But in a world where the specter of actual racism is fading, this tactic accomplishes two things. First, with national news coverage, it reinforces in blacks the idea that they are under attack; second, it tells whites that their racism is raging. It rubbed salt into both wounds, wounds that, if left alone, might be able to heal.

An episode like this shines light on why it is so important to the new Thought Police that people not feel comfortable discussing these matters. What was the politically correct thing to say if someone asked you about this incident? Well, you certainly knew what you *couldn't* say— that the kids deserved to be expelled. That would have indicated that you were "insensitive" to the "plight" of young black men. Perhaps you even think this about yourself. The speech code is so ingrained in our psyches that we tend to accuse *ourselves* if something crosses our minds that seems "wrong." But if we all talked honestly about such an event, each of us might just find out that we are not alone in our opinion, and we might conclude that we're not racists after all.

The Big Lie About the L.A. Riots

"[The broad masses] more readily fall victims to the big lie than the small lie." Intentionally distorting the truth for political gain was what Hitler had in mind when he defined the Big Lie in *Mein Kampf.* He reasoned that ordinary people, who often tell small lies in small matters, could not imagine someone telling massive falsehoods. Like the Tawana Brawley rape hoax, the 1992 Los Angeles riot was used by various Misery Merchants to reinforce a false view of reality—one of racism run amuck and a black community on the edge of justifiable revolution.

On April 29, 1992, four officers of the Los Angeles Police Department were acquitted of charges stemming from the beating of Rodney King. The rest is history. But whose history?

In the aftermath of those verdicts, Congresswoman Maxine Waters dubbed the riots a "rebellion." Other politicians and media commentators went along, pushing the idea that the riots were an act of righteous defiance by the victimized whole of blacks in Los Angeles against a corrupt justice system that had made their lives a living hell. "Injustice" was what propelled all those black people into an "uprising," burning down their neighborhoods, assaulting anyone who had the bad luck to be at the wrong intersection at the wrong time, and looting to make up for all that this vicious, racist society had denied them. You know this image—it has been seared in your mind so that you recall it whenever you think of Los Angeles. And yet it is the Big Lie. Here are the facts.

After the verdicts, Los Angeles was generally calm, with the exception of some not-so-unusual behavior by thugs in South Central Los Angeles. When white truck driver Reginald Denny was pulled out of his truck and beaten nearly to death, it was not by a random group of young black men. The assailants, caught on film by a local television crew, included known gang members. What we also saw was Denny being saved by other blacks in the community who were driving by or who saw the assault on television and heroically rushed to the scene. Those individuals are the true representatives of the black community in Los Angeles—not the gang members who make misery in all neighborhoods and whom the majority of Angelenos, black and white together, despise.

This is not merely my subjective impression. A RAND Corporation analysis a few months after the riot stated: "This was clearly not a black riot."[30] The celebrated think tank, which is based in Santa Monica, California, analyzed 5,000 court cases and found that 51 percent of the defendants were Latino. Only 36 percent were black, and 11 percent were Anglo. Yes, 11 out of every 100 arrested were white thugs participating in this fantasy "black uprising." Those arrested were mostly young men, RAND reported: "the biggest single group of eventual offenders were Latino men from 18 to 24 years old." Curfew violations and other "civil disturbance" offenses outnumbered arrests for looting.[31]

I'm a native Angeleno, and I remember the riot quite well. At the time, in addition to being president of Los Angeles NOW, I was working at a public relations firm. The day the Rodney King verdicts were expected, everyone in my office was glued to the television, our tension fanned by the news media and by the Misery Merchant alarmists warning that the city was "going to burn down" if the verdicts were "wrong."

As events unfolded, the opportunistic thuggery perpetrated on Denny and its airing on television sent a message to others. The newscasters repeatedly announced that there was no police response to the Denny assault, giving further encouragement to anyone who wanted to walk into the nearest Target store for a free TV.

Arriving home from work, as my local Taco Bell was burning down and my Big 5 Sporting Goods store was being shot at and looted, I noticed that most of the news footage of the mayhem was of Latinos. The expectation and the actual reporting of blacks trashing the city were simply wrong. As I began to shut my windows to keep out the ashes from the fires, my next-door neighbors (who are black) asked me if I'd like to come over and share their Ben & Jerry's (comfort food!). As we watched the riot coverage, the only difference from our normal soirees was our .38 Smith & Wessons on the table next to the ice cream in the event a hooligan thought it would be a good idea to come into the house.

Noncombatants in the Race War

The 1992 riot was the work of small-time hoodlums and thugs who took advantage of the Misery Merchants' race-war rhetoric. The vast majority of blacks in Los Angeles, ranging from single-mom families to the traditional nuclear family, were hunkered down at home, waiting like everyone else for the looting and violence to end. A *Los Angeles Times* poll taken a few days after the riot confirmed that a majority of African Americans—58 percent—condemned the rioting. The *Times* reported that almost half the blacks surveyed did not think the violence was inevitable, a view shared by the majority of city residents overall.[32] This is certainly not the picture of a city where a race war was looming.

Some black commentators were the most insightful about the media's portrayal of the riot. Thomas Sowell, a Hoover Institution scholar, made this comment in his newspaper column:

"It is bad enough when genuine racial polarization exists. It is unconscionable for the media to create it by depicting the actions of hoodlums, thugs and looters as representing either the actions or the views of the black community."[33]

Further evidence of how different reality is from the version the media and the chest-pounding black power elite presented to us is revealed in a 1997 national survey by the Joint Center for Political and Economic Studies, the nation's premier black think tank. One of the questions had to do with the political ideology of the respondents. The Joint Center's findings indicate that blacks are evenly divided (32 percent each) among self-described liberals, moderates, and conservatives.[34] In other words, 64 percent of the black community identify themselves as moderate to conservative. The Misery Merchants' depiction of the average black person as beholden to the Jacksons or Waterses of this world could not be further from the truth.

The black economist and social theorist Walter E. Williams sums it up best:

"The black leaders say one thing, and the people say something else. Black people have more in common with Jerry Falwell, while black leaders like Jesse Jackson and Maxine Waters have more in common with white hippies."[35]

Thought-Policing the Police

Now that we've seen how the public accepts the distortion of truth on a massive scale, let me mention one group that is particularly resistant to political correctness and mind control: the police. They can't afford to ignore reality—for them it's a matter of life and death.

Hence the Misery Merchants' latest mediagenic issue: racial profiling, commonly described as police stopping motorists solely on the basis of race. On the face of it, the practice of racial profiling does sound discriminatory. Why should the police even take the color of someone's skin into account?

Unfortunately, the crime statistics speak for themselves. According to the Justice Department, state correction bureaus, and the Census Bureau, 14 percent of black males are convicted felons.[36] Although African American men constitute only six per cent of the overall population, they account for roughly 40 percent of the country's violent crimes.[37]

Given these facts, it is more than appropriate for police officers on patrol to rely upon racial characteristics in predicting and seeking to prevent criminal activity. As the Eighth Circuit Court of Appeals noted in *United States v. Weaver*, "Facts are not to be ignored simply because they may be unpleasant . . . we [must] take the facts as they are presented to us, not as we would wish them to be."[38]

The Thought Police aren't buying it. Their solution to the disturbing arrest statistics is that we pretend the numbers mean something else. My favorite example of the Let's Pretend theory comes out of New Jersey. Besieged by Misery Merchant complaints of racial profiling, Peter Verniero, the then state attorney general, commissioned a report. Titled "Interim Report of the State Police Review Team Regarding Allegations of Racial Profiling," this document tells us, for example, that even though arrest and conviction statistics tell us it is primarily minorities who are involved in the drug trade, that's not because white people aren't selling drugs—it's just that they don't get arrested. Why? Because the white people selling crack are *doing it in their homes.*

Here is how Verniero's fable—er, report—put it:

> The vast majority of drug sales, for example, are accomplished in private or otherwise out of law enforcement's view and, thus, never lead to an arrest, prosecution, or conviction . . . It follows, therefore, that the fact that a disproportionate percentage of drug arrests are of minorities does not mean that any particular minority citizen is more likely than a non-minority citizen to be committing a drug offense. Minorities are disproportionately arrested for selling drugs largely because urban drug dealers tend to operate in open-air drug markets, making them far easier to identify and arrest than their colleagues who are operating more discreetly behind closed doors in suburban and rural jurisdictions.[39]

First of all, I—like you, no doubt—would like to know how Verniero knows that the vast majority of drug sales are occurring "in private or otherwise out of law enforcement's view," when in the very next clause he admits that there are no arrests, prosecutions, or convictions to prove his point.

Verniero also ignores the central role gangs play in the sale of drugs. After all, it's how they make their money. According to the report "Youth Gang Drug Trafficking," issued by the Office of Juvenile Justice and Delinquency Prevention (OJJDP) of the U.S. Department of Justice, two-thirds of local law-enforcement agencies report that

70 percent of drug sales involved gang members. Forty-one percent actually reported that gang members controlled *all* the drug sales in their jurisdiction. The report further states that "Caucasian and Hispanic gang members were significantly more prevalent in jurisdictions with *low* levels of gang member involvement in drug sales (0–33 percent) and that African American gang members were significantly more prevalent in jurisdictions with high levels of gang member involvement in drug sales (67–100 percent)."[40]

What could then–Attorney General Verniero have been thinking? Exactly what the Thought Police wanted him to think.

The OJJDP also reports that there are an estimated 29,000 gangs in the United States, with a combined membership of more than three-quarters of a million adults and juveniles.[41] The racial composition of these gangs is as follows: 46 percent Hispanic, 34 percent black, 12 percent white, 6 percent Asian, and 2 percent "other."[42] In other words, a stunning 80 percent of the gangs in this country are either black or Hispanic. Perhaps these groups represent such a high percentage of those arrested for trafficking in drugs not because some vast underworld

> **Perhaps these groups represent such a high percentage of those arrested for trafficking in drugs not because some vast underworld of white pushers operating out of their comfy homes in the suburbs are being ignored by the police, but because the gangs that control most of this country's drug trade are made up so heavily of blacks and Hispanics.**

of white pushers operating out of their comfy homes in the suburbs are being ignored by the police, but because the gangs that control most of this country's drug trade are made up so heavily of blacks and Hispanics.

What Were You Thinking?

As one would expect, the solutions offered by the opponents of racial profiling are downright Orwellian. These solutions center on documenting and controlling what police officers *think* when they're performing their duties.

In 1999, California Governor Gray Davis vetoed a bill that, somehow, was supposed to determine whether or not "racism" dictated who police stopped. The bill would have required police officers to record the apparent ethnicity of every motorist they stop. The officers would presumably not have asked the racial background of the motorists but would instead have relied on their own visual determination. Of course, the effort here is to suggest that the simple act of pulling a person of color over is in itself an act of racism. Even more important, it is an attempt to chill the officers' freedom of thought and control their minds.

In this scenario, all officers would have to report their actions to representatives from the Thought Police (some commission would no doubt be established), who would then determine what the officers were *thinking* when they performed their duty. And we know what the Thought Police, drawn from the NAACP and ACLU, would determine because the results are a foregone conclusion. Those organizations aren't *wondering* if the police are racist, *they already know*. If Governor Davis had signed the bill, officers would have been saddled with the Thought Police on every stop, serving as a constant reminder that they aren't trusted by others, nor can they trust themselves. Sounds familiar, doesn't it?

Although Davis's veto of the California bill was a good thing, the "racial profiling" issue will not go away. In 1999, President Clinton ordered all federal law-enforcement officials to collect information on the race and sex of people they stop. If you aren't convinced about police motives in general, you should at least raise an eyebrow at the federal government collecting information on people who are simply stopped by law enforcement—not arrested, not convicted—just stopped. A centralized collection of information on citizens is a hallmark of Stalinistic societies. It is no surprise that this assault on civil rights, *done in the name of civil rights*, would be demanded by the socialistic Left, with its goal of controlling our culture and our government.

The Magic Invisible Racism

We are a country that fought a civil war to bring an end to slavery, with tens of thousands of young men and, yes, women dying to change things for the better for black Americans. Since that seminal time, the progress this country has made on issues of race is undeniable. Actual racists in this country—the Klan and other white supremacists—are rightly shunned, and by now they are few and far between. Indeed, I believe that the progress made in the acceptance of those who are not in the majority is the greatest accomplishment of the twentieth century.

But if racism is becoming obsolete, how can the Misery Merchants hold onto their privileged positions? They have managed this by concocting the explanation that racism is now in our *subconscious*. We may be unaware of our racism, may even consciously reject it, but, alas, it's still there. In fact, it's stronger than ever. The Confederate slaver in you is hiding in your shadow.

The ultimate in brainwashing isn't getting you to believe that the Los Angeles riot—an external event—was a "black uprising." It's getting you to believe something about yourself that you know to be untrue.

> I believe that the progress made in the acceptance of those who are not in the majority is the greatest accomplishment of the twentieth century.

An op-ed piece in the *Los Angeles Times* by Halford H. Fairchild, a professor of psychology and black studies at Pitzer College in Claremont, California, exemplifies this new strategy. Fairchild tells us of a new phenomenon called "aversion racism." This is a subconscious racism that rears its ugly head in "support for the ideals of equality in human affairs."[43] That's right. You didn't misread it. "Support for the ideals of equality" is now the proof that you are a racist.

This fantasy approach would be funny if it weren't so dangerous—a harbinger of the new line being taken by the Thought Police. It is doubly useful because it not only perpetuates white guilt but also sends a chilling message to blacks. It tells them that even though they may no longer see racism as an issue, it still exists, hidden, in their white friends—disguised as respect, tolerance, and understanding.

Stepping Out of Line

There are so many stories of individuals who are attacked with the weapons of the Thought Police, but the story of Ward Connerly is one that deserves particular attention. It serves as a great example of how far the Misery Merchants are willing to go when someone, especially one of their own (black and/or progressive), steps out of line.

Connerly, a businessman and a regent of the University of California, is the man who led the campaign for passage of California's Proposition 209, to eliminate racial preferences. As a result of his efforts, he has been called a "houseboy," a "paid assassin," and a "freak of nature."[44] Jesse Jackson went so far as to accuse him of promoting "ethnic cleansing."[45]

In discrediting their targets, the Thought Police start by portraying them as one-dimensional paper cutouts existing for the sole purpose of destroying life as the Left likes it. Such a portrait is not a true depiction of any human being, and it certainly isn't true of Ward Connerly. Did you know, for instance, that he is the regent who fought for domestic-partnership benefits for the UC system's employees? For those of you who are liberal and/or gay, that gives Connerly another dimension, doesn't it? But you probably didn't know it before because you weren't told and you probably didn't think to inquire. You were told to hate Ward Connerly because he represents *ethnic cleansing*. You deserve to know the whole story so that you can make up your own mind about the issues and people in the news.

One of the attacks Connerly faced is quite novel. Publicly perceived as a black man but with a heritage that also includes Irish, Indian, and French Canadian, he has been repeatedly accused of trying to be "white." As an example, his black detractors have charged him with shortening his given name of Wardell to Ward because it sounds more "white." In my conversations with Ward(ell), he said he believes this attempt to ridicule and question his self-identity is meant to send a message to other blacks: If you stray from the party line or challenge what the supposed "community" feels is best, the very essence of who you are will be maligned. You will no longer *belong*.

> In discrediting their targets, the Thought Police start by portraying them as one-dimensional paper cutouts existing for the sole purpose of destroying life as the Left likes it.

However, Connerly's detractors didn't confine this charge to private conversation. In 1997, the year after Proposition 209 passed, then–State Senator Diane Watson, a black woman, suggested to Amy Wallace, a reporter for the *Los Angeles Times*, that Connerly's marriage to a white woman was just another indication of his desire to shed his blackness. Although Wallace ended up not using the quote in the story she was writing, she did mention it to Connerly.

Some time later, Connerly, as a UC regent, was invited by then–State Senator Tom Hayden to take part in a panel at a conference on affirmative action in the UC system. Senator Watson, who was also on the panel, arrived late, and when she saw Connerly, she asked loudly, "What is *he* doing here?" She then told Ward that "his kind" would never have been in his position were it not for the blacks in the state legislature. (She was referring to the legislature's confirmation of UC regents. By the way, Ward was confirmed 37–0.) Watson then referred a few more times to "his kind" and "your kind." Connerly, who had managed to maintain his composure throughout the Prop 209 campaign, had finally had enough, and he told the senator that she was a "lightweight" and a "bigot."[46]

The press in the room, not having been privy to Watson's earlier comments to Wallace, asked Connerly what he meant. He told them of her statement regarding interracial marriage, and when some of them spoke to Wallace, she confirmed it.

Still, in the stories that appeared in print and on the air, Connerly was expected to apologize for calling Watson a bigot, whereas nothing was expected of her for demeaning him and his interracial marriage.

What had Connerly done to incite so many vicious and personal responses by the black power elite? He had publicly stated his belief that affirmative action actually harms minorities, reinforcing the patronizing and debilitating concept that "they" can't succeed on their own. In a speech in Washington, D.C., he explained his viewpoint:

> We're not trying to eliminate preferences because we want to take opportunities away from women and minorities. We want to eliminate preferences because we believe doing so is the only way that we can have an America in which its people are aligned. We believe the

American people are fair people and will display their better nature if allowed to do so. . . . We believe the hard-working, high-achieving women and minorities should not have to live under the cloud of affirmative action, and it's an insulting premise that we are incapable of winning in an open competition. We want a better America, and we're convinced that affirmative action, as we know it, is now standing in the way of that objective.[47]

Ethnic cleanser? Paid assassin? Freak of nature? White man? Regardless of what you think about Ward Connerly's opinion on affirmative action, it is difficult to deny that the Thought Police were hard at work on him, and on you in the process.

CHAPTER

5

Not NOW

The Selling-Out of the Feminist Establishment

"The sudden acquisition of power by those who have never had it before can be intoxicating, and we run the risk of becoming absorbed in petty power games with our organization that in the last analysis can only be self-defeating."

—Toni Carabillo, founder of California NOW and of Los Angeles NOW, addressing a California NOW State Conference in 1973

I joined NOW in 1987, but my real activism began the following year. Appalled by the tactics of Operation Rescue (OR), a group of anti-abortion bullies who aimed to block a woman's access to her health care facility, I attended an organizing meeting for pro-choice clinic defenders in Los Angeles, jointly sponsored by Planned Parenthood and NOW. There was a decent turnout at the meeting, but I knew the more publicity the effort had, the better, and so I offered my public relations expertise (which is considerable) pro bono to NOW. I also had money (those were the days!) and wanted to make a sizable donation. I made my offer to the NOW representative and expected to be called. I never was.

Eventually, I attended the clinic defense action on my own. Two years later, I ran for the presidency of the Los Angeles chapter of NOW. Despite my lack of political experience, or perhaps because of it, I wanted to lead the chapter, knowing that I could do a better job than those in power. Seasoned leaders in Los Angeles NOW encouraged me to run, as did new activists like me who had gotten involved via the abortion issue. Everyone was dismayed by how badly L.A. NOW had organized its prochoice activities, and people wanted someone who could breathe new life into the chapter. I ran and won. Frankly, at first I considered my new post as a hobby. That attitude changed very quickly.

Once in office, I asked the representative of California NOW, whom I had met at the pro-choice organizing rally, why she had never called me. She replied that everyone was suspicious of me because I "didn't fit the profile" of someone interested in NOW—I was "professional, smart, aggressive, and offered just way too much." The NOW people determined that I "must have been sent as a spy by Operation Rescue."

I'm sure that when she was telling me this, it didn't occur to her how awful it sounded. By implication, this long-time NOW leader was saying that the organization had grown suspicious of professional and successful women because they just didn't see them any more. I didn't understand it at the time—my political naiveté getting the best of me again—and I would come to realize the importance of that revelation far too late.

I was president of the Los Angeles chapter of NOW from January 1990 to June 1996, and I also served on the National NOW Board of Directors for part of that time. I was 27 when I was elected the local chief and was thrust into a world that was anything but feminist.

Molly Yard's 'Concerns'

I approached my work in NOW with a sense of pragmatism that I had acquired in private business and with the goal of creating a more inclusive membership. I always felt that in order for feminism to work, men had to be brought along and the effort had to be truly nonpartisan. In fact, that's how NOW was presented to me in those early days—as a place where women and men worked together to improve the lives of all women. My first day as president of L.A. NOW, however, was a real eye-opener.

> I always felt that in order for feminism to work, men had to be brought along and the effort had to be truly nonpartisan.

I went to the NOW office that first evening, put the key in the lock, opened the door, and found an office full of Democratic Party workers using the space as though it were Party headquarters. At the time, I was a registered Democrat, but I was still disturbed by this. Not only did it endanger our tax status as a not-for-profit organization, but it also worked against our nonpartisan mission. I put a stop to it immediately.

What I didn't know at the time was that the activism history of National NOW President Molly Yard was in the Democratic Party. To say the least, my banishment of the Democrats from the office was not the kind of calling card Yard had hoped for from the new president of L.A. NOW.

It wasn't long before Yard and I got to know each other, and neither of us liked what we saw. During a trip to Los Angeles, she asked to meet with me to discuss "chapter issues." When we sat down for lunch, one of the first things she said was that National had been "reviewing" the L.A. chapter's membership list and had some "concerns."

When I took over the chapter, membership was at about 1,200. With some successful projects and aggressive outreach, membership was soaring (it would eventually reach 4,000). I couldn't imagine what kind of problem National could have with that, but Yard went on: "There seem to be a lot of men in your chapter. How do you explain that?" The question perplexed me. The thought of doing some kind of gender analysis of my membership was revolting, and I told her so. She then said that I must be doing something that was bringing in people who didn't fit "the profile."

I had run for office with a team that included a man, and there were men in the national office (not many, but they were there). I couldn't believe the real issue was how many men belonged to the chapter. In retrospect, I've suspected that the national officers, with their comfortable internal political positions, were somehow frightened by the increase in activity and the explosive membership growth, and that Yard needed a hook on which to assert her authority. Although clumsily put, the message that came through from Yard was that I must be doing *something* unfeminist. That theme, in one form or another, would be the drill against me for years to come.

Yard then asked me to explain why I threw the Democrats out of my office that first evening. "Democrats," she explained, "are our friends, and that's who we are." She then asked me what political party I was registered with. Although I actually was a Democrat, I refused to answer and told her that I would not run my chapter as though it was some Democratic Party club. I laid it on the line that my feminism was going to be a variety that welcomed men, Republicans, the religious, and anybody else who was feminist, agreed with us on the issues, and wanted to improve the quality of women's lives. My feminism transcends party politics, and so would the L.A. chapter's.

At the end of our lunch, Yard said it seemed to her that I wanted to "injure" NOW. She said that ever since my election, there had been concerns about whether or not I was going to be a "team player," and our current exchange only confirmed her "suspicions." Being a team player apparently meant being an arm of the Democratic Party, laying low, and not enlisting men in the struggle for women's rights.

No More 'Profile'

Although Molly Yard did not mention it at our lunch, the chapter's first project under my direction (which I detail in chapter 9) was a highly successful action against the book

American Psycho. Protesting the content of a book that sexualized violence against women, the project attracted national and international attention and generated scores of stories on violence against women and on women's image in the media.

One would have thought that National would have welcomed the widespread attention and the accompanying interest in NOW. It didn't. A few months after that meeting with Yard, and while the *American Psycho* campaign was still going on, the National NOW board of directors discussed a resolution titled, "Who Speaks for NOW?" A friendly board member confided to me that it had actually been nicknamed the "Gag Tammy Bruce" resolution. Although not passed, it was NOW's first official attempt to silence me.

Meanwhile, the activism and the true feminist theory that the chapter developed and promoted under my leadership were building it into the largest NOW chapter in the nation. We were attracting a whole new spectrum of people that included men, people of color, rich, and poor. Suddenly, there was no "profile" of a member, and Los Angeles NOW was regularly in the news, maintaining public awareness on issues of concern to women.

> This road ultimately, and most humiliatingly, led them to become apologists for a president who sexually harassed an underling and water carriers for the black power elite who continue to use the politics of race to condemn both black and white women to second-class citizenship.

NOW's leaders, however, were on a different road. This road ultimately, and most humiliatingly, led them to become apologists for a president who sexually harassed an underling and water carriers for the black power elite who continue to use the politics of race to condemn both black and white women to second-class citizenship. Clearly, today's feminist leaders are more concerned with pursuing a socialist agenda than with helping women achieve equality.

The Hijacking of Feminism

As a feminist who seeks to act on her principles, I believe that women, and the men and children who love and count on them, deserve nothing less than an effort concentrated on improving the quality of women's lives. In all its simplicity, this is the most basic of feminist ideals—but it is not the ideal of today's alleged feminist leaders. Do not be mistaken: what Gloria Steinem, Molly Yard, Patricia Ireland and all the rest have presented to you over the last 15 years (at least) has not been feminist theory.

Betty Friedan, a former Communist Party member, was only the precursor of the hijacking of feminism to serve other political interests. Some consider Gloria Steinem, the founder of *Ms.* magazine and probably the second most influential feminist leader, after Friedan, of the last 30 years, to be the one who began blurring the lines between gender and race issues. This might be surprising to those who are unaware of Steinem's involvement in socialist politics. In fact, she serves as an honorary chair of the Democratic Socialists of America, which boasts of being the largest socialist organization in the United States and is the principal U.S. affiliate of the Socialist International.[1] Good for her, but we should know this as we explore what factors influence those who are considered feminist leaders.

Steinem's influence, combined with the socialist sympathies of NOW's immediate past-president, Patricia Ireland, explain the co-opting of NOW by leftist ideologues. A 1996 article in *Ms.* quoted Ireland as saying that NOW "must offer a clear understanding of what it means to be a feminist organization *concerned with ending discrimination based on race, class, and other issues of oppression* [emphasis mine] that come from a patriarchal structure." Steinem then commented, "To be feminist, we have to take on the entire caste system."[2]

Ireland details her support of the Communist Party in her autobiography, *What Women Want.* She admits that her socialist sympathies and participation in pro-Communist rallies in Miami (of all places!) were due in part to the fact that her friend and future lover, Pat Silverthorn, was an activist in the Socialist Worker's Party.[3] There were problems, Ireland explains, with Silverthorn and her friends being Communists in Miami. "Later, after we'd become close," Ireland writes, "[Pat Silverthorn] would confide that she, too, had wondered how much more dangerous she'd made her life by openly professing communist convictions in that volatile, violent, commie-hating city. . . . Working closely with Pat opened my eyes about the reality of living as a political leftist in this country."[4]

I met Silverthorn on a couple of occasions. I liked her. She and Patricia seemed very happy together. My complaint here is not with someone being a Communist or a

Socialist—just don't do it in NOW. NOW has a responsibility to all women. When you insert a political ideology that shuts out the vast majority of the women, men, and children who support authentic feminism in this country, you do the theory, and NOW, a fatal disservice.

NOW's problems are far more complex than this, however. I wish that I could ascribe the slide away from Feminist NOW and into Socialist NOW purely to ideological agendas, but I can't. To differ ideologically from what I consider authentic feminism would require a different feminist vision. But in that respect, NOW's recent leaders—specifically, Molly Yard and Patricia Ireland—have been empty vessels. Inclined toward socialism and lacking in vision, Ireland became Jesse Jackson's Charlie McCarthy. Yes, she is able to tell anecdotes about the accomplishments of NOW, but she imparts those stories as an observer. In her autobiography, she writes of the battle for the Equal Rights Amendment (Eleanor Smeal's work), legal success on abortion rights with the *NOW v. Scheidler* case (Smeal's initiative, litigated by Faye Clayton of the Chicago law firm Robinson, Curley & Clayton), and success on the domestic-violence front during the O. J. Simpson case (my work). When it came to Ireland's own leadership initiative, it seemed that her main effort was to keep NOW from going under on her watch.

The Good, the Bad, and the 'Insensitive'

At no time was the allegiance of the feminist establishment clearer than in the O. J. Simpson case. During the trial, which lasted from January to October 1995, domestic violence became a dominant theme of the media coverage. Photographs of Nicole Brown Simpson's bruised face and recordings of her desperate 911 calls horrified the nation. But they apparently did not horrify National NOW. The silence from the feminist establishment was deafening.

One of the very few to speak up was Brenda Feigen. Feigen had served as national vice president of NOW from 1970 to 1972. In the early 1970s, she had, with Gloria Steinem, co-founded *Ms.* magazine and the National Women's Political Caucus. She exemplifies what the movement had been, with all its promise and enthusiasm. Fulfilling her potential, she became the kind of woman the movement could not keep up with. A lawyer, wife and mother, civil-rights activist, politician, Hollywood movie producer, and author, she is a feminist in the true sense of the word. Despite her ongoing friendship with Steinem, she has had the courage to challenge the increasingly unfeminist women's movement.

In her memoir, *Not One of the Boys*, Brenda Feigen had this to say regarding the concerns of purported feminist leadership in the Simpson case: ". . . after the verdict, some feminists actually seemed more concerned about issues of caste systems and race than about issues that specifically affected women, such as domestic violence. Certainly a paralysis had been created, so that feminists who would normally have taken to the streets in angry demonstrations against the verdict stayed home, quiet."[5]

Well, not every feminist. During the Simpson criminal trial and after the not-guilty verdict, I organized rallies and a march attracting over 5,000 people. The goal was to channel the frustration most people felt at an obviously unjust verdict into something constructive: keeping domestic violence and its victims in the spotlight. Three women in the United States die every day at the hands of a boyfriend, ex-husband, or husband.[6] I was determined that their plight not be eclipsed by Johnnie Cochran's false and exploitative racist rhetoric. As the brilliant feminist critic Andrea Dworkin notes in *Scapegoat: The Jews, Israel, and Women's Liberation:* "Cruelty inside the home, where women and children live, of course has no ethnicity, race or class."[7]

> **Three women in the United States die every day at the hands of a boyfriend, ex-husband, or husband. I was determined that their plight not be eclipsed by Johnnie Cochran's false and exploitative racist rhetoric.**

December 6, 1995, was the sixth anniversary of the murder of 14 women at the Ecole Polytechnique in Montreal, Canada. On that date in 1989, a man carrying automatic weapons entered an engineering class, screamed, "I'm going to kill all the feminists," and then opened fire. I first learned how Patricia Ireland observed the anniversary when I received a call from a Los Angeles reporter wanting to get my response. I was clueless, and the reporter had to fax me a copy of NOW's press release.

It turned out that Ireland had publicly censured me at a press conference in Washington, D.C., which, according to the press release, NOW had called to "apologize to people of color and to allies on racial justice issues" and to "apologize for national NOW's delay in repudiating racially insensitive statements made by or attributed to local NOW leaders, particularly NOW Los Angeles chapter president

Tammy Bruce."[8] (I was the only one mentioned by name.) I suppose I should be grateful that they only labeled me "racially insensitive" instead of using the favored Thought Police accusation, "racist"—perhaps as a bow to my activist history.

The national office did not call me before the press conference nor ever alert me that there was a problem. Afterward, when I placed calls to every National NOW officer, none of them took my call and none ever called back.

The *New York Times* reported the smear attempt:

> For months Ms. Bruce had been proclaiming loudly her contempt for Mr. Simpson—based on his history of abusing his former wife. . . . The protests have had strong support from many here. . . . Much of the local news coverage of Ms. Bruce has portrayed her as a crusader against social injustice. . . .[9]

The *Times* story included Patricia Ireland's claim that "never before have members been so offended and never before have political alliances been so damaged."

> "I deeply regret," Ms. Ireland said at a Washington news conference, that Ms. Bruce "has made public statements that clearly violate NOW's commitment to stopping racism." What had upset Ms. Ireland and other NOW senior officials were incidents in which they believe Ms. Bruce seemed to dismiss the views of blacks about the Simpson case. "What we need to teach our children," Ms. Bruce said in an interview on ABC's *Nightline* the day after the verdicts, is "not about racism but about violence against women."[10]

Another of Ireland's complaints focused on a comment I had made to the *Los Angeles Times* to the effect that our message about domestic violence was a "needed break from all that talk of racism." Which it was, but conveniently expunged from Ireland's statement was the rest of my comment and its context. As the *Los Angeles Times* had reported it:

> Bruce's anti-domestic violence message has fueled the media with what the 33-year-old women's rights crusader calls "a needed break from all that talk of racism. Ours was a clear position and certainly less contentious. We focused on anti-violence and on the victims." [11]

The Associated Press also reported a comment I made outside NBC's studios during a demonstration. After Simpson had canceled an interview, I said, "The new message to O. J. Simpson is that you're not welcome on our airwaves, you're not welcome in our society, you're not welcome in our culture. This is America's new message about domestic violence." Ireland once again edited my comments—this time excising the last sentence—and complained to the media that what I was saying to Simpson was: "Go back to Africa."

NOW veteran Toni Carabillo wrote about the conflict in *On the Issues*, a progressive women's quarterly: "This unprecedented censure by the national officers and board of NOW seemed to many of us—especially the old-timers—a rush to judgment, a process marred by lack of due process and based on highly ambiguous evidence. . . . Many of us suspected another agenda at work." [12]

Its Own Worst Enemy

NOW issued multiple press releases, one of which referred to the "dispirited, insidious and turbulent effects of the words and deeds of Tammy Bruce."[13] (I know—worthy of Shakespeare!) And yet, during a California NOW PAC meeting after the very public fight began, Ireland admitted to the PAC board that she knew I wouldn't have made some of the comments for which I had been censured. The whole thing became laughable, as Ireland's attacks began to be recognized as an odd kind of overkill.

A major element of the smear campaign was the suggestion that NOW's "alliances" with black civil-rights groups had been damaged. These "alliances" were formed with the intent of combining the strengths of various groups in the fight against racism and sexism. The only problem was that while NOW was working feverishly, like good little women, on the issue of race, none of the black civil-rights "alliance" groups were working on women's issues.

> The only problem was that while NOW was working feverishly, like good little women, on the issue of race, none of the black civil-rights "alliance" groups were working on women's issues.

This came up in a *Time* magazine piece about the battle over the Simpson case, where several prominent NOW members spoke up. "This is just some black leaders in NOW trying to intimidate the white leaders," said Michigan NOW member Tracy Ann Martin. The article also quoted Carabillo: "Is women's rights the priority issue for the NAACP? No, nor should it be.

NOW is losing its focus as the pre-eminent organization for women."[14]

More recently, although the NAACP protested the broadcast networks' discrimination against blacks, it did not speak up against the networks' rampant sexism.[15] Women have been protesting against Time/Warner and Warner Bros. Records because of their promotion of rap music that targets women,[16] but the black power elite has been AWOL on the issue. And, of course, none of us saw the Urban League, the NAACP, Maxine Waters, or Jesse Jackson take a strong position against the horrors of domestic violence during the Simpson debacle.

My experience in NOW serves as an excellent example of what plagues the Left in general. When an organization turns inward, focusing its anger on its own activists, believing the enemy is inside and needs to be purged, that's an indication that it has lost any belief that it can make a difference on the outside.

I had hoped that all this national media exposure would engender a new commitment to actual feminist policies. It did not happen. I resigned as president of Los Angeles NOW in June 1996 when I realized that NOW was too paralyzed by political correctness and groupthink to get done anything of any real consequence regarding women's issues. I was a feminist who wanted to make a positive difference in women's lives. NOW had begun to inflict actual damage.

O. J.'s Girls

The odd concern for Simpson on the part of NOW in particular and the feminist establishment in general exposed how deeply influential the black power elite really is. The "so-called feminist leadership," as Brenda Feigen termed it, had become a virtual satellite of the Misery Merchants. Even the Feminist Majority (FM), an organization founded by Eleanor Smeal in 1987 after she stepped down as president of NOW, was afraid to take on the Simpson apologists.

FM's national coordinator, Katherine Spillar, is the person with whom I worked most closely during the clinic defense efforts in the late 1980s. In fact, Kathy was one of those who encouraged me to run for the presidency of Los Angeles NOW in 1989. I liked her and trusted her.

The co-founding vice president of the Feminist Majority was my mentor, Toni Carabillo. In the sixties, Toni had been a founding member of NOW and the founder of California NOW and of the Los Angeles chapter. She too had encouraged me to run for the chapter presidency. Toni was an extraordinary role model—an example of what true feminism is and how one can remain a decent, thoughtful person even in an organization mired in groupthink and Thought Control.

As feminists, Toni repeatedly told me, *women* are our priority. Plain and simple. Not certain kinds of women, not certain colors. But *women*, all of them. As the Simpson trial dragged on, Toni warned Ellie Smeal that unless the Feminist Majority was planning on becoming the NAACP's version of Shari Lewis's Lamb Chop, the organization had a problem on its hands.

Following the Simpson criminal verdict, I got scores of media requests for interviews regarding domestic violence and the impact Simpson's acquittal would have on battered women and the men who beat them. On my way to one of those interviews, my car phone rang. It was Kathy Spillar. In a rather ominous tone, and clearly using a speakerphone, Kathy said, "We have to speak with you before you talk to anyone else about Simpson."

I had always looked up to Kathy, and I suppose she felt that because of our history she would have some sway over me. I told her I was actually on my way to an interview and she had better speak her mind. She was vague but dramatic. "I have to ask you not to say anything more about Simpson." Kathy's opinion mattered to me, but in this instance I was more curious than concerned. She refused to be more specific, and I, of course, refused to stop speaking about Simpson and domestic violence. I did agree to meet with her the next day at the Feminist Majority offices.

What transpired at that meeting remains the most unexpected and the strangest conversation I've ever had in my life. When I arrived, Kathy was alone in her office. As I sat down, she placed a call to Constance Rice, the western regional counsel for the NAACP's Legal Defense and Education Fund. At the time, Kathy and the FM had joined forces with Rice and the NAACP to defeat Prop 209, the anti-affirmative-action proposition that Ward Connerly was campaigning for (see chapter 4).

When Rice answered, Kathy put her on the speakerphone. Rice began: "I don't know if you understand the damage you're doing to the black community with your vendetta against O. J. Simpson. . . . He's a role model for the black community. . . . He's important to the black male . . . you're condemning young black men with your crusade." This went on for about 10 minutes. Occasionally, Kathy would nod her head in agreement with Rice, but she had trouble looking me in the eye.

Eventually, I had had enough. I reminded Rice and Kathy that if anyone was "condemning young black men" it was O. J. Simpson. As Rice continued to argue about "our responsibility" to black men, I explained that I was worried about the women whose batterers had just been told by Simpson's jury that you can beat up and kill your wife without repercussions. The Department of Justice reports that rates of nonlethal domestic violence are highest among black women, women in households in the lowest income categories, and women residing in urban areas.[17] I thought they, rather than the men who were beating them, were "our responsibility."

> As Rice continued to argue about "our responsibility" to black men, I explained that I was worried about the women whose batterers had just been told by Simpson's jury that you can beat up and kill your wife without repercussions.

The conversation ended with Kathy almost screaming, "You've just got to leave him alone! You've got to stop and leave him alone!" It was one thing hearing it from Rice but devastating to hear it from Kathy. That was the Feminist Majority's contribution to the issue of domestic violence, and the end of my friendship with Kathy.

One good thing did come out of the Simpson debacle. The Feminist Majority brought in leadership from the outside—a heretofore unheard-of event in the feminist establishment. The board of the Feminist Majority Foundation now includes producer Lorraine Sheinberg and Mavis Leno, writer and wife of *Tonight Show* host Jay Leno. Both women are creative feminists, and their fresh outlooks and lack of feminist establishment baggage have infused the FM with an energy that seems to be helping keep it focused and productive. The FM has been a key player in the introduction of the abortion pill, RU486, into the United States, and, with Mavis Leno's leadership, it has brought the plight of women under Afghanistan's Taliban regime to international attention. The cycle of groupthink has been broken, to the great benefit of those for whom the Feminist Majority speaks.

Bill's Girls

In a *New York Times* op-ed piece, Gloria Steinem set the pathetic tone for the "feminist" (actually socialist) elite's response to the revelations of Bill Clinton's sexual scandals. She characterized his encounter with Paula Jones, during which he exposed himself and asked for a blow job, as a "clumsy sexual pass."[18] Gosh, I imagine Clarence Thomas and Bob Packwood would have loved to have the sexual-harassment allegations against them characterized as such, but no. They were Republicans. As part of the Democratic Party elite, Steinem was exhibiting her commitment to her boss, not to feminism.

This kind of double standard is reprehensible and truly exposes the political hypocrisy in the feminist establishment. Brenda Feigen describes a press conference held by "feminist leaders" in support of Clinton: "On September 24, 1998, a few women, calling themselves feminist leaders and including in their number Betty Friedan, Patricia Ireland and Eleanor Smeal, president of the Feminist Majority, held a press conference to state that women supported Clinton because he'd been so good on all our issues."[19]

Feigen rightly pointed out that *any* Democratic president would have supported "choice" and made at least as many appointments of women. And that, really, is the point. The fan-like behavior of these so-called feminist leaders during both the Paula Jones case and the Monica Lewinsky scandal stems from their longtime allegiance to the Democratic Party. They were behaving like good party loyalists. Which, of course, has nothing to do with feminism. The only thing missing at this press conference was the kneepads.

Show Me the Money: Part III

There may, however, be more behind Clinton's seduction of the feminist establishment than its leaders' undeniable Democratic loyalty, let alone Bill Clinton's personal charm. As I made phone call after phone call in an attempt to get someone to speak with me on the record about a specific reason for NOW's odd silence, one courageous former NOW board member revealed what she felt was a serious conflict of interest.

I learned that in 1995, during Clinton's first term, NOW accepted federal money for the first time in its history. According to my source, California NOW was close to bankruptcy at the time. Meanwhile, Paula Jones's sexual harassment case had begun to pick up steam, as she fought for her right to sue Clinton while he was in office. The President himself was gearing up for his reelection campaign the following year. Instead of taking on Clinton as we had taken on Clarence Thomas, NOW may have opted instead to take on some money.

According to the Grants Management Office of the U.S. Department of Health and Human Services, California NOW was awarded more than half a million dollars in a grant from—get this—the Centers for Disease Control's Office on Smoking and Health. The grant was for what was termed "tobacco control." From the years 1995 through 1997—while NOW maintained its strange silence on Bill Clinton and on occasion actually issued a direct rebuke to Paula Jones—California NOW received a total of $543,636 in taxpayer money from Clinton's government, specifically the Donna Shalala-headed Department of Health and Human Services.

For an organization that had absolutely no history of leadership in the health arena, the grant was, to say the least, out of the ordinary. On the other hand, if the California organization—NOW's largest and most successful state satellite—had had to file for bankruptcy, it would have sounded a death knell for National NOW, exposing the depth of its troubles, financial and organizational.

But that's not all. In 1998, when the Monica Lewinsky scandal broke, the grant was *transferred* to National NOW in Washington, D.C. In 1998, National NOW received a modest $40,727 from the same CDC office for the same "tobacco control" agenda. Remember, in 1998, as Clinton's impeachment hearing loomed, silence wasn't enough from the feminist establishment. It was in September of that year that the so-called feminist leaders, including Patricia Ireland, reacted to the Lewinsky charges with their we-love-Clinton-because-he's-so-good-to-us press conference. The following year, National NOW received a whopping $182,736 for more "tobacco control." In all,

National NOW received close to a quarter of a million dollars from the federal government during the Lewinsky scandal. Taken together, California NOW and National NOW received over *three-quarters of a million dollars* ($767,099) during the Jones and Lewinsky scandals.

Is there hard evidence of a direct connection between the grants and NOW's bizarre reactions to the Clinton stories? No, but the acceptance of federal money for the first time, coupled with behavior that is so different from the organization's reactions to sexual harassment in the past, gives, to say the least, the appearance of impropriety.

NOW seems to recognize the problem of appearing to be beholden to those from whom you should be independent. Its Web site includes an answer to a Frequently Asked Question, "Is NOW funded in any way by the federal government?" The answer? "No, NOW is a nonprofit organization which receives all its operating funds from private donations and membership dues." Does the organization specify "operating funds" because it has accepted federal money for specific projects? Is this just semantics? I don't know about you, but for the life of me I don't recall a "tobacco control" project launched by NOW. And one would think that three-quarters of a million dollars would fund one heck of a campaign.

NOW's Dr. Laura

As these stories show, NOW is able to overlook wife-beating and murder in the case of someone who's a role model for young black men and the sexual exploitation of subordinates in the case of someone who can help the organization politically and financially. Some things, however, cannot be overlooked—like the opinions expressed by Rush Limbaugh. NOW's principal Thought Police campaign at present is the Flush Rush project, aimed at taking Limbaugh off the air. NOW regularly sends out mass mailings explaining how dangerous Limbaugh is and asking for money to continue its campaign against him. Apparently emboldened by the gay community's crusade against Dr. Laura, NOW is using Limbaugh to reinvigorate its own speech- and mind-control efforts.

> NOW is able to overlook wife-beating and murder in the case of someone who's a role model for young black men and the sexual exploitation of subordinates in the case of someone who can help the organization politically and financially.

"NOW believes that Rush Limbaugh is truly a dangerous man," one of NOW's letters says. "We need the help of every progressive person to expose the hateful, divisive fanaticism of Rush Limbaugh." (Sounds a little like the "dispirited, insidious and turbulent effects of the words and deeds of Tammy Bruce," doesn't it? When it comes to rhetoric against its enemies, NOW seems to be in a bit of a rut.) The letter exhorts its recipients to pressure radio stations and advertisers to cut off support for this "dangerous bigot" who spews forth "reactionary rhetoric" and "venom" and who is in tune with the "messages of intolerance and violence that dominate television. . . ." "It's astonishing," the letter continues, "that Rush Limbaugh gets so much airtime" with his "hate-filled show."

Either the people who wrote these letters are naive or they hope their readers are. The reason Limbaugh gets so much airtime is pretty obvious: people *like* him. He is a principled conservative with a populist foundation, and he discusses issues that hit people where they live. For those who are of a different political persuasion, he offers an invaluable window on what Republicans are thinking. Personally, I find him witty, funny, and often wrong. If NOW finds him too wrong to ignore, then countering his *ideas* would be the principled and feminist thing to do. But, alas, NOW has nothing of substance to say. Instead, its Flush Rush campaign just gives Limbaugh more proof that the "feminazis" are alive and well.

The Pretenders

Brenda Feigen asks, "Why is it that most women will fight to save anyone with less power than they have?"[20] However it manifests itself, there is a feminine tendency to try to save others before we save ourselves. Perhaps our nurturing skills have made it difficult for us to put ourselves first. NOW's devolution into a "social justice" organization focusing on "race, class, and other issues of oppression," as Ireland put it, and Steinem's taking on "the entire caste system" are examples of women who seem to believe that women's issues are less worthy of fighting for than the issues of others.

In any political organization, the leaders project their own issues onto the landscape. Under Patricia Ireland's leadership in the early 1990s, NOW passed a resolution stating that "NOW commits itself to intense examination of its own residual racism." I was a member of the National NOW Board of Directors during part of Ireland's tenure. At that time, the board met only once a quarter for a weekend, which some of us thought was already too little; but then part of that time was reserved for "sensitivity trainings" addressing our "internal racism." Participation in these "trainings" was mandatory for every board member at every meeting. The self-flagellation was unending.

Could this self-condemnation and obsession with race be reflective of Ireland's personal concerns? Are Steinem and Ireland victims of racial guilt, or social guilt? Are they dealing with their inner demons or working out other political agendas at the expense of the feminist movement? I think those are questions that both women should ask themselves.

It's only fair to ask me in turn why I feel so passionately about what I'm doing. In my activism directed at helping women and improving their lives, I'm probably still trying to save my mother, who led a difficult life as a single mother of two girls, abandoned by my father, periodically dependent on welfare, and addicted to valium during most of my childhood. I'm also probably still trying to save my first partner, a woman who committed suicide at the age of 36. I understand that in my drive to help women I'm probably still trying to help the women in my life who are lost. I'm determined, however, to transform the events that wounded me into something positive. Activists need to find how best to put their compensating drives to work, transforming pain into, yes, power.

This country is not at a loss for organizations working for black civil rights, but we are starving for a truly feminist effort that devotes strict, focused attention to women's rights. For me to join a black civil-rights group and force my issue onto it would not be the most productive thing to do. By the same token, if Steinem and Ireland are compensating on racial issues, they should do their work with the Urban League or the NAACP and stop projecting their issues onto NOW. The Thought Police have made their mark, however. By now, many feminists still associated with NOW probably fear that working exclusively for women's rights is a racist thing to do.

This fear, combined with the practically instinctual (albeit conditioned) response that makes a woman place the needs of men before her own needs, is expertly exploited by some men all across the color spectrum. Think about it—united we stand, divided we fall. If women can be divided, there will be no real threat to the male-dominated status quo. Paint feminists as lesbians, and straight women will stay away. Add that feminism is racist, and you can deter black women from working with women from other communities on the truly color-blind issues that make all women sisters—rape, domestic violence, reproductive freedom, and male responsibility.

The only way women's lives are going to change is if new feminist leadership emerges—leadership prepared to challenge the hypocrisy of the posers now in charge and to reintroduce self-esteem to a movement that needs to believe, once again, that women deserve attention and concern. How can we, as activist feminists, tell women of all generations that they deserve better when the movement itself doesn't believe they deserve action and representation?

In July 2001, NOW elected a new president. Due to term limits, Ireland was unable to run again, but she endorsed Kim Gandy, a woman who has been part of the NOW bureaucracy since 1973 and has been a national officer in one capacity or another for the last 14 years, actively participating in NOW's sad decline. Obviously, this was not an election that indicated any commitment to bringing in new blood; instead, it was more a rearrangement of the deck chairs. Or, as Ireland said to a newspaper reporter regarding the transition, "I don't want to talk about passing the torch, but I'm happy to share it."[21]

How unfortunate not only for NOW but also for everyone who would have benefited from an authentic feminist effort as we enter the twenty-first century.

6

Multiculturalism
Thought Police in Costume

"The price paid for intellectual pacification is the sacrifice of the entire moral courage of the human mind."

— *John Stuart Mill*

Black people have always been here as different. People need to stop saying that there is one way to be—and then the issue will disappear. I don't tell Navajos they can't speak Navajo. I don't tell Asians they can't eat noodles. Because black people have refused to eat potatoes and cabbage, white people are terrified. Now that we're saying "I'm talkin' Zulu, I'm changin' my name, my child's goin' to a black school with Muslims," white people get upset and have to call it something. Multiculturalism isn't about culture, it's about power.[1]

Finally, it is said. The speaker here is Ntozake Shange, born Paulette Williams in Trenton, New Jersey. She rose to national prominence with the 1975 production of her play *For Colored Girls Who Have Considered Suicide/ When the Rainbow Is Enuf: A Choreopoem*, and she has received acclaim over the past two decades for her work as a poet and novelist. With the above quote, Shange gives us a great example of the use of a concept to divide and rule—in this case, the concept is the demonization of any attempt to foster common values and mores.

Multiculturalism—the claim that minority cultures and ways of life should be protected through group rights and privilege—amounts to the Balkanization of this country into blacks, Asians, Native Americans, Hispanics, and so on. It highlights differences and obscures similarities, and it gives each group the idea that it has a special knowledge about itself that no one else can share. How many times have you heard that you have no right to criticize a black (or Latino or Bengali) if you aren't black (or Latino or Bengali)?

Multiculturalism is the antithesis of the American melting pot, and quite deliberately so. I've heard black nationalists argue that the melting-pot theory, with the assimilation it demands, is just another racist attempt to "disappear" the black man in America. Multiculturalism is heralded specifically because it keeps people in separate groups. Ironically, if actual multiculturalism—an appreciation for diversity—were in effect today instead of the warped balkanization we have under that label, each of us would be free to embrace a culture *other than our own*. As a black woman, Paulette Williams would have been celebrating multiculturalism much more distinctly by keeping her own Anglo name. Or perhaps she could have changed her name to Mary O'Reilly or Edna Ferber. Now *that* would have been *real* multiculturalism.

The melting pot has served us through generations, making the heritage of every person who has ever immigrated to this country an element in the mixture we know as American culture. The way we speak the English language is uniquely American. How is that? It's a blending of the languages, accents, and histories of all of us. And the same goes for every aspect of our culture. The black experience is central to American music, film, dance, food, and sport.

> **Multiculturalism—the claim that minority cultures and ways of life should be protected through group rights and privilege— amounts to the Balkanization of this country into blacks, Asians, Native Americans, Hispanics, and so on.**

The Irish brought their special brand of humor and melancholy (without the one you don't get the depth of the other), their literature, and the best whiskey and cheekbones on the planet. Without the French there would be no Statue of Liberty and New Orleans would be boring, our language monotonous, and our food lifeless. For that matter, without the French there would *be* no United States. The Italians? What can you say? Love, food, Enrico Caruso, Joe DiMaggio, the discovery of America (by both Amerigo Vespucci and Christopher Columbus), football (the precursor to American football is a game called *calcio*, a Florentine game that goes back to the sixteenth century), and the Bank of America (founded by an Italian and originally called the Bank of

Italy). Jews, Catholics, Muslims, Lutherans, atheists, Buddhists—you name it, different faiths (and rejections of faith) have also shaped the experiences of everyone in this country.

Right now, you're probably thinking of a hundred things that your ethnic group has contributed to American culture. This is true diversity and an indication that the great experiment actually worked. American culture is made up of contributions from everyone who lives here, and therefore it belongs to all of us. The culture exists *as American,* however, only because of assimilation. As in a terrific Irish stew, every ingredient flavors and is flavored by all the others. Multiculturalism seeks to destroy this unique American culture by dividing groups into separate tribes, each celebrating only itself and viewing other groups—especially anything Western—as the enemy. The melting-pot relies on individualism for its content and character. If the multiculturalists had their way, group stereotypes would necessarily erase the uniqueness of each one of us.

Diversity has always existed in the United States, so why the sudden defense of mini-cultures now? Because these constituencies are seen as power bases for the Left. Ntozake Shange and her fellow multiculturalists are the Thought Police in costume. They do not truly value diversity—which would, of course, include the European background of the majority of Americans—but instead promote "victimized" cultures exclusively. In so doing, they condemn to isolation any new immigrant who is unlucky enough to arrive here while they are in charge.

They also seek to shield non-European cultures from moral judgments. In the mind of today's multiculturalist, the cultural practices of minority groups are above reproach, no matter where they lead.

Beat the Hell Out of Her

When police arrived at the tony address in Century City, a community of million-dollar condominiums and towering office buildings on the west side of Los Angeles, they found Kyuang-Ja Chung dead, her body covered with bruises and abrasions. Sixteen of her ribs were broken, her heart was crushed against her backbone, and her kidneys had failed. The muscles of her abdominal wall were deeply bruised, and sections of her intestinal tract had shut down and were showing the first signs of gangrene. The medical examiner said the damage was comparable to that of being run over by a car.[2]

In fact, the injuries had been inflicted by Mrs. Chung's husband and another man, who had repeatedly beaten and stomped on her abdomen and chest. The two men were tried and convicted . . . of involuntary manslaughter. Mr. Chung was sentenced to two years in state prison, his accomplice to four years.

How is this possible? Despite the prosecution's argument for second-degree murder convictions, Los Angeles Superior Court Judge James A. Albracht was swayed by the "cultural defense" put up by the two men, who claimed that Mrs. Chung's death was an accident that occurred during a *demon-cleansing ritual*. Judge Albracht ruled that Mr. Chung and his accomplice had behaved recklessly, *but not maliciously*. He found that although the men, both Korean Pentecostal Christians (as was the victim), may have been misguided, they were focused on "saving her from demons they believed possessed her."[3]

How did the men know that Mrs. Chung was possessed? Dark spirits, they said at the trial, were making her arrogant, leading her to disobey her husband and interfere with his work.[4]

Possessed? Baloney. In every culture, from the beginning of time, men (and sometimes women) have found some kind of excuse for barbaric behavior. Blaming events on someone or something other than yourself is commonplace. Now, with the multiculturalists in control, blaming "culture" is the easiest, and potentially the most successful, way to dodge personal responsibility.

> Multiculturalism is not about exotic restaurants and charming street fairs. Accepting the notion that all ideas and systems are equal precludes a willingness to think critically about what surrounds us.

Multiculturalism is not about exotic restaurants and charming street fairs. It is a code word for moral relativism. Accepting the notion that all ideas and systems are equal precludes a willingness to think critically about what surrounds us. It is the cornerstone of our inability to come to judgments about events such as the murder of Kyuang-Ja Chung.

Unfortunately, while Mrs. Chung's killing was unusually brutal, it was far from an isolated case. Patt Morrison of the *Los Angeles Times* drew back the curtain on the dark side of multiculturalism: the Iranian medical student who shot his wife in the head because she had worn trousers and left their Encino home after he ordered her not to; the Yemeni teenager in Visalia who loved Michael Jackson and makeup and who was shot to death, allegedly by a brother who felt dishonored by her conduct; the Thai man who killed a Laotian man at a Los Angeles restaurant because the Laotian had put his foot on a table as the Thai was singing—a deadly insult in his culture.[5] Even though morality and religion in most parts of the world tell us that murder is wrong, multiculturalism gives an excuse for placing killings like these outside the definition of murder.

Multiculturalism is also bad for women, forcing them to remain cloaked in their old culture. These women are left out of the opportunities and the support systems that would otherwise be available to them in America—like the Japanese woman who, after learning her husband had a mistress, walked into the Pacific Ocean off Santa Monica with her two children. She was rescued; the children died.

Although this woman's despair was very personal, the method she chose to resolve it was cultural and very Japanese. In their paper "Cultural Dynamics and the Unconscious in Suicide in Japan," Drs. Yoshitomo Takahashi and Douglas Berger remark, "Although she had lived in the United States for 14 years, she remained Japanese in her thinking and lifestyle, isolated from American culture. She did not drive, spoke little English, knew nothing of her husband's business, and had no hobbies or close friends outside the family."[6] Somehow, she felt she had "dishonored" her husband, which led to his infidelity. Japanese culture provided a way out: *oyajo shinju*, or parent-child suicide[7]. Although American women have also been known to kill their children out of despair or depression, it's safe to say that had this woman been assimilated into American culture, murder-suicide, a culturally unacceptable course of action, would have been at least a less appealing choice.

Unfortunately, the abuse of women and children is so commonplace around the world that it could be argued to be a cultural practice. But our own values would make us reject any suggestion that this practice should therefore be "tolerated," wouldn't they? Not quite. You see, multiculturalism and the relativism it invites offer one more opportunity for the Left to reinforce the idea that personal responsibility is just too simplistic a concept for today's world.

Where the Lines Are Drawn

The "cultural defense" put forth by Chung and his accomplice can only succeed if we are willing to suspend common sense and reason, which is exactly what the Thought Police have conditioned us to do. While tolerance is an important virtue in American life, there must be some sense of where the lines are drawn. We are becoming so hypnotized by the mantra of "tolerance," however, that we are losing sight of our moral compass and are mindlessly embracing anything that's "different."

We need to recover the balance between tolerance and values. Admittedly, that can be a scary prospect for some of us, considering that many of the more appalling acts in history were committed in the name of morality. But not to work for that balance dooms us to being a society that can't figure out that stomping a woman to death is in fact murder, not involuntary manslaughter, and not an act that cultural differences can make acceptable.

Immigrants and minorities should be especially suspicious of standards that essentially say they are too backward or simple-minded to become part of their new country. Whatever Mrs. Chung's killers said in court, I would guess that most Koreans know the difference between providing spiritual help and beating someone to death. The Koreans I know would be insulted by the implication that their "culture" was responsible for such a gruesome act.

In his book *On Toleration,* Princeton political philosopher and social critic Michael Walzer muses about the potential backlash against the "postmodern tolerance" (multiculturalism) that is running amuck in our society. Although he rightly regards toleration—making room in society for people whose beliefs and practices you don't share—as the principal work of democratic citizens, he nonetheless issues a stern warning: "People have begun to experience what we might think of as a life without clear boundaries and without secure or singular identities." Walzer also worries about "the processes that produce dissociation and are its products," including high rates of divorce and illegitimacy, the increase in reports of child abuse, the decline in voting rates, and the rising tide of random violence.[8]

Walzer cites multiculturalism as a reason for citizens' declining participation in society. He's almost on target. Where his argument fails is in not recognizing that the individual's dissociation from society is not a *symptom* of multiculturalism but its DNA.

The more we are told that every "culture" is on an equal footing, the less comfortable we feel thinking critically and challenging the problems in our society. If our values tell us that Kyuang-Ja Chung's killing was murder, but our multiculturalist society tells us it wasn't, what are we to do? Confusion and revulsion make retreat from the public sphere—Michael Walzer's "dissociation"—the inevitable next step. Multiculturalism creates little hermetically sealed pockets of "culture" that are the antithesis of the classical liberal vision of individual promise and contribution to society as a whole.

Deconstructing History

In 2000, Interior Secretary Bruce Babbitt decided to hand over a 9,300-year-old skeleton known as Kennewick Man—one of the oldest and most significant set of human remains ever found in North America—to a coalition of the Umatilla, Yakama, Colville, Nez Perce, and Wanapum Indian tribes of Washington State. The five Columbia Basin tribes claimed that these were "ancestral remains" to which they were entitled under the Native American Graves Protection and Repatriation Act (NAGPRA), enacted in 1990. They knew that Kennewick Man was one of their ancestors because they've occupied the area where he was found "for millennia." How did Babbitt know the tribes' claim was true? Because of their "oral histories."[9]

The bones were discovered on July 28, 1996, along the banks of the Columbia River in Kennewick. Anthropologist James Chatters performed an initial examination of the skeleton on behalf of the county coroner's office. The 40-to-55-year-old male had a long, narrow skull, a projecting nose, receding cheekbones, a prominent chin, and a square mandible.[10] These traits would have made this ancient fisherman stand out in a crowd of modern American Indians. Chatters thought Kennewick Man raised the possibility that Europeans or Asians had lived in North America before many of the "Native American" tribes.

A custody battle immediately ensued between the coalition of tribes and a group of scientists. The tribes did not want research conducted on the bones to determine the ethnic origins of someone who may have been one of the first New World settlers. They preferred to have their "oral histories" serve as proof that their own people have, after all, been here from time immemorial. In a press release, the Confederated Tribes of the Umatilla Indian Reservation put it this way:

> If this individual is truly over 9,000 years old, that only substantiates our belief that he is Native American. From our oral histories, we know that our people have been part of this land since the beginning of time. We do not believe that our people migrated here from another continent, as the scientists do.[11]

It must be a pretty heady thing to believe that "your" people and culture have populated an area from "the beginning of time" and that they are a distinct group, unrelated to anyone else, particularly anyone from Eurasia. This attitude is perfectly suited for a multicultural society, which encourages and rewards arrogance, pride, and separatism.

Meanwhile, a group of scientists filed suit in Portland, Oregon, seeking to block repatriation. They argue that a treasure trove of information about the lives of ancient Americans would be lost if the bones were turned over to the Indians. The scientists believe that learning the truth is preferable to suspended disbelief when it comes to investigating how the world was populated.

NAGPRA, however, in describing what constitutes a "Native American," states in so many words that reality must take a backseat to fantasy in order to maintain the myth of a preferred "culture." A memo from the Interior Department titled "Determination That the Kennewick Human Skeletal Remains are 'Native American' for the Purposes of the Native American Graves Protection and Repatriation Act (NAGPRA)" explains how Kennewick Man, despite James Chatters's initial findings, was determined by the government to be a "Native American":

> As defined in NAGPRA, "Native American" refers to human remains and cultural items relating to tribes, peoples, or cultures that resided within the area now encompassed by the United States prior to the historically documented arrival of European explorers, *irrespective of when a particular group may have begun to reside in this area, and, irrespective of whether some or all of these groups were or were not culturally affiliated or biologically related to present-day Indian tribes* [emphasis mine].[12]

In other words, even if a skeleton of the appropriate age is determined to be of completely different ethnic origin, such as Asian, European, or North African, it will, in the name of multiculturalism and political correctness, be declared Native American.

This outlandish standard had to be created in order to maintain the tribes' fantasy that their people had been the Adam and Eve of North America, and perhaps Seattle the Garden of Eden. In fact, independent scientific analysis of Kennewick Man's bones indicates that he resembled people from Asia, particularly the Ainu of northern Japan and the Polynesians.[13]

At this writing, the scientists' lawsuit is still winding its way through the courts. More recently, a California man of Polynesian descent filed a second suit, claiming to be Kennewick Man's "next of kin." Whatever the eventual result, we can clearly see the Thought Police at

In other words, even if a skeleton of the appropriate age is determined to be of completely different ethnic origin, such as Asian, European, or North African, it will, in the name of multiculturalism and political correctness, be declared Native American.

work here, declaring the untrue true, effectively deconstructing history to suit a protected group.

Cultural Group Rights

Will Kymlicka, a leading proponent of multiculturalism, describes the logical extension of the movement: cultural group rights. "Such rights," he has written, "which I call 'external protection,' can take the form of language rights, guaranteed political representation, funding of ethnic media, land claims, compensation for historical injustice or the regional devolution of power."[14]

This one sentence carries a lot of left-wing baggage. "Guaranteed political representation," for example. This doesn't mean the right to vote—it means the right to vote for people of your own ethnic group. Remember, a black can only be represented by a black, a Latino by a Latino, an Aleut by an Aleut (but don't expect Kymlicka to say: a WASP by a WASP, an Italian-American by an

Italian-American . . .). "Language rights" means the right not to learn the language of the oppressor class, English. Not only is this bad for society—resulting in a modern-day Babel, where no one understands anyone else—but it also places the immigrants themselves in the untenable position of being perpetual strangers in a strange land.

"Compensation for historical injustice" means reparations for slavery, a proposed transfer of wealth on an unimaginable scale. I'll come back to this in chapter 8, but for now, let's ask who is to pay these "reparations." Most present-day Americans are descendants of post–Civil War immigrants who had nothing to do with the antebellum South. As the social and political commentator David Horowitz points out, "The two great waves of American immigration occurred after 1880 and after 1960. Is there an argument worth considering that would, for example, make Jews (who were cowering in the ghettos of Europe at the time) or Mexicans and Cubans (who were suffering under the heel of Spain) responsible for this crime? What reason could there be that Vietnamese boat people, Russian refuseniks, Iranian refugees, Armenian victims of the Turks, or . . . Polish, Hungarian, and Korean victims of Communism should pay reparations to American blacks?"[15]

The Bilingual Trap

For over three hundred years, people have left everything behind in their native lands, sometimes even risking their lives, in order to come to America and explore the dream and the reality of freedom. They did not come here to live in a little isolated version of their homeland. And yet American culture (and we do have one!) became a major target of the Left in its grab for power.

Historically, immigrant groups were expected to assimilate into this Great Experiment, as excited and willing contributors to American culture. Certainly, assimilation did not require forgetting about your origins, but it did mean becoming an American—learning English, obeying the laws, and doing your best to participate. And no matter how aggressively the Left markets its politics of division, the reality of immigration to the United States is still one of pride and excitement. As an example, according to a Latino National Political Survey, 90 percent of Hispanic Americans in the 1990s were "proud" or "very proud" of the United States.[16]

Alison Dundes Renteln, an associate professor of political science at the University of Southern California (USC) and a contributor to a book titled *Cultural Issues and Criminal Defense*, has found a standard that she believes balances reason with diversity. She states, "For things which are innocent, like folk medicine or what kind of animals people eat or what kind of religious symbols they wear—why should the assumption be that people should become Americanized?"[17]

Folk medicine? Why not? (As long as we aren't talking about lethal demon-cleansing ceremonies.) The wearing of religious symbols? Americans have always embraced that. But notice how Professor Renteln slips "what kind of animals people eat" into this list. We are doing immigrants a serious disservice if we fail to tell them that Americans have a special feeling for certain animals and that eating Fido for dinner or spit-roasting a Shetland pony for a special feast are not ways to make friends with your new neighbors.

Even more central—and something more complex than understanding that Sadie the Cat is not a snack here—is *language*. Learning English is in the interest, both personally and financially, of every person who immigrates to this country. To deny the benefits of assimilation to our newest immigrants because of our own games of racial politics is unforgivable. But we do it every day, and children are the first victims.

> **Learning English is in the interest, both personally and financially, of every person who immigrates to this country.**

Bilingual education is a classic example of an experiment that was begun with the best of intentions, as a special effort to help immigrant children learn English so that they could catch up with their English-speaking classmates and receive an equal educational opportunity. Now turned on its head by the multiculturalists, "bilingual" education is too often actually *monolingual* in the child's native language, imprisoning youngsters in linguistic isolation. The multiculturalists no longer even try to hide this fact. According to José Gonzalez, director of bilingual education in the Carter Administration and now a professor at Columbia University Teachers College, Spanish "should no longer be regarded as a 'foreign' language." Instead, he writes in *Reinventing Urban Education,* Spanish should be "a second national language."[18]

Linda Chavez, president of the Center for Equal Opportunity, sums up the situation perfectly: "[F]ailed policies such as bilingual education and multicultural curricula are not being demanded by Mexican laborers or Chinese waiters. Instead they are being rammed down immigrants' throats by federal, state and local governments, at the behest of native-born political activists and bureaucrats. . . ."[19] She is astute in examining the motives behind retaining these policies: "The purpose in many cases is no longer to bring immigrant children into the mainstream of American life. Some advocates see bilingual education as the first step in a racial transformation of the United States into a nation without one common language or fixed borders."[20]

How did this nightmare begin? The hijacking of children's education by the multiculturalists can be traced back to a now mostly forgotten 1989 report commissioned by the New York State Education Department. Titled *A Curriculum of Inclusion, Report of the Commissioner's Task Force on Minorities: Equity and Excellence,* the report argued that "cultural differences" must be a part of every subject and every class:

> [N]o topic is truly culture-free . . . by ostensibly omitting cultural references from science and mathematics materials, a subtle message is given to all children that all science and mathematics originated within European culture. Thus, there is a clear need to include in the science and mathematical curricular materials references to the many contributions made by people from a variety of cultures.[21]

But even multiculturalists can't include *everybody* in their embrace of tolerance and inclusion. Here is how the

Catholic Church fares in Section IV of the *Curriculum of Inclusion:*

> European Conception of the World in 1500 is not satisfactory. It fails to reflect the conflict, chaos, and war which characterized Europe after the Crusades and the corruption of the Roman Catholic Church. This situation in Europe contributed directly to the development of negative values and policies that produced aggressive individuals and nations that were ready to "discover, invade and conquer" foreign land because of greed, racism, and national egotism.[22]

Wow! So much for tolerance and inclusion!

English First, a 150,000-member grassroots lobbying organization founded in 1986, is working to make English the official language of the United States. English First describes its members as people who are "tired of seeing the government use their tax money to divide Americans on the basis of language or ancestry." The group advocates giving every child the opportunity to learn English and ending costly and ineffective bilingual education. Jim Boulet Jr., the executive director of English First, eloquently sums up the repercussions of multiculturalism in the classroom: "Children who are both denied a chance to learn America's language, English, and indoctrinated in the offenses of this nation against their ancestors will grow up to be both underemployed and bitter. That's not the future we want for any of America's kids."[23]

Show Me the Money: Part IV

No discussion of bilingual education would be complete without a mention of Ebonics. The debate over this proposed language classification had faded by the end of the 1990s, but it is worth recalling, as it sheds considerable light on the actual reasoning behind many efforts that are swathed in the banners of "civil rights," "tolerance," and "culture" but that actually come down to a recurring theme in the establishment Left: money.

In 1996, the school board of Oakland, California, declared that the pattern of speech used by most of the black children in the school district was not slang or substandard English but instead a separate language, which the board called "Ebonics" (a combination of the words "ebony" and "phonics").[24] This newly discovered "language" sounds suspiciously like English but with elements such as dropping final consonants—so that "good" becomes "goo"—and using verb forms in creative ways—as in "She been married" for "She has been married for a long time," or "He be goin' to work" for "He goes to work."[25]

This would be a good time to remember Ntozake Shange's admonition quoted at the beginning of this chapter: "Multiculturalism isn't about culture, it's about power." Some observers wondered if the Oakland School Board's decision to declare Ebonics a language was really about money.

You may not be aware of the fact that schools receive additional federal funding if they have to provide bilingual education. Keep that in mind as we consider two elements of the Oakland School Board's resolution:

"African-American pupils are equally entitled to be tested and, where appropriate, shall be provided general funds and state and federal (Title VIII) bilingual education and ESL [English as a Second Language] programs" and "All classroom teachers and aides who are bilingual in Nigritian Ebonics (African-American Language) and English *shall be given the same salary differentials and merit increases* [emphasis mine] that are provided to the teachers of the non-African-American pupils."[26]

Are you surprised that linguists found "Nigritian Ebonics" had no relation, grammatically or phonetically, to any African language? Even the Clinton administration did not hesitate to declare that Ebonics is a form of English slang that does not belong in the classroom and does not qualify for federal bilingual-education funds. But meanwhile, for anyone who didn't see the agenda at work here, one more instance of oppression had been created. Is it cynical to believe that moves made in the name of children are often about something else entirely, such as pay raises? No. It's called critical thinking and being wise enough not to be taken on another ride by the Left—who do not have your, or your children's, best interests in mind.

> It's called critical thinking and being wise enough not to be taken on another ride by the Left—who do not have your, or your children's, best interests in mind.

Color as Culture

Thanks to the multiculturalists, black racism has come a long way from the "Get Whitey" days of the 1960s. Now race itself doesn't even need to be mentioned—the argument can be framed entirely in terms of culture.

The best example I have seen of the gobbledygook of multiculturalism comes from a New Jersey organization called the Center for the Study of White American Culture. It sounds too nutty to be real, but make no mistake—it *is* real, and it's very serious. It's a perfect example of what the New York *Curriculum of Inclusion* was actually aiming to do.

The first page of the Center's Web site immediately assures us: "Not an organization for white supremacists, as some people might infer, we are instead a multiracial organization that looks at whiteness and white American culture."[27] One of the Center's projects is "The Whiteness Papers," which "is a series of occasional papers looking at whiteness and 'white culture' in the United States and throughout the world. Papers published in the series may be used in classroom and organizational settings to promote discussion of whiteness."[28] Here's a sample:

> The authors [of the paper] believe that whiteness and white culture form the center of society in the United States. This circumstance is unfair and inequitable. The center, which includes power and resources, should be accessible to people from all racial backgrounds. Whiteness therefore needs to be removed from the center. The center cannot be left to a vacuum. Instead, the center should be multiracial. Decentering whiteness and centering a multiracial culture are interdependent goals. Whiteness can not be decentered unless something else takes its central place. A multiracial center can not exist so long as whiteness is central. . . . [29]

The white-as-demon-culture argument was inevitable once society had come to accept the black-as-culture construct. The arguments of "The Whiteness Papers" may seem absurd, but history offers us a warning that should be taken seriously. The demonization of certain cultures and complaints that people of those cultures are controlling society can be, as most notably in Nazi Germany, the opening salvos of tragic and violent attacks. Let's say it once more: "Multiculturalism isn't about culture, it's about power."

Framing arguments about race as arguments about culture has the additional advantage for the Left of *removing the individual from the scene entirely.* Ironically, it also reinforces what is supposedly being resisted: the isolation of people because of their race. By defining society not as an entity made up of individual people but as a collection of cultures—such as white culture, black culture, Hispanic culture—the Left effectively isolates us, whether we like it or not, into special-interest groups. The culture has the identity, eclipsing the individual. We're no longer individuals with unique minds and talents; we're defined instead by the color of our skin, by the country in which we were born, by the religion we practice.

Speech codes, the New McCarthyism, and public attacks on those who dare to challenge the status quo are effective tools to condition people into silence and subservience, but they are time consuming, and they don't rule out the reemergence of someone who will proclaim that the emperor has no clothes. True socialism works best when *everyone* has been conditioned to identify as part of a group instead of as an individual.

The only way for the Left to actually accomplish this is to control how you view reality, through a flood of definitions. Jesse Jackson stated it clearly for the Thought Police:

> Definition is power. When a photographer takes a picture, he or she decides what is in the picture, and what is left out, what is highlighted and what is blurred. Two photographers shooting the same scene can create totally different images of it. The same is true with issues. If you have the power to define an issue, you go a long way to determining what is relevant and what is not. In doing that, you can have a huge effect on who wins and who loses.[30]

"Who wins and who loses"? Jackson clearly believes that someone has to "lose" in this culture war. But why? If the Left's "definition" is best for everyone, why would someone have to "lose"? Of course, it is individuals—of all colors and both sexes—who lose. The Left's aim is to eliminate the individual, not only from public discourse about social issues but also as a factor in society itself.

Striving for Mediocrity

Jackson's comments also highlight the reality that the Left's grab for power relies not on merit but on manipulation, not on excellence and performance in competition but on the expectation that the Left can doublespeak its way into defining the issues.

Lowering society's standards for success has become a major element in this effort. In a political essay in *Mother*

Jones—a magazine, named after a labor organizer of a century ago, that describes itself as being for "independent thinkers" but which is actually of interest only to overaged hippies and anarchists—Louis Menand put it right out on the table:

> [It is] liberalism that established sham categories like "merit" and "excellence," which have served as high-minded excuses for the exclusion, disparagement, and marginalization of "other" ways of knowing and achieving. [And it is] liberalism that insists on the majoritarian principles that permanently prevent minority groups—who will always be outvoted—from wielding power in America.[31]

Of course, the "liberalism" he refers to is of the classical variety. Did you ever think you would hear the concepts of merit and excellence called a "sham"? Neither did I, but if the effort is to redefine our social objectives, the only way to do it is with a straight face. "Marginalization of 'other' ways of knowing and achieving" is a code phrase to tell you that the inability to succeed in a merit-based system is not the fault of the person but is the fault of the entire "white" culture and its unfair and biased standards.

The argument here is that somehow, some way, people who do not do well in a competitive environment—provided the people in question are not white males—are experiencing some kind of "knowing" other than that of the patriarchal, racist culture. There need to be special protections and benefits for those who belong to an oppressed, marginalized, and otherwise disfranchised "culture." In other words, what the Left has been advocating for a very long time but trying to disguise—quotas, race-conscious hiring practices, judging men and women by the color of their skin—is now comfortably out in the open under the guise of multiculturalism.

The concepts of "new knowledge" and "other ways of achieving" are dependent on the concept of group rights. Only by grouping people together in a "culture" can the argument be made that an entire mass of people, such as all blacks or all women, have different ways of "knowing" and "achieving." A generation ago the suggestion that some Americans, such as women and minorities, are so significantly different from everyone else that they even *think* differently would have been met with swift rejection. The argument that certain kinds of people can't or don't think like others has been used throughout time to justify the *oppression* of those same people. Now it is the previously marginalized who have decided to use their victimhood to reap the rewards our society has pledged to the allegedly oppressed.

> **Now it is the previously marginalized who have decided to use their victimhood to reap the rewards our society has pledged to the allegedly oppressed.**

The Looking Glass

In *The Atlantic Monthly*, Stanley Fish, lawyer, literary critic, and multiculturalist, explained why certain "cultures" should be treated differently in higher education:

> If the skills that make for success are nurtured by institutions and cultural practices from which the disadvantaged minority has been systematically excluded, . . . then words like "fair" and "equal" are cruel jokes, for what they promote and celebrate is an institutionalized unfairness and a perpetuated inequality.[32]

This doublespeak has one objective and one only: to redefine standards, in this case, academic standards, into a kind of never-never land devoid of merit and excellence. In this way, it is the Thought Police who, while accusing everyone else of racism, purposely and disgracefully deprive blacks and other "protected" groups of the chance for development and condemn them to isolation, distrust, and paranoia. Humpty-Dumpty and Jesse Jackson are right: definition is everything. Stanley Fish and other multiculturalists are working hard to get us to believe that "fair" is "unfair" and "equal" is "unequal." In the looking-glass world of the Thought Police, black racism is not bad like white racism because blacks have a good reason for doing it, and words mean the opposite of what they have always meant.

Orwell once again had it right: it is not actually behavior that the Thought Police care about, *it is what you are thinking*. If racism were the issue, then "reverse racism" would be equally condemned by the multiculturalists.

But we're not dealing with principles here, we're dealing with *thought processes*. As Fish admits, "The difference is not in the outcome but in the ways of *thinking* [emphasis mine] that led up to the outcome."[33]

The Politics of Otherness

In a 1998 article in *Civilization,* the Smithsonian Institute magazine, Václav Havel characterized the situation in global terms. Havel is the great Czech writer and humanistic human-rights activist whose literary plays helped lay the groundwork for the Prague Spring of 1968. In August 1968, Soviet tanks crushed that move to lessen the repressiveness of the Communist regime, and over the next two decades Havel was in and out of prison repeatedly. As the Soviet bloc started to crumble, he became a leader of what was termed the Velvet Revolution in 1989. He was the first president of post-Communist Czechoslovakia and, later, president of the Czech Republic.

In his 1998 article, Havel wrote:

Humankind is actually entering a world whose characteristic features are multipolarity and multiculturalism. And so far, it would seem that the more tied the various civilizations, cultural, and religious groups are by the bonds of a single global civilization—exerting unavoidably a unifying influence—the more they emphasize their sovereignty, inalienable identity, specificity or simply things by which they differ from the circle of the other groups. It's as if one lived in an epoch of accentuated spiritual, religious, and cultural "otherness." This growing accent is indeed another large threat to this world.[34]

Havel saw the threat to individuality that Soviet domination posed to his country, and spoke up against it.

Ironically, after the collapse of that depraved system, he sees the politics of otherness, a hallmark of socialism, continuing to grow. Havel is a great example of how critical, independent, and creative thinking can prevail even in the ultimate of oppressive environments. Our responsibility to the next generation demands that we do as much.

CHAPTER

7

Control the Image and Control the Culture

The Thought Police in News and Entertainment

*"Ideas are more powerful than guns.
We would not let our enemies have guns;
why should we let them have ideas?"*

—Josef Stalin

would be happy to give him [Clinton] a blow job just to thank him for keeping abortion legal. I think American women should be lining up with their presidential kneepads on to show their gratitude for keeping the theocracy off our backs."[1] This little gem comes from Nina Burleigh, a reporter who, for a while, covered the Clinton White House for *Time* magazine. And to think that some people still complain that the press has a liberal bias!

Winning the Spin

Time's assignment of Nina Burleigh to cover the White House is a symptom of a much larger problem: news media, in all forms, that have a decidedly left-wing agenda. This is certainly a statement you've heard before, but I say it not as some think-tank egghead but as a publicist and a feminist activist who experienced the media's bias firsthand. I *had* to learn how the media really operate in order to use journalists to further my client's or my organization's agenda.

During my seven years as president of Los Angeles NOW, I worked constantly with journalists to ensure that the stories making the newspapers and the radio and television news shows were sympathetic to our issues. My office would send to reporters and news editors "information packets" designed to influence the labels attached to us and to our opponents—in essence, to win the spin. For example, when the abortion wars were hot and heavy in the early 1990s, I wanted to make sure that reporters got used to calling us "pro-choice" instead of "pro-abortion," and calling anti-abortion activists "anti-choice" instead of "pro-life."

During the Clarence Thomas confirmation hearings, while I was driving to an appointment one morning, I heard a radio reporter deliver a story to the effect that "12 percent of women admitted to sexually harassing men in their office." Why was *that* the spin on the story? I called the station from my car phone, demanded to speak with the reporter, and told him that the *real* story was that 88 percent of women *did not* engage in sexual harassment at the office.

The reporter had read the story the way it came off the news wire. He wasn't thinking about the spin. I was. In the next news segment, the reporter actually apologized (!) and delivered the *real* story (that is, my version of it).

I also made sure the media knew I was available for background information on any issue that was of concern to feminists. In other words, reporters could call me not just for an interview but if they needed research on issues such as abortion, equal pay, domestic violence, violence against women, sexual harassment—you name it. You see, if I was the one providing research and background, the reporters would be getting the kind of information that I thought important.

At L.A. NOW, we arranged meetings with the editorial boards of leading newspapers, we faxed en masse press releases about events of concern to us, and we helped reporters find interviewees and commentators who would tell our side of the story. You get the picture. In general, the fact that journalists are usually on the Left has been a good thing for me and any other feminist. The issues I've worked on, such as abortion and women's rights, have historically been well received and supported by the Left. I've felt lucky that I was on the same side as those who program the "news." If the Right were in control, it would be safe to say that moving certain projects and issues through the media would not have been so easy for me, if possible at all. But that makes all the more frustrating the denials we hear from the Left that the news is controlled by, well, them.

On the Wrong Side

Since my days with NOW, I've found out what it's like trying to get your message out when you're on the "wrong" side of an issue.

As the attacks on Laura Schlessinger began to escalate, I learned from conversations with friends and colleagues that there was widespread concern in the gay community about this search-and-destroy mission. Someone had to speak up, so I nominated myself and wrote an opinion piece intended for the editorial pages of the *Los Angeles Times*.

During my 10 years as a feminist activist and commentator, whenever I submitted an opinion piece to the *Times*, it was published. I had always offered a piece that was relevant and moderately well written and that gave another viewpoint on an issue the newspaper had covered. All of those factors were present with this piece, and I expected the same response. I was wrong.

When I had submitted an opinion piece to a newspaper in the past, the editors had contacted me within a few hours, and at the most a few days. Well, I submitted the story, a few days came and went, and I heard nothing. Not even a rejection. After a few more days, I called the person who was assigned to handle query calls from submitters (she was not the editor), and she assured me that I would have an answer in a few days.

This was a simple 600-word commentary, not a volume that needed to be pored over. Furthermore, time is important with a piece of this sort: it's been written in response to a particular current event, and the more time passes the less relevant it becomes. The additional "few days" went by, along with more phone conversations with the editorial staffperson, but still no decision. After three weeks had passed without either a "yes" or a "no," even the woman I was dealing with seemed perplexed by the delay.

I came to the conclusion that the *Los Angeles Times* was unwilling to respond because on the one hand the editors did not want to publish a piece supporting Dr. Laura, but on the other hand it would have been difficult to say no to such a piece submitted by a credible gay feminist when their coverage had been obviously anti-Laura. So, hold, hold, hold, until it gets too old or the writer withdraws it.

> Since my days with NOW, I've found out what it's like trying to get your message out when you're on the "wrong" side of an issue.

Ultimately, I did withdraw it and faxed it cold (without a contact) to the editorial desk of the *New York Times*. Within an hour, an editor from the op-ed page called to say yes, it was a good piece and they'd love to run it. *Voilà!* Back to the real world, with a newspaper that knows how to make a decision.

My *Times* liaison on the piece seemed sincere and hardworking; she checked in with me occasionally over the next few days for clarification on one point or another. It gradually became clear that there were several people involved in "editing" and "clearing" my piece. E-mails and telephone calls to me, however, consistently expressed the editors' intent to publish, despite an increasing delay.

Eventually, I was e-mailed an "edited" version of the piece that bore little resemblance to what I had originally submitted. It was now replete with sentences I never wrote and moved in a direction that was arguably *anti*-Laura.

In the past, none of the edits on any of my opinion pieces had been such as to warrant a protest, but someone at the *New York Times* had actually added the line, "Not everything Schlessinger has to say is offensive." This was so contrary to the intent of the piece that I asked for the line to be removed. The editors refused. Rather than let myself be positioned as some sort of apologist for comments I deemed to be offensive, I once again withdrew the piece.

Two months had now passed, and it was the premiere week of the *Dr. Laura* television show. In the meantime, two more anti-Laura stories had run in the *Los Angeles Times*. I decided to resubmit to them, but this time to "Counterpunch," the opinion page of the entertainment section, "Calendar."

The editor of "Counterpunch," Lee Margulies, called promptly and said, "Gosh, this is good, but it sounds like you wrote it months ago." He was right. The article had become obsolete. I constructed a new piece, making essentially the same arguments but using fresh examples that updated the material. Still, it only worked because *Dr. Laura* had premiered the week I submitted the piece to "Calendar." A week later and it would have been dead.

I must give credit to Lee Margulies. He never indicated to me his own position on the issue, but the prevailing opinion around him was presumably much the same as in the paper's editorial offices. Nonetheless, he had the integrity to print a pro-Laura piece.

There was one deeply disappointing editorial decision, however, which proved that the Thought Police mentality has seeped in everywhere, affecting even those who are inclined to operate on principle rather than on politics. In reference to the gay community assailing Dr. Laura while ignoring rapper Eminem, one of the key points I made was that the gay male community needed to address its own misogyny. I put it this way:

> These are important questions that should be asked, especially by those with the double standard in a community that needs to address its own misogyny. Tragically, it should be obvious to most people that those responsible for the murders of people like Brandon Teena and Matthew Shepard are living in a milieu created in part by people like Eminem, not Laura "Go-Take-On-The-Day" Schlessinger.

That paragraph, the heart of the piece from my point of view, revealing what I believed to be the genesis of the attacks against Dr. Laura, was excised in its entirety by the *Los Angeles Times*.

Meanwhile, the delaying tactics used by both newspapers had kept an important part of the story—the rejection by some gay individuals of the new Left establishment's attempt to silence Schlessinger—from becoming a part of the debate until the issue had already formed itself in the minds of the public. If it happened in this case, you can be sure it happens in others.

Who Needs James Carville?

We know what to expect from magazines such as *The American Spectator* and *National Review*. They have a specific political persuasion, and they make no bones about it. Some of my friends consider them "sneaky, untrustworthy rags," and yet you know what you're getting when you read them: conservative opinion and conservative columnists with their particular spin on the news. I actually enjoy magazines like these. I've always had an easier time trusting people (or entities) that are honest, even if I disagree with them.

If honesty is your standard, then suddenly the truly sneaky, untrustworthy rags are *Time* and *Newsweek*—publications that purport to be objective and nonpartisan while taking you along for their ride.

Consider a comment Evan Thomas, then Washington bureau chief for *Newsweek* and now the magazine's assistant managing editor, made in 1994. Thomas said this about Paula Jones's sexual-harassment charge against Bill Clinton: "Yes, the case is being fomented by right-wing nuts, and yes, she is not a very credible witness, and it's really not a law case at all. But Clinton has got a problem here. He has a history of womanizing that most people believe is a problem. . . . That's a dangerous attitude to have. It leads to things like this, some sleazy woman with big hair coming out of the trailer parks. . . . I think she's a dubious witness, I really do."[2]

Gosh, with Evan Thomas on your side, who needs James Carville?

Some of my friends, proud of their refreshing honesty, admit they see a liberal bias in news coverage but believe it's okay because, according to them, it represents the way the majority feels. Really? That is one of the foundational arguments of the Thought Police: they aren't trying to control what people think, they're just giving people what they want.

In the first place, considering the outcome of the 2000 presidential election, it's safe to say that what the Left provides is *not* what at least half the people of voting age want. More important, if the news outlets are "just giving people what they want," why do they insist that there is no political spin in their coverage? Why is it so important to appear unbiased?

> **That is one of the foundational arguments of the Thought Police: they aren't trying to control what people think, they're just giving people what they want.**

It's because they are in the business of *influencing* us in the direction of guilt, shame, and retreat on socially important issues. Influencing us would be so much more difficult if we knew that what we were seeing was, for all intents and purposes, propaganda and certainly *not* news.

The issue isn't whether or not you agree with Burleigh and Thomas or what you think of Bill Clinton—the important point of these examples is that they are not anomalies. Burleigh, Thomas, and the industry of which they are a part have led us to believe that they are above the politics of the Thought Police, when in actuality they are its technological foot soldiers.

'F—ing Idiot'

Sometimes even journalists themselves see the bias. In a column titled "Honest Bias," William Saletan, a senior writer for the Internet magazine *Slate*, discussed the impact of reporter bias on the coverage of the 2000 presidential campaign: "Politically, while nobody at *Slate* toed the Democratic line in this election, most of us heartily criticized Bush. Yes, Bush deserved it. But often, so did Gore. The reason Gore got less grief than he deserved is that most of us shared his ideology. His assumptions were as invisible to us as our own."[3]

Saletan makes a cogent argument that reporter bias is subconscious. I believe some of it is, but plenty isn't. Regardless of its genesis, the end result of bias is what we should at least be aware of—whether it's Dan Rather gushing over Hillary Clinton, Bryant Gumbel silently mouthing "F—ing idiot" about a guest from the conservative Family Research Council on CBS's *Early Show*,[4] or Saletan's colleagues subconsciously giving their candidate a free ride. The reality is that the majority of news outlets are telling you that they're objective, know you believe it most of the time, and then proceed to do the bidding of the Thought Police. "Dr. Laura Schlessinger is a bigot and a homophobe." "The Los Angeles riot was a race-based rebellion." "Racism is running rampant." "Vast right-wing conspiracy . . ."

A study conducted by Drs. Robert and Linda Lichter and Stanley Rothman confirms the apparent connection between journalists' personal political beliefs and their coverage of issues. In *The Media Elite: America's New Powerbrokers*, Lichter, Lichter, and Rothman report that more than 60 percent of journalists described themselves as "liberal." On specific issues, the percentage tilts further to the left; for example, 90 percent of journalists identified themselves as pro-choice.

Since, as the Lichters and Rothman put it, journalists are the "gatekeepers for the messages contending groups and individuals wish to send to each other and to the general public,"[5] recognizing their perspective helps us understand what happens to information as it moves through these middlemen. (Some of my feminist friends would want me to say *middlepeople*, but I just can't be that politically correct!) Understanding who is influencing what we

> **Understanding who is influencing what we think, and how they are doing it, is of utmost importance in maintaining our true individualism.**

think, and how they are doing it, is of utmost importance in maintaining our true individualism.

UnFAIR

The Lichter/Rothman findings, both in that study and in other, more recent ones, are considered controversial, particularly by the Left, which is resistant to any questioning of the idea that the media are totally objective and honest. I wish that was true about the media, but it's not.

Taking special issue with the study and its authors is Fairness and Accuracy in Reporting (FAIR), which describes itself as a national media watch group that offers criticism of media bias and censorship. A FAIR Research

Memo complained about a study by the Lichters that found PBS's programming to be biased toward the Left. The FAIR Web site quotes the Lichters as stating, "On the social and political controversies addressed by PBS documentaries across a full year of programs, the balance of opinion tilted consistently in a liberal direction."[6] FAIR (certainly a convenient acronym) claimed that the Lichter study was selective, ignoring PBS documentaries that did not support its conclusions. FAIR gave no specifics of documentaries omitted, however; and the Lichter study certainly appears to be comprehensive.

Especially revealing was FAIR's charge that the Lichters are not to be trusted because they are "academics" and "conservatives." FAIR specifically complained about Robert Lichter's "conservative worldview" and about what it described as "conservative" funding sources for the Center for Media and Public Affairs (CMPA), which the Lichters founded and for which they serve as president and vice president.

If FAIR's position is that any study generated by the Lichters is suspect because they have their own political beliefs, then FAIR must be subjected to the same rigorous criticism. Ironically, FAIR seems quite proud of its efforts as agents of the Thought Police.

Here's the way FAIR reported on its campaign to get New York's WABC Radio to fire vitriolic talk show host Bob Grant: "FAIR's Bob Grant Success. Thanks in part to activists from all over the country who contacted ABC and Disney, FAIR's campaign against the bigotry of talk show host Bob Grant has been a success."[7]

Before taking on that project, FAIR was worried about someone *not* being able to speak his mind: Mumia Abu-

Jamal, the convicted murderer of a 25-year-old Philadelphia police officer. Under the headline "Mumia Abu-Jamal: Silenced on Death Row," FAIR complained: "The Philadelphia Fraternal Order of Police, which succeeded in getting National Public Radio to drop Abu-Jamal's series of commentaries, failed in its efforts to get [his] book [deal] canceled . . . it is a violation of his First Amendment Rights, which do not vanish simply because someone is convicted of a crime and incarcerated. . . ."[8]

Personally, I'm disturbed by the idea of either Grant or Abu-Jamal, a convicted cop killer, having free rein on the airwaves. There are compelling arguments for both of them to be heard, however. My point is that it is hypocritical to decide that the First Amendment applies to some people and not to others. If Abu-Jamal deserves to have a radio show, then Bob Grant does, too; you can't have it both ways. But FAIR thinks it can. What it's saying in effect is, "We can handle freedom of speech because what we have to say is right. You are weak and stupid, and need to be silenced." Welcome to the party of tolerance and inclusion.

I'd Rather Not

Bryant Gumbel's typically juvenile response ("F—ing idiot") to a conservative guest is so obvious that it loses most of its power to influence. The spin on the evening news is a more insidious matter. Here, courtesy of Dan Rather, anchor and managing editor of the *CBS Evening News*, is a prime example of how an editorial edge is woven into your "news":

This was President Bush's first day at the office, and he did something to quickly please the right flank of his party: he reinstituted an anti-abortion policy that had been in place during his father's term and the Reagan presidency but was lifted during the Clinton years.[9]

Rather is telling you in no uncertain terms that President Bush used this important issue to make a political payoff in his first act as president. Compare that to Rather's characterization of Bill Clinton's first day as president:

On the anniversary of Roe versus Wade, President Clinton fulfills a promise, supporting abortion rights. . . . Today, with the stroke of a pen, President Clinton delivered on his campaign promise to cancel several anti-abortion regulations of the Reagan-Bush years.[10]

A cynical player of partisan politics versus a man fulfilling a promise to voters—two very different ways of characterizing men, each of whom was both appeasing a wing of his party *and* fulfilling a campaign promise. Although I was personally thrilled with Clinton's decisions on abortion rights, I can't pretend, as Dan Rather chose to do, that it was a matter of pure principle. Spin is that simple, that insidious, and a part of your nightly news.

Rather will take his editorials disguised as news as far as he can, but sometimes he needs to resort to other means to spin a story. Consider the Chandra Levy/Gary Condit mystery. As of this writing, Chandra Ann Levy, the 24-year-old alleged lover of Democratic Representative Gary Condit, is still missing. At the time of her disappearance, on May 1, 2001, Chandra was living her dream, finishing an internship in Washington, just weeks shy of graduating from the University of Southern California, and probably thinking she was in love. Then, she vanished.

No matter how you spin it, Condit is in trouble. Although he has not been named a suspect, he has comported himself oddly ever since the story broke, from his initial denial to everyone, including the police, that

> I can't pretend, as Dan Rather chose to do, that it was a matter of pure principle. Spin is that simple, that insidious, and a part of your nightly news.

he was romantically involved with Chandra to the publicity stunt of taking a lie-detector test without police involvement. Condit is behaving, well, like a man with something to hide.

This is obviously a bona-fide news story. Our country just went through months of wondering whether a president would be removed from office for sexual involvement with an intern who, however, was unquestionably alive and well. Surely the *disappearance* of an intern merits some coverage.

Most of our news outlets agreed. Cable news and network programming alike covered the story, with the one exception of the *CBS Evening News with Dan Rather*. For 11 weeks Rather refused to report on the Levy/Condit case. Even when the police searched Condit's home, Rather decided not to report the story. His own producers prepared a segment on it, but it was never aired.[11]

Jim Murphy, Rather's executive producer, tried to explain the bizarre decision making to a reporter from the

New York Times: "What we were seeing, what we were hearing, wasn't always solid. Often it was rumor or gossip. We chose not to report that until we had something that we thought was important to the story."[12]

That's funny, because when it comes to reporting a story replete with gossip and innuendo about a Republican, Rather and Murphy's principle-laden news program has a different standard. The August 18, 2000, edition of the program featured a full report from Bob McNamara, who began, "As the spotlight zeros in on George W. Bush's front-running campaign, over and over now comes the 'Did you ever?' question. Again today, he was asked if he ever did cocaine and refused to answer."[13] So much for choosing not to report something that may be rumor or gossip.

Finally, on July 18, 2001, the *CBS Evening News* decided to report on Chandra's disappearance. What did Rather think was important to the story, something that wasn't rumor or gossip? The one angle that would be seen as clearing the California Democrat. Rather reported that the FBI's cold case unit had taken over the investigation—an indication, Rather explained, that there were no serious leads and no suspects in the case. After Rather's story ran, other news agencies reported that the FBI denied assigning the investigation to a cold case unit, or indeed taking it over at all.

Unfortunately for Rather, his story was . . . gossip.

On July 19, 2001, Rather was a guest on the syndicated talk radio program *Imus in the Morning*, and Don Imus asked him about his odd decisions on the Levy case. Imus also brought up Rather's inconsistencies—for example, the fact that nine years earlier he had reported with vigor on the Bob Packwood story. Rather had this to say about himself: "Well, you know, I've been a dumbass all my life, why would anybody expect me to be different about this?"

A little something you should know about a man who has the power to decide what millions of viewers will and will not hear. Regardless of whether we agree with Rather politically or not, most of us don't want a dumbass giving us the news.

Sauce for the Goose?

The Media Research Center (MRC), the nation's largest and most respected conservative media watchdog organization, tapes more than 150 hours a week of shows aired on the broadcast networks and cable news channels. MRC is the only organization in the country that has a complete tape library of network news and entertainment shows dating back to the late 1980s—more than 160,000 hours' worth so far. Every day, teams of MRC analysts enter data from these shows into a customized computer database, identifying bias in the process. Analysts also comb through the nation's most influential newspapers and news magazines.[14]

Recently, MRC compared the way journalists reported on Hillary Clinton's $8-million book advance and Newt Gingrich's $4.5-million book advance. The least this research reveals is how right the Lichters are. (I wish I could bring you this information from a source not considered conservative, but for now it seems that it's up to the conservatives to tell us when the Emperor has no clothes.)

Typical of the coverage of Newt Gingrich's contract with HarperCollins was the suggestion by CBS reporter

Eric Engberg, on February 1, 1995, that the embattled new Speaker of the House ought to surrender his advance: "Speaker Gingrich, who could end the controversy by scuttling the book deal, is standing fast."

Dan Rather chimed in during the CBS Evening News: "More tonight about whether Australian-born and -centered communications billionaire Rupert Murdoch is trying to buy influence with politically connected authors." HarperCollins is part of Murdoch's multibillion-dollar communications empire, which, not for the first time, was facing regulatory questions in the United States.

When Gingrich did give up his advance, Rita Braver, filling in as host of CBS's Face the Nation, asked Bob Dole, "You don't think he'll be called 'The Four-and-a-Half-Million-Dollar Man' any more?"

Who engineered Hillary's book deal with Simon & Schuster six years later? Bob Barnett, Rita Braver's husband.[15] And CBS? It is part of the Viacom empire, which also includes MTV, Nickelodeon, VHI, BET, Paramount Pictures, Paramount Television, Infinity, Country Music Television, Showtime, Blockbuster, Madison Square Garden, various sports franchises, and . . . Simon & Schuster. I wouldn't recommend holding your breath as you wait for Engberg, Rather, or Braver to inquire if Viacom, with various regulatory interests in front of Congress, is trying to "buy influence with politically connected authors."

A comment by Time columnist Margaret Carlson on CNN's Capital Gang pretty much summed up the prevailing media attitude about the Clinton book deal: "Unlike Newt Gingrich and his book deal, Hillary Clinton isn't getting her $8 million advance from Rupert Murdoch with his billions of dollars' worth of legislation before the

House, which, unlike the Senate, banned such deals. If Hillary were to utter her first spontaneous word and answer the burning question—Is the Senate worth all you had to put up with?—the book might be worth it. Anyway, since the independent counsel impoverished her, let's let her trick some publisher into paying her legal bills. It takes a Senator."[16]

What Carlson ignored—and she's a smart, informed woman, so she had to have chosen to ignore it—is the remarkable similarity between the two deals. Yes, the House of Representatives and the Senate have different rules about outside income. But the main difference between the two is that Representative Gingrich ultimately gave up his entire advance. As of this writing, Senator Clinton is refusing even to let her new colleagues review her deal.

From the Horse's Mouth

Still not sure? Okay, don't take it from me; take it from *Newsweek*'s Washington bureau reporter Howard Fineman. On November 28, 2000, he was a guest on *Imus in the Morning*. Discussing the election fiasco in Florida, Don Imus asked, "What if Gore had won and Bush—what if the roles were reversed? How would, I wouldn't want to include you in this, but how would the liberal weenies of the news media be treating this if the roles were reversed?"[17]

Fineman's response? "Oh, my God. Are you kidding? That George Bush was a crybaby, that he was the spoiled son of a failed President. You know, you could just hear, the personal attacks on Bush would be just absolutely vicious."[18]

Tim Graham of the Media Research Center notes,

But, as Fineman knows, the networks aren't calling Gore a crybaby or subjecting him to vicious personal attacks. Monday, all of the broadcast networks interrupted prime time to carry Gore's plea for patience; Sunday, NBC refused to give the certified winner, George W. Bush, a similar chance to speak live and unedited to the entire country. Instead, in the Eastern and Central time zones, NBC showed *Titanic*, starring Leonardo DiCaprio and Kate Winslet. For those who missed the movie so they could watch the finale of this historic election: the ship sank.[19]

Why is all of this an issue? Because people like Burleigh, Rather, and Braver are the vehicles through which the Left speaks to us. The way controversial ideas are disseminated makes a big difference in what we think of someone or something and whether we even feel comfortable thinking freely about an issue. My beef with the news media is not that they represent a point of view on the issues that contradicts mine. Actually, the views promoted by the news media are usually in sync with my own. The problem is that journalists share much more than a link with the establishment Left

> The way controversial ideas are disseminated makes a big difference in what we think of someone or something and whether we even feel comfortable thinking freely about an issue.

on the issues—they are also the Thought Police's most important resource.

I am not concerned about people or entities that are *honest* about their agenda. Many on the Right, perhaps even you, consider, for example, Geraldo Rivera a honcho of the Thought Police because of the obvious liberal bias in his work. In fact, Geraldo is no more involved in thought control than Rush Limbaugh is. Both present programming that is opinion-based, and do so proudly. Both are understood and admired by their audiences for what they are. Neither is pretending to be Walter Cronkite. The Thought Police, in order to influence the public, must operate within what is considered mainstream, objective news media. Geraldo is not considered either.

I have a confession to make, which will also shed some light on what I'm talking about. In spite of his unwavering left-wing commitment, Geraldo was one of the first people to stand up and support me publicly during the NOW fight. Geraldo put principle before politics. He was there, bucking the left-wing establishment when it really counted.

In any case, the problem is not Geraldo, Bill O'Reilly, Rush Limbaugh, or anyone else with a program that runs on attitude and opinion, liberal or conservative. The problem is entities and individuals that have an agenda but attempt to hide it.

News . . . Not

The problem for anyone who battles for our minds is how to reach us without allowing us to put up any barriers.

When are we the most vulnerable to accepting someone's message uncritically? Common sense suggests, and research confirms, that our level of skepticism changes depending on the format in which information is presented. We're more skeptical of a commercial's claims than we are of what our local television news anchor tells us. We're more suspicious when we read the editorial and opinion pages of a newspaper than when we read the "news" reports.

Why? We've all been brought up to believe the news is real and can't be tampered with. Newspaper reporters don't write in the first person; they seem to be just recording "what happened." The pioneers of television news, Edward R. Murrow and Walter Cronkite, exhibited an air of honesty that created a belief that if they said it, it must be true.

Benefiting from such expectations, the Thought Police make use of television and print news to shape what we think. Where do you suppose print and broadcast journalists get many of their ideas and much of the information for their stories? From the press releases sent to them by publicists, activists, and politicians—who are all battling for our minds.

As a publicist, my expertise was in the electronic segment of advertising and marketing. My job was to get material about my corporate client's product on the news *as a news story.* That's right: corporate America—like political activists—knows that taking out ads in newspapers or buying commercial time on television is only one, and in many ways the weakest, way to reach the public.

I worked with material known in the industry as "video news releases" (VNRs), which are exactly what they sound like: press releases in video form (note, incidentally, the phrase *news release,* which suggests more credibility than *press release*). Let me tell you about one of my most successful campaigns. It was the campaign that made me understand exactly how powerful television news is and how remarkably easy it is to manipulate. This was a lesson I would use throughout my years as an activist.

The client company, which will remain nameless, had its product brand anniversary coming up and wanted the news media to cover it not as a corporate event but as news. Of course, in order to place what is effectively an ad in the news, you have to give the news producers what they need: great visuals and something that at least sounds as if it could be actual news. With these requirements in mind, the clients and I decided to throw a "birthday celebration" for this particular product. We brought in several children (the target of the product), a huge puppet version of the product mascot was in attendance, and we filmed the whole darn thing. *Voilà,* a video news release!

With great video footage of a completely contrived "news" event, we sent every television news station in the country a fax that made a pitch about the event and included the satellite coordinates for downlinking the video. A staff person then personally called the assignment editor at every network station in the top 50 television markets, pitching the story one on one. If an assignment editor liked it (meaning, if we had done our job right), she'd downlink the material from the satellite and place it somewhere in the newscast. As news.

My favorite part was that everyone in the chain knew exactly how the symbiotic relationship worked. Newscasts have a never-ending need for content. Corporate and special-interest America have things they want us to buy—with our money and our minds—and so they are happy to provide the content. (Here's another difference, by the way, between the Murrow/Cronkite period and today: Then, the networks each had only one newscast per day, and it was 15 minutes long; today's newscasters have hours of broadcast time to fill. Perhaps we should go back to the days of time constraints!)

In any case, the whole project—mascot, kids, and all—worked beautifully. The video aired in almost every one of the top 50 markets in the nation. It was a coup, and our client was thrilled. This may seem to you especially blatant—pitching a product as news. But consider the way protests and demonstrations by special-interest groups are arranged exclusively to receive media coverage. What is pitched is different—a product brand versus an issue—but the method is the same. In each case, the critical thing is not to let the public know how it is done.

The Thought Police in Hollywood

There are two closets in Hollywood: one for gays and the other for conservatives. These days, the conservative closet is more jammed than the gay one. As Michael Levine, a Los Angeles–based publicist, puts it, "It's easier to declare yourself a gay, drug-addicted kleptomaniac than to call yourself a conservative in Hollywood."[20]

If we were to accept appearances, Charlton Heston and Arnold Schwarzenegger are the only two conservatives in Hollywood. Well, don't be fooled. It's not that actors are somehow genetically predisposed to be on the

Left, it's that it is perilous to be anywhere else. What Heston and Schwarzenegger have in common is a level of power that outweighs what would be a dangerous position for a less successful actor.

What *are* the dangers for an actor who is thought of as conservative, anti-abortion, or, God forbid, a Republican? Obviously the big one is not getting picked for plum assignments. Less serious, but wearing over the long haul, is social ostracism and innuendos about your professional standing. It's difficult to get people on the record about their other-than-Left politics in this town. Still, a few stories have emerged that provide some insight into the way the backlash works.

> There are two closets in Hollywood: one for gays and the other for conservatives.

Actor Bo Derek has been very vocal about her conservative politics. During the 2000 presidential campaign, she even attended the Republican National Convention in Philadelphia, provoking ridicule such as this pearl from Argus Hamilton in the *Los Angeles Times:* "Movie star Bo Derek was one of the speakers before the GOP convention in Philadelphia. She really feels at home in the Republican Party. They've both been looking for their next big hit since [the 1980s]."

This may not sound like a big deal—after all, it's only a joke. In fact, it's not merely a joke; it is reflective of a tendency in Hollywood to dismiss and ostracize those who don't parrot the Left's party line. Talking with Chris Matthews on CNBC's political program *Hardball*, Derek remarked that admitting to Republican leanings in Hollywood can indeed be a poor career move. She later told an interviewer for the *New York Post*, "They [Hollywood liberals] are very adamant and almost militant about their views. It's tough to have a nice, open conversation of any kind. People get really angry, and they treat me as though I'm some hateful monster." Derek went on to say that she's been warned by peers to keep her mouth shut if she knows what's good for her. She said, "I've been told that I'll never work again."

Sharon Lawrence of *NYPD Blue* had the bad luck simply to be pictured in *People* magazine on the same page as President George W. Bush and other well-known Republicans. A lifelong and active Democrat, Lawrence happened to be in Washington, D.C., attending an event that had no connection with the Bush inauguration.

After the photo was published, she received hate mail and was confronted irately on the streets of Los Angeles about "being a Republican."[21] Gossip maven Liz Smith reported in her column, "In a recent business meeting, Lawrence was chilled when a producer said, with heavy emphasis, 'I have to ask you, are you really a Republican?'"[22] Lawrence, reportedly "shaken" by the experience, told Smith, "If one is even *perceived* [emphasis hers] to be a Republican in Hollywood, there can be an excluding reaction and people genuinely resent you!" Smith ended her column by reassuring her readers (who include Hollywood's elite), "So let's set the record straight: Sharon Lawrence is *not* a Republican."

Whew, Lawrence's career is probably safe after all. She's high enough on the industry ladder that a Liz Smith column can make her pure again. But from the way the producer asked her that question in the business meeting, it was pretty clear that if she had said yes, the "business" they were there to discuss would not have happened.

Consider how this must affect the kind of product the entertainment industry makes and promotes. In enforcing a code that punishes personal deviation from the Left's norm, the Thought Police simultaneously eliminate any ideas for projects that challenge the status quo. If it's dangerous to admit that you're a Republican, what do you think would happen if you went into a "business meeting" suggesting a film that was anti-abortion?

Doug Urbanski is a veteran producer and manager who, teamed with actor Gary Oldman, made the British Academy Award–winning film *Nil by Mouth*. Urbanski also produced the Oscar-nominated film *The Contender*, starring Oldman and Joan Allen. In Hollywood, however, Doug has a problem. He's a conservative. Despite his talent and his decades of success in theater and film (including projects, such as *The Contender*, that reflect other political points of view), he still had to be reminded by his wife, producer Diane Wilk (she executive-produced the hit television show *The Nanny*), what to say and what not to say when they attended Hollywood parties. "We would always have to have a conference to remind ourselves what not to say," Doug confessed to me. "The last thing you wanted to do was say something conservative, or praise a conservative politician, in a room full of entertainment honchos. There was too much risk of being completely isolated."

Although Doug is open about his conservative worldview, Gary Oldman has made the personal decision to not discuss his politics, refusing to answer questions by colleagues and others about his political beliefs. Because of his refusal to announce his allegiance to the Left, however, the Thought Police in Hollywood have labeled Gary either an "arch" conservative or a "neo" conservative (these days someone like Gary could never just be labeled a plain "conservative"). It is a reputation that has stuck, despite the fact that even Doug, his close friend and colleague, doesn't know Gary's political leanings, and certainly neither do any of the McCarthyite labelers.

Summing up the experience of having to announce allegiance to the Left or face ostracism by being labeled "conservative" by default, Gary, who is British, mused, "And I thought Americans were finished with making lists." Apparently not.

Doug and Gary survive in Hollywood because they're talented, of course, but also because they established themselves and garnered power before they challenged the Left's status quo. Even so, it isn't easy. Doug told me that when Gary appeared on PBS's *Charlie Rose Show* to promote *Hannibal,* he made this comment: "Isn't it sad that the most popular word in America is 'abortion' and the least popular is 'Jesus.'" Rose, who knows when an interview is about to get good, continued his discussion with Gary, which revolved around issues of spirituality, not abortion. It was that kind of remark, however, that, while not exposing whether or not Gary is pro-choice, has been used to reinforce the labeling of Gary as "neo" conservative, furthering attempts by the very-powerful in Hollywood to keep both he and Doug professionally isolated. Gary was right. Uttering "Jesus" in reference to the man is indeed a risky thing to do in Hollywood.

Keep in mind, we're not talking about political extremists who support Taliban-like public policy, the killing of abortion doctors, or the blockading of clinics. We're talking about good people facing hostility and potentially career-ending blacklisting because they are Republican, personally anti-abortion, or have simply refused to announce their allegiance to the Left.

A Woman of Courage

What about an actor who isn't generally conservative but is "incorrect" on an issue? It takes a certain amount of courage and principle to admit in Hollywood that you're against abortion. Actor Kate Mulgrew has done just that, describing herself as a liberal Democrat and ardently pro-life. I think Mulgrew's story is worth sharing with you, to demonstrate that despite the pressure of the Thought Police and the potential repercussions in a very small industry where everyone knows everything, there are people who are willing to be honest about their values.

An extraordinary actor who is best known today for her portrayal of Captain Kathryn Janeway on UPN's *Star Trek: Voyager* series, Mulgrew has worked in theatre, television, and film for more than 23 years. Raised in a large Irish

> **Despite the pressure of the Thought Police and the potential repercussions in a very small industry where everyone knows everything, there are people who are willing to be honest about their values.**

Catholic family, she came into her own holding some beliefs that many probably share in Hollywood but are
afraid to admit publicly.

In 2000, *The American Feminist* magazine—the quarterly publication of a group called "Feminists for Life"—
ran a feature article on Mulgrew that included this
passage:

> "Life is sacred to me on all levels. Abortion does not
> compute with my philosophy. . . . I practiced my belief
> at great cost to myself," said Mulgrew, who became
> pregnant at an early age and placed her baby girl for
> adoption. They were reunited two years ago. Mulgrew
> believes that losing a child through "adoption or abor-
> tion almost always promises the mother a legacy of
> shame and regret. I have to be frank about my experi-
> ence. I survived it. Women often don't believe that they
> can survive nine months of pregnancy and place the
> child with an adoptive family. Life is not always easy."[23]

Personally, I love the pro-choice status quo, and I believe that the pro-choice argument for society will always
prevail as long as complete debate can take place and
people can freely participate in the process. The pro-
choice argument allows for Kate Mulgrew to make her
choices and for every other woman to make her own decisions based on her religious beliefs and personal values.

Even so, many of my pro-choice friends are upset at
what they term my "sympathetic" portrayal of Mulgrew's
pro-life beliefs. In fact, it's not necessarily Mulgrew's beliefs that are sympathetic, *she* is. Her statements about
abortion and adoption are not the kind that even invite

agreement or disagreement. They invite respect and admiration for someone willing to share her own painful story in support of her values.

What Art Is

The heroes in our stories are individuals who dare to take their responsibility in life seriously. For an artist like Mulgrew, this can mean speaking up about an important social issue that happens to be separate from her work. For other artists, it can mean choosing or creating projects that have something to say at an infinitely personal level—something that, although it may be shocking, strengthens both artist and audience by showing us another side of our humanity. One actor who takes seriously this responsibility to her art is Charlotte Rampling.

It should not go undiscussed here that the very nature of film—its ability to draw us in and to move us—makes it vulnerable to the Thought Police. In recent years, it has most often been the far Right that has organized to protest films and television it finds threatening because they portray life in unconventional ways (*Ellen,* for example) or because they challenge a prevailing belief system (*The Last Temptation of Christ*). Of course, the films regarded as the most threatening are those that have the most potential to shake us out of our unconscious, habitual lives.

Charlotte Rampling was originally celebrated as one of the great faces of the sixties. Her role in *Georgy Girl* (1966) made her famous, and she has acted in more than 40 films since, including Visconti's *The Damned* (1969), Dick Richards's *Farewell, My Lovely* (1975), Woody

Allen's *Stardust Memories* (1980), Sidney Lumet's *Verdict* (1982), and most recently François Ozon's *Under the Sand* (2001).

Despite all her other work, her image remains fixed for many people as the seductive and disturbed young woman in probably the most controversial of her films, *The Night Porter* (1974). In this film, Rampling starred as the Jewish mistress of her former Nazi captor, played by Dirk Bogarde. Then considered sexually explicit (though it is certainly not by today's standards), the film was actually shocking because it dared to explore "forbidden" love—in this case, a sado-masochistic relationship. Rampling made a similar decision when she made *Max Mon Amour* (1986), a story about a bored Parisian housewife having an affair with an orangutan. Shocking? Certainly, but brave as well in its willingness to face areas that most of us would prefer to leave hidden in the dark recesses. There was nothing explicit in the film; it was the *idea* that took center stage.

In a world where creative freedom is supposed to reign, Rampling answered a question about how she handled the uproar over *The Night Porter*, which included attacks on her for taking the role: "What you have to do is somehow turn off the sound of all the stuff that's going on when a film like *Night Porter* comes out, and just move on, knowing what you've done. And I knew what I'd done in that film with Dirk Bogarde. Whether people saw it or not remained to be seen, but we knew we'd done something—so with that knowledge, I moved on. You just don't have to listen to all those personal insults from everybody. I was shat upon. . . ."[24]

Rampling's eschewing of the ever-tempting big Hollywood machine, which today continues to embrace mindless violence while rejecting films that challenge our emotional and sexual lives, didn't come out of the blue as some grand theoretical commitment to her art. Rampling's personal resolve to make films that do more than entertain came at the age of 21, when the death of her 23-year-old sister devastated her life. "My mother almost died out of grief," she told an interviewer from the *Guardian.* "I think that's when I tried to understand what the hell was going on, and took parts like *Night Porter,* and other parts that sort of delved into the human psyche—they weren't just entertainment films. I didn't want to entertain any more. I became very aware of the other side of life, not just having fun."[25]

There is an irony to the fact that Rampling is not the kind of actor that today's (or yesterday's!) Hollywood establishment understands. Sure, she's made some Hollywood movies, but Rampling has found more acceptance in Europe, where sexuality and strong women are celebrated. "We all have loads of emotional information; what an actor does is bring it to the surface. I jump without a net because that's how I am," she says. "The information comes out because I am brave enough to allow it. I'm not brave as a human being in everyday life. I'm brave when I'm acting."[26]

Ultimately, for all of us it comes down to the personal. What project an artist chooses, and how we in the audience react, is an individual matter. Being an individual doesn't necessarily mean being *different* from everyone else—it means being free to make choices that best suit us.

"I love people, but . . . there are a lot of things I haven't been able to let out, and I'm able to let them out through the screen and this medium," Rampling continues. "I think that all us people who perform and are called artists are usually very crippled people, and we use this to uncripple ourselves for a little bit of time. When people want to see your film, you're over the moon because you've actually made real contact. That's something very special."[27]

> Being an individual doesn't necessarily mean being different from everyone else—it means being free to make choices that best suit us.

Despite her protestations, you know that Rampling is in fact a brave human being. A woman of enduring, self-possessed beauty and among our era's most gifted actors, she is also one of our heroic individuals. Both Kate Mulgrew and Charlotte Rampling—two women who could not be more different—challenge us and the status quo, one personally, the other professionally. Both have been and remain at risk in a culture guided by the Thought Police. Their personal courage provides us with much-needed benchmarks of what it means to be a unique individual.

CHAPTER
8

The Thought Police in Academia
Indoctrinating the Next Generation

"I never taught language for the purpose of teaching it, but invariably used language as a medium for the communication of thought; thus the learning of language was coincident with the acquisition of knowledge."

—*Annie Sullivan (Helen Keller's teacher), speaking to the American Association to Promote the Teaching of Speech to the Deaf, July 1894*

In his autobiography, *Creating Equal: My Fight Against Racial Preferences*, Ward Connerly tells of being shouted down during a speech about affirmative action at Emory University. Ward is not alone. The heckler as censor became commonplace on college campuses in the 1960s, when speakers who supported the Vietnam War or opposed the Black Panthers were shouted down, presented with dead pigs, and occasionally forced to leave the campus accompanied by armed guards.

Sometimes the speaker never even makes it to the lectern. In addition to heckling speakers and shouting them down, other tactics at the academy include the cancellation of speaking engagements and the "uninviting" of panelists who may challenge the Left's status quo.

The Politically Uninvited

My experience with this was vicarious until the fall of 2000. That is when I joined the ranks of the Politically Uninvited.

During the height of the attacks on Dr. Laura Schlessinger, I was asked to participate in a panel for a class at the University of Southern California. The professor explained that she needed a "conservative" who could represent Dr. Laura's point of view. (It's now inevitable, of course, that if you come out against oppression and intolerance and for freedom of expression, you're the "conservative." Who would have predicted *that* turnaround?)

The professor explained that the other panelists would be a representative from the Web site that had targeted Laura, a representative from GLAAD, and a representative from the ACLU; in other words, representatives from two groups that had directly participated in the attacks and a third group that had supported the other two with its assurances that freedom of expression didn't apply to Dr. Laura (see chapter 3). So, three against one.

No problem—I've handled worse. I thought speaking before a class would be fun and a terrific opportunity to discuss the issue, considering the press's biased coverage of the assault. I accepted the invitation.

A few days later I received a rather cryptic phone message from the professor saying, literally, that she had to "uninvite" me from the panel. When I called her back, she explained that the other panelists had said they would refuse to take part if I were involved. She said she was rather shocked by their reaction, but she had put so much time into the project that she didn't want to risk it "falling apart," and so was forced to eliminate me from the discussion.

The *Los Angeles Times* had already published my opinion piece in support of Dr. Laura, with my arguments about the speciousness of the attacks and the hypocrisy of the gay community. At first, I was actually pleased that the anti-Laura people were being so blatant in their effort to keep a dissenting voice from being heard, and I didn't believe that the professor would easily acquiesce to a so obviously childish demand. I reminded her that she was setting up a panel with people who were involved in the project of silencing someone and implored her not to let them speak without counterpoint. Their demand that no opposition be represented on the panel was in and of itself part of the story. *This* was the topic that needed to be discussed with the class.

Unfortunately, my belief that the professor would be committed to having all sides heard was misplaced. Not only did she acquiesce to the Thought Police bullies, but also she apparently was so intimidated that even the idea of my showing up unofficially (which I never indicated I was intending to do) panicked her. She asked me to *not even consider entering the building*, in the event I was planning on attending the discussion as an onlooker. I suggested that she at least tell her students what had transpired. She declined. I was deeply disappointed but, sadly, not completely surprised.

This incident was my first experience on a campus of phenomena I had come to know all too well in NOW: groupthink and the placing of "group rights" over the individual's freedom of speech. Joining the ranks of the Politically Uninvited confirmed for me what I had been learning about the Left during the previous decade. To borrow Gertrude Stein's description of the city of Oakland, *there is no there there*. The Left implements speech and mind control because they know they cannot truly persuade on the issues; silencing the opposition becomes their only recourse.

> The Left implements speech and mind control because they know they cannot truly persuade on the issues; silencing the opposition becomes their only recourse.

In all fairness to USC, this was not an event arranged by the university as a whole or by the administration. It was one professor in one department who was unwilling to stand up to the bullies whose goal it was to keep a true discussion of events from her students. It was far too typical, however, of what we are seeing on campus after campus around the country. Ironically, colleges and universities, once the champions of freedom of expression and the leaders in encouraging genuine dialogue and inquiry, are now implementing the opposite. The liberal university culture has turned into, as one valiant professor put it, "the slithering gargoyle it once fought against—the oppressive Establishment."[1]

Bonfire of the Humanities

Novelists, such as George Orwell, with *1984* and *Animal Farm,* are often our most visionary writers, the ones who do the most to warn us about the reality of totalitarian regimes. In *Fahrenheit 451,* Ray Bradbury's frightening vision of the future published in 1953, firemen don't put out fires—they start them in order to burn books. In this prophetic novel, Bradbury describes a society that has achieved happiness by becoming a place where trivial information is good and knowledge and ideas are bad. Fire Captain Beatty explains it this way: "Give the people contests they win by remembering the words to more popular songs. . . . Don't give them slippery stuff like philosophy or sociology to tie things up with. That way lies melancholy."

Bradbury's story was written as a fantasy; it is becoming reality. Today on campus, "wrong-thinking" newspapers sometimes simply disappear; in other cases, they are officially "confiscated" by university administrators. And sometimes they are literally burned.

On September 27, 2000, "Nazi!" "Fascist!" and "White mother-f—er!" were among the verbal attacks hurled at Dan Flynn as he tried to deliver a speech at the University of California at Berkeley. Flynn is the author of *Cop Killer: How Mumia Abu-Jamal Conned Millions into Believing He Was Framed.* The students did not want anyone to hear his views regarding the leftist icon Abu-Jamal, who currently sits on death row for murdering Philadelphia police officer Daniel Faulkner in 1981.[2]

In the week leading up to the scheduled speech, hundreds of fliers posted around campus to promote it were ripped down, sidewalk chalkings were scribbled over, and a banner in the student union was seized.[3] At one point, a member of the Student Senate even suggested that the police should arrest Flynn if he attempted to speak.

Name-calling and flier theft weren't the only things in the arsenal of the Berkeley precinct of the Thought Police. Unable to continue his speech because of the hundreds of interruptions, Flynn found that the demonstrators set fire to the remaining copies of his book that were on display. In true Thought Police fashion, several book-burners then held up signs that exhorted others to "Fight Racial Censorship."

At Cornell University, Flynn has company. The conservative *Cornell Review* is in the distinctive position of so angering the Misery Merchants that two separate editions were stolen and burned by the Black Student Union in 1997. The *Review* had committed the crime of printing an editorial that questioned what was being taught in the school's Black Studies Department. The dean of students attended the bonfire, and Cornell spokeswoman Linda Grace-Kobas declared, "The students who oppose the *Cornell Review* have claimed their First Amendment right to be able to have symbolic burnings of the *Cornell Review*."[4] With Cornell and its Black Student Union, who needs Fire Captain Beatty?

Syracuse University certainly doesn't. In 1998, Pat Buchanan was invited to speak at the school's chapel.

Protesting students disrupted his speech by shouting, staging a "kiss-in," burning Bibles, and threatening to burn down the chapel itself.[5]

WorldNetDaily.com, an Internet news service that accurately describes itself as "fiercely independent," has reported extensively on the *Fahrenheit 451* incidents on campuses all across the country. At one point, WorldNetDaily.com interviewed Wesley Wynne, program director of the Collegiate Network, a nonprofit organization that "has helped establish more than 70 independent campus publications over the past 15 years." In the interview, Wynne commented, "We've seen these things happening more and more to our member publications. The trend does not bode well for free speech on campus."[6]

'Disappearing' the Messenger

Not all newspapers or books that challenge the Left on campus get burned—some just get "disappeared." In 2000, Chris Lilik was the editor of a Villanova University student newspaper called the *Conservative Column*. One day he received an ominous voicemail message from, ironically, the school's director of student development. The message? "We obviously have some concerns about the content of the *Conservative Column*. Therefore, I will be removing all the issues of the *Conservative Column* that I see."[7]

When Lilik checked, he found that, indeed, every copy of the newspaper had been confiscated. What awful thing had he printed that caused the university administration to "disappear" the paper? Lilik and his colleagues had run a parody advertisement for a local bank's ATM services.

Unfortunately, that bank was the one that provided Villanova's ATM services.

Lilik should have seen it coming. It's not just opinion about controversial social issues that puts original thinkers in jeopardy—it's any opinion. And parody, the ultimate in political commentary, is especially at risk.

> It's not just opinion about controversial social issues that puts original thinkers in jeopardy—it's any opinion.

The Student Press Law Center (SPLC), as quoted by the *Chronicle of Higher Education*, reports that 205 major student-newspaper thefts have occurred since it began recording them in 1993. At the University of Pennsylvania, a group called the "Black Community" stole 14,000 copies of an issue of the *Daily Pennsylvanian* to protest student-written columns that criticized affirmative action and questioned whether Martin Luther King Jr. was a national hero.[8]

In 2000, student activists stole Yale University's *Light and Truth* newspaper because the editors had objected to a freshman "safe-sex" program that they felt promoted risky sexual behavior. The fact that students are employing the theft tactic suggests that the Thought Police have indoctrinated the next generation quite well. But the students weren't alone in the Yale case. It was revealed that one of the university's deans had helped in the theft.[9]

At UC Berkeley, copies of the student paper were stolen six times in the 1996–97 academic year and once in 1997–98, each time apparently because of debates over ending affirmative action in California. Students who backed affirmative action stole as many as 23,000 copies each time, arguing that the newspaper was not supporting their cause.[10]

Horowitz's 'Racial Assault'

In February 2001, David Horowitz, editor-in-chief of FrontPageMagazine.com and president of the Center for the Study of Popular Culture, created a campus newspaper advertisement titled "Ten Reasons Why Reparations for Slavery Is a Bad Idea—and Racist, Too." Horowitz's ad has contributed some significant numbers to the SPLC's statistics.

Papers bearing the ad were burned at the University of Wisconsin at Madison and shredded at Berkeley.[11] But shredding was not enough: Berkeley students stormed the editorial offices of the *Daily Californian* to demand an apology. The paper in fact published a front-page apology, expressing regret that it had become "an inadvertent vehicle for bigotry."

After the *Brown Daily Herald* (the student newspaper of Brown University in Providence, Rhode Island) ran the ad, protestors promptly stole 4,000 copies and then stormed the *Daily Herald*'s editorial offices. When the matter came up at the next Brown faculty meeting, Lewis Gordon, chair of the Afro-American Studies program, suggested that the seizure of the newspaper was valid civil disobedience against "hate speech."[12] Gordon later compared the publication of the ad to "spray-painting the word 'nigger' on a campus wall" and added, "The ad wasn't speech. It was a racial assault, and we should admit this."[13] Asmara Ghebremichael, a senior majoring in Afro-American

Studies and architectural studies, who was a member of the "coalition" that stole the *Herald*, says of the ad, "If students were more educated, they'd be able to know the ad's contents were lies and propaganda."[14]

What caused such panic and outrage at universities all across the United States? What kind of "lies and propaganda" deserved the shredding, burning, and disappearance of campus newspapers? Did Horowitz defend slavery? Did he suggest that slavery is not a stain on the American Republic? Far from it. The following are three of Horowitz's "Ten Reasons Why Reparations for Slavery Is a Bad Idea—and Racist, Too," which are representative of his tone and line of argument.[15]

Three

Only a Tiny Minority of White Americans Ever Owned Slaves, and Others Gave Their Lives to Free Them

Only a tiny minority of Americans ever owned slaves. This is true even for those who lived in the antebellum South, where only one white in five was a slaveholder. Why should the non-slaveholders' descendants owe the slaves' descendants a debt? What about the descendants of the 350,000 Union soldiers who died to free the slaves? They gave their lives. What possible moral principle would ask them to pay again, through their descendants?

Five

The Historical Precedents Used to Justify the Reparations Claim Do Not Apply, and the Claim Itself Is Based on Race Not Injury

The historical precedents generally invoked to justify the reparations claim are payments to Jewish survivors of the Holocaust, Japanese-Americans and African-American victims of racial experiments in Tuskegee, or racial outrages in Rosewood and Oklahoma City. But in each case, the recipients of reparations were the direct victims of the injustice or their immediate families. This would be the only case of reparations to people who were not immediately affected and whose sole qualification to receive reparations would be racial. As has already been pointed out, during the slavery era, many blacks were free men or slave-owners themselves, yet the reparations claimants make no distinction between the roles blacks actually played in the injustice itself. Randall Robinson's book on reparations, *The Debt*, which is the manifesto of the reparations movement, is pointedly subtitled "What America Owes to Blacks." If this is not racism, what is?

Nine

What About the Debt Blacks Owe to America?

Slavery existed for thousands of years before the Atlantic slave trade was born, and in all societies. But in the thousand years of its existence, there never was an antislavery movement until white Christians—Englishmen and Americans—created one. If not for the antislavery attitudes and military power of white Englishmen and Americans, the slave trade would not have been brought to an end. If not for the sacrifices of white soldiers and a white American president who gave his life to sign the Emancipation Proclamation, blacks in America would *still* be slaves. If not for the dedication of Americans of all ethnicities and colors to a society based on the principle that all men are created equal, blacks in America would not enjoy the highest standard of living of blacks anywhere in the world, and indeed one of the highest standards of living of any people in the world. They would not enjoy the greatest freedoms and the most thoroughly protected individual rights anywhere. Where is the gratitude of black America and its leaders for those *gifts*?

Newsweek called the ad "intentionally inflammatory." Perhaps *Newsweek* is right. We know that shedding light on the Left's orthodoxy does indeed inflame . . . those who would rather keep everyone in the dark. But racial assault? Hate speech? I don't think so.

Free Speech for Me

The totalitarian cadres who shout down speakers, burn books, and disappear newspapers on today's campuses look in only one direction. "Feminists" at Penn State provided one of the most unfortunate examples of how absurd the double standard is.

On the one hand, the Penn State's Young Americans for Freedom invited Star Parker, a black conservative and former welfare mother, to speak. Her speech, titled "From Entitlement to Empowerment," was interrupted by demonstrators who, determined not to allow her to finish, blew whistles and marched to the front of the room in military clothing. They then continued to disrupt the speech by performing a skit.[16] The situation became so chaotic that Parker was forced to leave the building through a back door.

On the other hand, Penn State's "feminists" put together a program titled "Cuntfest," sponsored by Womyn's Concerns and Ellie Smeal's campus outreach effort, the Feminist Majority Leadership Alliance. "Cuntfest" also received $10,000 from the university committee responsible for promoting student activities; the committee's funds come from student fees, plus some state tax dollars.[17]

Frankly, I felt uncomfortable even repeating the program's title, and many of the exhibits were indeed too vulgar to describe here. In one of the *milder* ones, a woman threaded strings through her pierced nipples so that she could maneuver her breasts like puppets as she stood behind a prop to make it appear as though her breasts were talking to each other. At one point, the audience was treated to a film called "Butt F—ing Bunny," which featured paper puppets engaging in various sexual acts, including the one described in the title.

> There is a twisted war being waged on campus when a woman giving a speech about individual empowerment has to flee for her safety out the back door.

There is a twisted war being waged on campus when a woman giving a speech about individual empowerment has to flee for her safety out the back door, while those who degrade and objectify women in the name of feminism prosper—and on the students' and taxpayers' dime. This is not a legacy of which the Left should be proud.

Get 'Em While They're Young

What power could possibly have led college students, who we think of as challenging the status quo with wild individuality and expansion of their minds, to become foot soldiers for the Thought Police? Young people in their late teens and early twenties don't just wake up one morning and decide that burning books would be a fun thing to do. No, the conditioning begins early, and in ways that may at first seem innocuous or perhaps even appropriate. I submit that the following story gives us an important insight into how the indoctrination begins. You see, the fear of offending and the reinforcement of victimhood begin very early.

In February 2001, it was reported that an 8-year-old girl in Boulder, Colorado, had prepared a project titled "Does Skin Color Make a Difference?" for her third-grade science fair. The day before the fair, officials of her elementary school pulled her project.[18]

The officials insist they did the right thing because the issues the girl (whose name news accounts did not supply) raised might "hurt" minority students. Veronica Benavidez, executive director of elementary education for the county school district, whined, "The question is, Are we being responsible to all our children when we put up something that is potentially hurtful to a limited number of them?"[19] As far as the Thought Police for Little Kids were concerned, the answer was obviously "no."

What shocking thing had the little girl done? She had shown a pair of Barbie dolls to two groups of 15 adults at her father's office, then to two groups of 15 fifth-graders at her school, asking each person which doll they liked better. One doll was white, the other brown. This was much like the survey a social scientist conducted decades ago, in which black children expressed a preference for a white doll (which the social scientist used to demonstrate the psychological damage done by segregated schools). In the Colorado girl's project, while almost all the adults picked the doll wearing the prettier dress (regardless of skin color), most of the children—24 out of 30—picked the white doll.

School officials apparently panicked over the wording of the girl's stated conclusion: that the children "liked" the white doll better. It was a message, Benavidez told the *New York Times*, that might have led a minority student to infer that classmates liked white children better and, therefore, that the minority student was somehow inferior.[20]

And so the indoctrination begins. The 8-year-old receives the devastating message that she did something wrong. She learns early that she had better watch what she says because, God forbid, someone's feelings might get hurt. At the science fair there is debate and discussion among and between adults and kids. There would have been plenty of opportunity to point out that minorities are not inferior. In classic Thought Police (and Misery Merchant) fashion, however, Benavidez and her colleagues decided that people of color are so sensitive, so vulnerable and clueless, that they must be protected from an 8-year-old's science project.

If you think this absurdity is limited to professional members of the Thought Police, here's what one parent thought. Michael Webster, described by the *New York Times* as "an African-American aerospace researcher," applauded the school's decision to ban the project, saying, "For my kids or any elementary school kid of color who may not be strong enough to be comfortable with who they are or where they came from, it could quite possibly have a devastating effect on them somewhere down the line." Nevermind the parents' responsibility to make their kids proud of who they are. To prevent this "devastating effect," it can never be too early to teach white kids the importance of self-censorship when it comes to issues of race, and to infuse black and Hispanic kids with a victim mentality that they may never be able to shake.

After threat of a lawsuit, the school apologized to the girl and her parents, but her project never made it to the fair. Her compensation? She was given credit for participating in the project. The girl's father summed up the problem, "Race is a messy subject. It could be that people's feelings get hurt. But if it is only discussed in a sterile manner, we cannot address all the aspects of race that the entire American culture is facing."[21]

The power the Thought Police wield at universities and schools is indeed disturbing, but at least it gives us a clear view of what exactly the Left wants. In an environment under their ideological control, the Thought Police have free rein to silence opinions, squelch debate, and punish dissent. It's everything we're experiencing in the real world—just with a little less dressing.

Nude Handsprings

At least the Thought Police aren't elitist—yes, they're active in the Ivy League schools, but they also have troops at North Hennepin Community College in Minneapolis.

Just ask Jon Willand, who has taught there since 1966. A few years ago Willand hung on his office door a poster of General George Custer in an "Uncle Sam Wants You!" pose inviting the public to join the cavalry "to help put down the militant Sioux." The poster remained on Willand's door for two years, until Robert Alexander, then the associate dean of liberal education (of course), removed it, citing a complaint and his desire to "avoid students, employees, or visitors being offended."[22]

This wasn't Willand's first brush with the Thought Police. He had been reprimanded twice in the past for "making comments and using phraseology which do not manifest a clear concern for student sensibilities and which may promote student misunderstandings."[23] What had Willand said that earned him this rebuke? Among other things, that Stalin was responsible for more murders than Hitler, that Pocahontas did nude handsprings through Jamestown, and that "Native American" is an inaccurate term to describe any race.[24] These comments are of different orders, but what they have in common is that all three challenge the prevailing orthodoxy, which is Willand's real crime. After all, if speech of this sort was permitted, people might find out that Stalin *did* murder tens of millions more people than Hitler and that, unless the Garden of Eden was in North America, there is no such thing as "Native" Americans. As far as Pocahantas' alleged extracurricular activity, I wish I had been there!

Boorishness, Not Harassment

One argument for speech and thought control suggests that it is needed to end sexual harassment on campus.

While there is no denying that sexual harassment exists at universities, implementing speech codes to protect women is redundant, as well as ineffective. I don't know of anyone who doesn't understand that sexual harassment, in addition to being rude, can get you sued.

The federal law that prohibits sex discrimination in higher education is called Title IX. That is the law that mandates equal funding of women's and men's sports, but it also has a provision prohibiting "conduct of a sexual nature" that is "sufficiently severe, persistent, or pervasive to limit a student's ability to participate in or benefit from the education program, or to create a hostile or abusive educational environment." Title IX defines "sexual harassment" as "unwelcome conduct of a sexual nature," which "can include unwelcome sexual advances, requests for sexual favors, and other verbal, nonverbal, or physical conduct of a sexual nature." Title IX allows for civil recourse against harassers who do not stop and do not take "no" for an answer.

No, these legal prohibitions have not stopped harassment entirely—but neither will calling in the Thought Police. Even the Office for Civil Rights admits that ". . . the good judgment and common sense of teachers and school administrators are important elements of a response that meets the requirements of Title IX."[25] And at least sticking with the law is not so likely to foster a debilitating sense of perpetual victimhood.

One of the better examples of how Thought Police tactics are being utilized in the otherwise legitimate arena of combating sexual harassment involved a student at the College of the Canyons in Los Angeles. Sophomore Kelly Friscia, 19, accused speech professor Fred Martin of creating a "hostile learning environment" by allowing a male student to give a speech in class on how to perform oral sex on a woman.[26] A reasonable person would consider that the speech was offensive and that allowing it was certainly not a scholarly, civilized thing to do. But did it rise to the level of sexual harassment?

Ultimately, an investigative panel at the school found Martin not guilty. Title IX demands that the occurrences be such as "to limit a student's ability to participate in or benefit from the education program." Friscia's lawyer, however, said that school officials should have used a different standard: whether a student would have been *offended* by such speech.

This is where the warping of a valid idea becomes obvious. Many of us have been offended by something that someone said in our presence. There must be differentiation between what simply offends and what *injures*. Where that line is drawn is what the battle is all about.

When is using the name "Monica Lewinsky" really sexual harassment? Inbal Hayut is suing political science professor Alex Young and the State University of New York at New Paltz for allegedly creating a "sexually hostile environment." Her complaint? Young constantly referred to her as "Monica," observed that she wore the same color lipstick as Lewinsky, and, in front of the entire class, made comments such as "How was your weekend with Bill?" and "Shut up, Monica, I'll give you a cigar later." Eventually some of Hayut's fellow students started calling her "Monica."[27]

Young, who has since retired, admits to making the references but said that he was "joking and teasing."[28] Not good enough. If these charges are proved true, this really is the kind of thing that sexual harassment laws were meant to combat. Hayut was targeted with speech meant to sexualize her in front of her classmates. She complained, but Young continued despite her complaints. His behavior affected the environment, causing her peers to join in; she alleges that it affected her morale and her grades, eventually forcing her to drop out. The legal action Hayut took is appropriate, but a Speech Code banning the words "Monica Lewinsky" would be both too much and too little.

Vision 2000

In their book *The Shadow University*, Alan Charles Kors and Harvey A. Silverglate analyze the attacks on academic freedom and freedom of speech that continue to occur within American universities. Among the things banned by speech codes on various campuses are comments that cause loss of "self-esteem or a vague sense of danger" (Colby College in Maine), "intentionally producing psychological discomfort" (University of North Dakota), "insensitivity to the experiences of women" (University of Minnesota), "feelings" about gays that evolve into "attitudes" (West Virginia University), "inconsiderate jokes" (University of Connecticut), and the telling of stories "experienced by others as harassing" (Bowdoin in Maine).[29]

These examples set the stage for "Vision 2000," a program jointly designed by women's studies officials at the University of Massachusetts at Amherst and the New England Land Grant University Women.[30] Vision 2000 is pure Thought Police in action. The danger is that it will be taken as a product of feminism.

The plan calls for the complete transformation of the university curriculum. It includes some genuinely progressive suggestions, such as the holding of an annual seminar on gender issues and the introduction of gender into "all pertinent programs of institutional research"; but then, perhaps predictably, things get nutty.

"Recommendation #7," for example, deals with ending "Gender-bias and Discrimination Against Women in the Curriculum of Each University." According to this proposal, faculty would be held account-able if their pedagogies (teaching styles) and content were not "woman-friendly."[31] In the first place, how would this be determined? "Faculty whose students identify their courses, teaching styles, and mentoring as failing to be inclusive do not receive teaching prizes, satisfactory teaching evaluations, or merit raises." That's right. It would be the students—who presumably come to college knowing quite a bit less than their professors about what needs to be taught and how it should be taught—who would be the final arbiters.[32]

> **Some so-called feminists have argued that women resent and don't respond well to teaching styles that involve argument, debate, and competition.**

Furthermore, what are "woman-friendly" content and pedagogies? The theory seems to be that women learn differently from men—the multicultural argument again—and need to be taught material that has been "feminized" in some way. Some so-called feminists have argued that women resent and don't respond well to teaching styles that involve argument, debate, and competition. If accepting this theory isn't a prescription for disaster in the real world, I don't know what is.

These establishment feminists like to talk of feelings, consensus, and cooperation as the hallmarks of women's leadership. In my experience, those qualities are certainly more common in female than in male leadership, but women leaders strive for hierarchy and power just like their male counterparts. These feminists are simply loath to admit that power is power and leaders are leaders, and that men and women are more similar than different in those departments. Women may come to different conclusions about power and related issues because of their life experience, and they may have a different outward style, but for those of us who seek to gain and maintain power, we are certainly no more genteel in our efforts than are men.

The supposed feminists who drafted this proposal are promoting an insidious line of reasoning—that most things are woman-*un*friendly—that reinforces a woman's internalized expectation of victimhood. Wasn't the fight for women's rights based on our demand to be treated the *same* as everyone else? As we've seen regarding the gay, black, and feminist establishment outside the academy's walls, demands for *special* treatment lead to the marginalization and patronization of the constituency at issue.

Although a program like Vision 2000 is startling, the Petri dish that is campus life is invaluable; it allows us to see attempts to curtail freedom of speech in their most shameless form. Ironically, the modern university itself "stands as a refutation of all justifications for curtailing academic freedom," notes Daphne Patai, a professor at the University of Massachusetts at Amherst. "It was the existence of academic freedom that allowed feminists to establish a foothold in the academy. It was academic freedom that contributed to scholars being able to pursue their interest in African-American and ethnic studies and queer studies."[33] Patai is right. While she is a critic of women's studies and feminism, her understanding of the importance of freedom and her unapologetic use of her own voice to move her message make her more of a feminist than some of those who wear that banner across their chests.

Speech Zones

An emerging effort of the left-wing campus establishment, designed to keep its speech codes while appearing to support free speech, is to construct "free-speech zones." The first recorded "zone" was established at Tufts University in 1989, in response to a male student selling T-shirts with the amazingly "insensitive" legend "Why beer is better than women."[34] The Tufts administration swung into action, establishing zones within which "racist" and "sexist" speech would be permitted. The student body erupted, and the "zone" idea was dropped just a few days later.

Despite the complete failure of this early effort to make it appear as though free speech exists when it doesn't, the Thought Police have dusted off the idea, hatching zone plans at campuses all across the country. Of course, some students have quickly recognized that this new device is not a creation of areas *for* free speech but in fact an elimination of their right to discuss the issues *everywhere else* on campus.

Even within the zones, students face a whole host of restrictions. The *Chronicle of Higher Education*, reporting on the sudden popularity of the phenomenon among college administrators, notes that Pasadena City College in California wants to know *what* you're going to say before you're granted permission to say it. At New Mexico State University, you are permitted to distribute fliers, but you must remain in the designated area;[35] this rule makes fliering impossible, since distribution requires moving around. Georgetown and Kansas State Universities, the University of California at Berkeley, and the University of Mississippi have adopted similar policies, and other schools are considering them.

The good news is that some students are rejecting this doublespeak granting of "freedom." One student at the University of Mississippi was arrested for failing to obey a police officer: the student had refused to move his protest against the campus newspaper to the designated area.[36] Students at other universities, including Tufts, the University of South Florida, and Oklahoma State University, have held protests and actions that have disrupted campus life enough to get the policies rescinded. Two students even filed suit to get New Mexico State's policy declared unconstitutional.[37]

The vast majority of students, however, are vulnerable to the messages of the Thought Police. This should not be surprising. Day after day, through speech codes, censorship, and "memos" banning dissent, through star-chamber indictments of wrong-speakers like Eden Jacobowitz and arrests of misbehavers like the young man at Ole

Miss, students are indoctrinated with the message that they need to be controlled, that free speech is bad, that they must be restricted for their own good. That is, after all, the whole point of getting to individuals early. It is so much easier to prep them in the closed environment of the academy so that once they enter the real world they will accept totalitarianism as if it were a regular, everyday part of life. Because it has been.

Equal-Opportunity Mind Control

The situation that students at historically black colleges face is particularly ominous. At least most colleges *have* a college paper, even if it is occasionally confiscated and destroyed. About 25 percent of the black colleges, however, do not have a newspaper, and even at those that do, there are increasing concerns about censorship.[38]

In February 2000, the Black College Communication Association sponsored a conference specifically to address this problem. In some instances, it was reported, campus administrators halted students' efforts to start newspapers. Many students experience some kind of restriction on their reporting of campus news.[39] Most shocking was the revelation that at many of these colleges the faculty must approve a student's reporting *prior* to its publication. One academic

> **Many students experience some kind of restriction on their reporting of campus news.**

has argued that "proofing" material before it is printed is necessary because outside journalists write negative articles complaining that students, "can't write a sentence."[40] So much for faith in the institution and support of your students!

Many students and faculty at black colleges are convinced, however, that the issue is not about the quality of students' grammar but about silencing their voices. There are reports of the confiscation of yearbooks and of college newspapers being stripped of funding because of investigative stories that showed the college in a bad light. The result is student editors willing to write only happy news to please administrators. Dena McClerkin, a student editor at Clark Atlanta University's *The Panther*, states, "Our reporters have no fire or drive, because we know our voices will not truly be heard."[41] On campus, mind control is indeed equal opportunity.

Feminist Eggheads

My own undergraduate experience at USC gave me my first real insight into the rivalry between different branches of feminism, of which I had seen only one side throughout my activist career. Certainly a "nontraditional" student, I decided to go back to college in my thirties, after I stepped down as president of L.A. NOW. I came to USC with a wealth of knowledge about how the real world works. I also knew that for all their differences, the academic world and the real world are both competitive environments, as they should be. So with my age and experience, I arrived with an advantage but also with preconceived feminist establishment ideas about the inequity and general unfairness that women were supposedly experiencing in college.

I was prepared to fight through a maze of misogyny on my way to a degree while also facing the academic feminists whom I had repeatedly heard derided as "out-of-touch egghead theorists." Gloria Steinem has been more than willing to share her rantings about academic feminists. During an interview with *Mother Jones*, the interviewer commented to Steinem, "From a distance, a fair bit of academic feminist writing and argument seems pretty near impenetrable." Steinem's response? "Yeah, but that's stupid. Nobody cares about them. That's careerism. These poor women in academia have to talk this silly language that nobody can understand in order to be accepted, they think. If I read the word 'problematize' one more time, I'm going to vomit."[42]

Steinem's characterization of academic feminists could not have been further from the truth, at least at USC. Although I chose not to become involved in the women's studies department or the feminist clique on campus, I was impressed by my interactions with USC's feminist professors, women and men alike. Some were more leftist than others, but there was an overall intellectual appreciation of one another, regardless of where an individual fit on the political spectrum.

Even during my activism, I was somewhat suspicious of establishment feminists' depictions of academic feminists, considering how wrong the former were in their views of other women in general. Academic feminists, you see, were considered the Opposition. It's completely contrary to authentic feminism, but there are a few women in the feminist elite who consider the movement their own and resent the "presumption" of other women who involve themselves in the shaping of feminist theory. You can hear the resentment in Steinem's attack. Even Pulitzer Prize–winning author Susan Faludi is seriously resented by a certain nationally recognized feminist leader, not because Faludi didn't do a great job with her book *Backlash* but precisely because she *did*, and influenced the movement as a result. Groupthink through and through: there is to be one ideology, maintained by control, conformity, self-righteousness, and the rejection of new or different ideas.

When feminism succeeds on campus, it's because it is genuine feminism—women's studies departments, for example, that are serious academic programs, presenting a great diversity in styles and points of view. But those departments that serve as group therapy and become consumed with working to End-the-Patriarchal-System-of-Oppressed-Peoples-Everywhere are as dysfunctional as the establishment feminist organizations that succumb to socialism, groupthink, and the controlling nature of the Thought Police at work.

Opposition to Opposition

Despite the forbidding nature of the "rules," not all students are willing to go meekly into subjugation. Growing pockets of resistance are one of the more exciting developments in this culture war.

Brown University, its Ivy League cup brimming over with Thought Police, once again serves as our setting. On December 4, 2000, more than eight years after the U.S. Supreme Court decision banning speech codes, Brown's Dean of Student Life sent an "Important Message to All Students," stating that "Dialogue is to be owned by the person(s) involved. The Office of Student Life opposes the use of anonymous actions to give voice to hate, *opposition or dissent*" (emphasis mine).[43] Notice what you're reading here: at Brown University, "opposition" and "dissent" are now lumped together with "hate," to be stigmatized equally. What brought on this opposition to opposition at Brown? Someone had written on a residence hall memo board and on a posted advertisement the words "whores" and "sluts" and "You're gay." Offensive and juvenile? Yes. But worthy of an official decree opposing "hate, opposition or dissent" and barring anonymous statements? In fact, it is the efforts at speech and mind control on campus that drive those with certain opinions to express them anonymously.

This time, however, the Thought Police at Brown did not have it all their way. Tom Hinckle, a gay student and a columnist for the *Brown Daily Herald*, noted:

> The fact that the [Office of Student Life] singles out "dissent" and "opposition" rather than opposing all anonymous speech makes the goal of the policy frighteningly clear: the erasure of dissenting voices.[44]

Another student, named Sarah Fick, sent in this reader comment:

> Unfortunately, you can't change someone's opinion by silencing them, and it seems that a lot of people hold these opinions. If this is true, and if, as we know to be the case, they continue to hold blatantly wrong opinions, then there must be some problem with the way we discuss the issues. . . ."[45]

Brava, Ms. Fick. You have realized what so many of your elders have not: the danger of the attempts to "protect" you into mindlessness.

The problem *is* in the way we discuss the issues—or, more precisely, in the fact that we don't discuss them at all. Students are not to question the supposed reality that is spoon-fed to them. They are not to express themselves, ask questions, or investigate the state of relationships between the sexes or the races because, God forbid, they might come to conclusions and form opinions that don't mesh with the Left's version of reality.

One of the many severe drawbacks to censorship is that it drives feelings and opinions underground. Eventually there is a backlash, and the experiencing of the forbidden becomes the goal. The banning of certain books makes them all the more interesting; the banning of certain speech will compel some to utilize it even more. Why would people at the university level—people such as Professor Alex Young—use epithets or denigrating words? Perhaps it isn't racism or sexism but rather rage against the social machine. As I suggested earlier, dissenting ideas and opinions, if not allowed to breathe, only fester. They do not go away.

> One of the many severe drawbacks to censorship is that it drives feelings and opinions underground.

Education and the Open Mind

The damage that identity politics and group rights do on campus goes well beyond issues of expression. These systems of control are truly contradictory to what education is all about: creating a community of the educated and celebrating the heroics of the individual mind.

The academy should, in fact, deliberately take people away from what is familiar and comfortable, giving them an entirely new world of ideas and possibilities. Through their education students become different citizens and members of society than they were before, exploring new values and principles and thinking for themselves more than they may have done in their previous environments. The result—or at least this is the way it *should* be—is a community of educated people necessarily creating a *new* culture of individuals with similar ethics and principles. This is one of the most important roles of higher education, and the best possible weapon against the Thought Police.

9

Protest and Freedom
An Activist's Diary

"To know what you prefer, instead of humbly saying Amen to what the world tells you you ought to prefer, is to have kept your soul alive."

—*Robert Louis Stevenson*

As we wade through instance after instance of speech and mind control disguised as political action, you might start to fear that any protest risks falling into the Thought Police trap. Nothing could be further from the truth. There are many ways to protest the decisions of our cultural gatekeepers without trashing freedom of speech and thought in the process.

We are blessed with a culture that is based on freedom. Freedom, however, with all its benefits, also has its share of problems. Freedom of expression, for example, opens the door to the Thought Police and the Misery

Merchants. The antidote to thought control by a narrow segment of our society is broad public participation that influences the direction of our culture and exercises the muscle of our individuality. This exercise is necessary, for without it we will lose our awareness, our freedom, and, ultimately, our selves.

At the core of individual liberty is responsibility. We know that liberty is not something that will simply be given to us. The historical reality is that the power elite will do whatever they can to eliminate the rights of the individual, usually in the name of the "group." Activism is necessary to remind the elite that the citizenry is alive and well and has every intention of participating in our society's political and cultural life. Activism tells the elite that they are answerable to those of us who reap what *they* sow. Our duties, lifestyles, and blessings, the kinds of lives we are lucky enough to enjoy, give us a responsibility to engage in activism.

It might seem that activism would be at odds with individual liberty. Doesn't what we mean by "activism" require collective action? Sure it does—but collective action is not the same thing as group-identity politics and enforcement. Americans have a long tradition of uniting for a cause while retaining their remarkable individuality.

The Land of the Free

Economic freedom, which gave birth to capitalism, is the means by which people become politically free; it has been the flameholder of the promise for which people by the millions have left their native countries to seek freedom in the United States. What capitalism ultimately represents is an equal chance for all the members of society to improve their own lives. Where we've gotten bogged down is in the socialist insistence that everyone deserves not equal opportunity but equal *results*. The Soviet Union demonstrated how eliminating competition and depriving people of the fruit of their labor destroys ambition and, hence, the quality of life. And yet that is what the Misery Merchants would wish on the United States.

It's time that we admit the failure of socialism and embrace the benefits of capitalism and competition. No, not everyone will end up at the top of the heap, but most of us will land in a pretty comfortable place. And

> Our duties, lifestyles, and blessings, the kinds of lives we are lucky enough to enjoy, give us a responsibility to engage in activism.

because we Americans are a generous people, we take care of those who are truly unable to make it on their own. The least we can expect, though, is that everyone *tries* to participate, giving honest effort.

Socialism has had its appeal because it offers, albeit falsely, an environment that appears to be safe and consistent. The free market does not offer those comforts; it demands constant effort. The marketplace of ideas demands the same kind of effort. We talk all the time about the amount of violence on television, the proliferation of pornography, and the advent of shockingly violent video games for children. One part of you may believe that respecting others' freedom of expression requires you to stifle your own, to keep silent, and just accept the disintegration of your culture. In fact, each one of us has a duty to play a role in the shaping of society, and our free marketplace gives us the means to do that, via the protest of the pocketbook.

When the cultural gatekeepers are criticized for the violence and sexism of their products, they tell us that their decisions on what to give us are based on our own buying patterns. This does not compute. What the gatekeepers—the heads of studios, television networks, and publishing houses—conveniently do not figure into the equation is their own publicity and promotion campaigns, designed specifically to affect our buying patterns. Furthermore, while we can refuse to buy material we find dangerous or offensive, we can't buy material that isn't offered. Some "sleepers" do break through—films from small independent producers, books that aren't promoted—but those are few and far between.

> Activism has an important role to play when the gatekeepers start thinking that we, the marketplace, have no choice but to accept whatever they offer us.

Activism has an important role to play when the gatekeepers start thinking that we, the marketplace, have no choice but to accept whatever they offer us. If we are silent, they can argue that the state of our culture, its lack of values, simply reflects what the public wants. That is when we have to take action. We need to do so, however, in a way that is anathema to the Thought Police—that is, not hiding behind some false agenda but making our opinions crystal clear. The following is an example.

Mainstreaming Porn

My favorite activist project was also my first as president of Los Angeles NOW. In 1990, Knopf published a book titled *American Psycho* by Bret Easton Ellis. Ellis was one of those young authors who were thought to have their finger on the pulse of the new generation. He supposedly knew the heart and soul of what we wanted—and to judge from this book, what he "knew" we wanted was a book that sexualized violence against women in the most pornographic of ways.

Ellis's hero used a variety of methods to murder women. In one case, he attached battery cables to a woman's breasts to electrocute her. In another, a rat was inserted into a woman's vagina; Ellis described how it consumed her as it moved through her body. I believed the publishing of this book was an attempt by Sonny Mehta, Knopf's publisher, to introduce violent pornography into mainstream literature and get a share of the vast amounts of money reserved by some consumers (those we would not invite to dinner) for hard-core porn.

I first heard about the book when CNN asked me for an interview about its impending release. The book had come to CNN's attention because women staffers at Simon & Schuster, the house first scheduled to release it, had protested internally against being associated with such a violent and pornographic book. They thought their house deserved better. Apparently, management saw the light; in any case, Simon & Schuster dropped the book.

After the CNN story broke, I received a number of anonymous telephone calls from women (and some men) in the publishing industry who were shocked at the impending publication. Through one contact, I received a copy of the working proofs of the book. These proofs had handwritten edits, additional paragraphs, and other changes—presumably the author's own, although I don't know that for a fact. There were also doodles, including little monsters drawn next to the paragraphs describing women being tortured and mutilated.

Most of my information at this early stage came from sources in the New York publishing world. I was impressed by the courage, not only of the women at Simon & Schuster who put their collective foot down but also of the massive network of people in the industry who knew that this book was smut and were willing to help do something about it.

But what? How do you protest a book without becoming the Thought Police? That concept hadn't even formed in my mind when I designed a project that I believe offered the best combination of protest and respect for freedom of expression.

Genuine Consumer Action

Some activists favored asking Knopf to cancel publication of the book, but that was out of the question for me, no matter how horrific the material. At the same time, I believed the marketplace had every right to react. Those in control at Knopf seemed to feel that it would be just fine with the bookbuying public if they threw acid on the fabric of our culture. The protest we organized was a way of telling them that we actually noticed what they were doing, and it was not fine at all.

A simple boycott of the book wouldn't work because our supporters would not buy the book anyway. So what we did was to initiate a one-year consumer action (a genuine one, not like GLAAD's campaign against Laura Schlessinger). We suggested that bookbuyers could send a message indicating their displeasure over *American Psycho* by not buying any Knopf book for a year. That meant if you wanted a mystery, a cookbook, nonfiction, whatever, you would stick with other publishers for a year. What I liked about our campaign was that it was structured, it had an endpoint, and it would remind Knopf that the marketplace does have a say.

I also liked the fact that our plan empowered the individual. Far too often, corporate America—including television and the publishing industry—seems to be an impenetrable monolith. This project offered perfect ways to involve the individual and shatter that myth. People could choose to do a little or a lot. Even by *not* doing something—not buying Knopf books—they would be sending a message. And if they chose to do a little more, they could dial the phone or write a letter to explain why they weren't buying Knopf.

Meanwhile, there had been scores of news stories about the book and our campaign, and the phones at L.A. NOW were ringing off the hook. On a shoestring budget, we set up an "*American Psycho* Hotline"—one phone line connected to one answering machine with a taped message suggesting how the individual could "activate." Courtesy of insiders, we had every internal phone number at Knopf. This was important because it was becoming more and more difficult to get through Knopf's main switchboard. Also, most of America's corporate elite are, shall we say, sheltered from the common man. Normally, Sonny Mehta wouldn't take calls from someone he didn't know even if that person did manage to reach the switchboard. Now, he was being called on his private line.

Binky's Bad Day

One of the funniest and most revealing moments was provided by Amanda "Binky" Urban, Bret Easton Ellis's agent at International Creative Management (ICM). Binky had told a number of interviewers that she was "proud" of the book. We thought she should hear what other people had to say. So Binky's telephone numbers, fax numbers, and other contact information went on the hotline as well. Binky, like Sonny Mehta, got unsheltered very quickly. Apparently, people from all across the country started calling to tell her what they thought of her protégé and his handiwork.

I found this out the morning after we put Binky's numbers on the hotline. When my crew of volunteers and I arrived at the office, the first thing we did was to check the 30-plus messages that had come in early that morning from the East Coast. It seemed that Binky was not having a good day. The first several messages were from her, and I have to admit that I enjoyed listening to them. I didn't write down the exact wording, but I remember the substance of the messages quite well: "This is Amanda Urban. My name is not *Binky*! [Actually, it's her well-known nickname.] Stop calling me that. Stop telling people to call me that! You are to call me *immediately*. I demand that you take my numbers off your little hotline. You people don't know what you're doing. You better stop it right away." She then left her number.

As I listened to Binky's messages, I recalled my efforts to get through to her before the protest began. She had refused to take my calls then. No doubt to her dismay, I was now too busy to call her back.

Binky left several more messages, including the one that ended up being my favorite: "Why don't you return my calls? I told you to stop calling me Binky!! *Don't you know who I am??!!* Why aren't you calling me back? I am a very important person at ICM! Take my number off your hotline. This is ridiculous!" Yes, Binky, we did know very well who you were.

Booksellers Have Choices, Too

Targeting bookstores with pickets or asking them not to carry the book was also out of the question. Bookstores were not responsible for what was happening. We did ask the booksellers to follow a few guidelines, however: place *American Psycho* on shelves over four feet high to keep it out of the hands of children; do not place the book in the impulse-buying section at the register; do not promote or publicize it.

Many booksellers, both management and staff, called us during the campaign, expressing their disgust with the book but saying they felt they had a responsibility to carry it. At the same time, they appreciated the suggestions we gave them. It had never occurred to some of them that a book like this, written simply, could easily be understood by youngsters if it fell into their hands.

Some bookstores had staff meetings to decide what to do, voting on whether to carry the book. Some voted not to carry it at all, while others decided to offer it only on special order. Still others carried the book but followed our guidelines. Some feminist bookstores became part of the effort to educate about the image of women in the media by distributing leaflets and information about the campaign. Apart from what happened in the marketplace, this aspect of the campaign reminded booksellers that they, too, can make these kinds of decisions; they do not have to be just passive observers.

I'm still so pleased with the success of that project. The book did not do well. After the campaign, Sonny Mehta told a reporter he would rather be "lit on fire" than talk about what had happened with *American Psycho*. People from all across the country wrote to me and expressed their appreciation for being given "permission" to speak their mind. The campaign serves as a perfect example of how to protest: empowering individuals while not trampling on freedom of expression. Ellis had his book published, did book signings, and went to parties. Knopf distributed it, bookstores made it available to consumers, and librarians decided to carry it. It was even eventually made into a (widely panned) movie.

At the same time, more stories about the image of women in the media and about violence against women were generated during that campaign than in the several years previous. I was told by my continuing industry contacts in New York that *American Psycho* had one of the largest "returns" for the year (bookstores returning unsold copies). It is worth noting that in the decade that has followed, a mainstream publisher has issued nothing similar.

In the meantime, Ellis did have another book published, from which, I am told, his editor decided to excise a particularly brutal scene of a woman being disemboweled. I'm sure Ellis is still having fun, and Binky is still probably, oddly, proud.

Talking Back to Howard Stern

I never liked Howard Stern. His attitude toward women is abusive, condescending, and objectifying. In 1992, when I heard that the then-fledgling cable network E! Entertainment Television had signed him to do a television show along the lines of his radio show, I knew something needed to be done.

My goal was to tell E! that although it was their right to air Stern, Los Angeles NOW felt there should be programming that countered his sexist attitude. Since E!'s programming ran the gamut from gossip to gossip, we knew we had a challenge on our hands.

I contacted E! and expressed our concern, and their management team quickly agreed to meet with us. I was rather surprised by their speedy response, but I later found out that they had done a little research on Yours Truly and the NOW chapter, coming up with the press coverage of our *American Psycho* campaign. Succeeding with a project like that is like getting your black belt— once you have it, you may never have to use it again.

We also did our own bit of research. At that time, E! was well below the 30-million-subscriber mark, a make-or-break point in the cable world. Like all the players in our wonderful capitalist market economy, E! wanted to increase its market share, and it thought that airing Stern would do that. But engaging in a battle with us could turn a good thing into a bad thing.

During our meeting at the E! production offices in Los Angeles, I expressed my concern that their first program with editorial comment (as opposed to movie news or gossip) was a decidedly sexist one. I told them I couldn't blame them for attempting to increase their base, but I wanted them to know that they were *partners* in a social community that had an interest in what was going to fill our airwaves. Yes, they were in the decision-making seats, but they were not alone.

We were in a strong position, and if I were the Thought Police, I would have "demanded" that E! reverse its decision and not air the Stern show. But I'm not, so I didn't. What I asked for instead was what we all say we want from our airwaves: a balanced mix of information and ideas.

> **We were in a strong position, and if I were the Thought Police, I would have "demanded" that E! reverse its decision and not air the Stern show.**

Our request that E! offer program material that would counter Stern's was readily agreed to by their executives, with the first effort to be a program produced by Los Angeles NOW. It was a special titled *Women on the Verge*, which focused on the work and successes of women in the entertainment industry and the obstacles they had faced. Valerie Harper hosted the show, which featured a panel of women actors, writers, and directors. It aired many times over a period of several months.

Some activists wanted to punish E! for airing Stern by launching a full-out boycott of its advertisers or by intimidating local cable carriers into dropping it. Others accepted our strategy but complained that one feminist production was not enough.

The goal, however, could not be to "control" E! and extinguish anything that did not meet with feminist approval. I also knew that E!'s executive programming staff, including the *woman* who had engineered E!'s deal with Stern, had received an education about the impact of the programming decisions. Did we need to punish or destroy them to make that point? No. Would it have been more exciting to do something other than talk with them and influence them to run some additional programming? Probably. But I was not in the Thought Police business then, and I'm not now.

The Night Nicole Brown Simpson Died

Many people think that activist work is glamorous and exciting, particularly when they see the leader of a not-for-profit public-policy group on television. Most of what an activist does, however, is behind the scenes. More than 95 percent of the work of those who toil in not-for-profit civil-rights groups is unknown to anyone but their colleagues. "Organizing," that thing which leads up to rallies, legislation, and social change, involves administrative work, phone-banking for donations and to spread the word about issues, meeting with politicians and legislators, and so on. It is this anonymous work, carried out by a handful of leaders and many volunteers, that makes the machine run.

Then there is the aberration, the event that is like no other. The O. J. Simpson murder trial was one of those events.

I, like so many others across the country, had been working in obscurity on the issue of domestic violence (DV) for years. Prior to the Simpson killings, however, getting anyone to pay attention was next to impossible. DV wasn't a "sexy" crime. It is hard to feel sympathy for the victims when, as often happens, they defend their batterers. It is difficult in general to educate the public about matters such as battered-woman syndrome and the dangers a woman faces when she *does* leave her batterer.

The murders of Nicole Brown Simpson and Ron Goldman outside Nicole's condominium on Bundy Avenue in Brentwood are now etched in the American consciousness. I recall very clearly that night in June of 1994. I was in my fourth year as president of Los Angeles NOW. That evening I had gone to see the movie *The River*, starring Meryl Streep, with the vice president of the chapter, Nicole Perlman. I was driving home at about the time the killings occurred, and my route actually passed right by Bundy. Of course, we all speak about never knowing what the next day will bring, but for the people of Los Angeles that night, it was an understatement.

I know that for those of you who don't live in a big city it's difficult to imagine a place like Los Angeles or New York being a community. But we are. I was born here and have always loved Los Angeles. The riots did dim my romantic vision, but I still really love this city and the people in it. We have all been through so much together, and despite our size, there is an undeniable feeling of family—a big, dysfunctional one, but family nonetheless. As a result, Los Angeles' reaction to the murders did not surprise me. We responded like a small-town community, at first sympathizing with O. J. in what we thought was his grief (even though he and Nicole had been divorced for two years), and then being horrified as we learned that one of our favorite sons had desperately betrayed us.

One way Los Angeles and New York are different from a small town is that we have murders. Lots of them. Famous people are killed here, and so are homeless people. Husbands murder their wives, and boyfriends their girlfriends. Gang members shoot each other to death and occasionally kill a toddler who gets in the way. There was even a while when drivers were shooting each other on the freeways. I know it sounds sordid, and it is, but we *know* murder. Although we are far from desensitized (thank God!), we are, unfortunately, not shocked when it happens. That was the attitude in town when Nicole and Ron were found.

> **Beating and stabbing are the most personal ways to kill someone. This did not sound like a robbery gone wrong.**

What was odd, though, was *where* they were found and how they had been murdered—beaten and stabbed to death. Murders like that don't happen in Brentwood. Also, beating and stabbing are the most *personal* ways to kill someone. This did not sound like a robbery gone wrong.

Enter the Misery Merchants

I watched the proceedings—the bizarre televised slow-speed chase and the eventual arrest of Simpson—with considerable interest. I had always been impressed with Los Angeles District Attorney Gil Garcetti. Now, his office was making very strong statements linking the murders with Simpson's history of jealousy and domestic violence.

I felt that a comprehensive exposure of the plague of domestic violence was finally upon us. Although Simpson claimed he was innocent, his attempt to flee told a different story, reinforced by the fake beard, thousands of dollars, and passport he had with him. He claimed he was going to kill himself at Nicole's grave. Funny thing—I didn't think you needed a passport to make that kind of departure.

While just about everyone recognized this as a case of a battered woman finally being murdered by her batterer, the Misery Merchants had another idea. Los Angeles, like any diverse city, has its share of racial tension. It was the race issue that Simpson's defense team decided to exploit. Actually, the attempt to portray Simpson as a man targeted by the LAPD because of his race was absurd. If Simpson was targeted for anything, it was for autographs and the use of his hot tub.

Simpson lived in a white area, had married a white woman, was now dating another white woman, and belonged to a country club that was mostly white. Everyone in town—black, white, Asian, Jew—knew that the race issue was bogus and that domestic violence was *the* factor in the killings. I was determined to make sure that wasn't forgotten as Johnnie Cochran and the others played the race card.

Throughout the trial, my offices were swamped by journalists, volunteers, and women looking for help in getting out of their own abusive relationships. My officers and I did interviews about domestic violence, and I wrote opinion pieces on everything from domestic violence to prosecutor Marcia Clark's custody issue during the trial.

Judge Ito's Response

As the trial went on, I, along with many others, noticed that Judge Lance Ito seemed to be treating Marcia Clark with much less respect than he was according the other attorneys in the case. I decided to contact him and let him know that a sexist and dismissive attitude toward Ms. Clark could send a message to the jury that she was not worthy of being listened to. Here's a segment of the letter I sent to Judge Ito on February 2, 1995:

> Something has come to our attention that we think you would be interested in knowing . . . it has become rather apparent that you are treating Deputy District Attorney Marcia Clark with a different level of respect than the other attorneys on both the prosecution and defense teams. . . . She seems quite capable of taking the heat in your kitchen. We are concerned however with the impact your perceived attitude may have on the jury. After all, if Your Honor appears not to take Ms. Clark as seriously as Mr. Cochran, why should *they*?

Judge Ito responded to my letter immediately. I hadn't expected him to because I knew that judges were not permitted to discuss a trial in progress. But Judge Ito asked for dates and times of what we considered troubling and said he would look them up in the transcript. He seemed genuinely surprised by our perception of a negative attitude toward Clark on his part and anxious to correct any behavior that could lead to such a perception. He set up parameters for communications with us that observed the Canon of Ethics for judges, the most important being that we must never discuss specifics of the case.

We told him that we didn't think the transcripts would convey the extent of the problem. Tone of voice and body language affect the nature of a statement. We felt he should see and hear what he was doing. Fortunately, with the trial being televised, I was able to compile a video log with corresponding notes about comments that appeared to be derogatory or condescending.

Although that event did not have an impact on the trial's eventual outcome, it's an example of a kind of activism that can and must be engaged in.

When I had completed the video, my mentor, Toni Carabillo, a chapter board member, and I met with Judge Ito in his chambers during a lunch break in the trial. We discussed the material and were pleased by his open response to our criticism. On the way back into the courtroom, I was thrilled to be able to give Simpson the Evil Eye. If only Judge Ito had handled the trial as well as he handled us, we might have seen a guilty verdict.

Watching the trial coverage in the days following our meeting, we noticed that Judge Ito's treatment of Marcia Clark was distinctly more respectful, comparable now with his treatment of the male attorneys. It was so obvious, in fact, that reporters who knew nothing of our communication with Judge Ito noted his change in attitude.

Although that event did not have an impact on the trial's eventual outcome, it's an example of a kind of activism that can and must be engaged in. Women attorneys face sexism all the time in court. It's systemic, and most of the time the male judges and attorneys are oblivious to it. With Judge Ito's attitude being watched around the world, I felt that getting him to treat Clark with respect would send a much-needed message to his colleagues.

Not Guilty

Those are two words I didn't expect to hear. I suppose I still believe in the good guys winning.

As well as I know this city, I still did not predict its reaction to the verdict. In fact, to my dismay—and contrary to my experience of the Rodney King riots—reactions tended to divide along color lines. One of the most disgusting things I saw was blacks sitting around the Los Angeles County Courthouse waiting for the verdict and then erupting in elation when it was announced. It was even more pathetic to hear our local Misery Merchants suggest that blacks in Los Angeles really believed that Simpson was innocent. To believe that you would have to be clueless. The black community in this city is not clueless.

Some observers speculated that most blacks in Los Angeles and elsewhere in fact knew Simpson to be guilty but wanted payback for the times when black men who actually were innocent had been jailed. That is a more realistic and honest appraisal, and certainly less insulting than the Misery Merchants' image of a black community too confused to follow basic evidence.

While the misguided and the malevolent cheered the verdict, the phone lines at Los Angeles NOW were swamped. At one point, our system crashed. As the thirteenth juror, a majority of Angelenos had reached the opposite verdict from the 12 jurors in the box. The callers wanted something, *anything*—a demonstration, a vigil, some event where they could express their frustration.

Our first step was to ask people to come in and volunteer. As a result of the *American Psycho* campaign and several other projects, our membership had soared and so had our resources, but we were still overwhelmed by the number of calls that came in from across the country and around the world. Nicole Perlman, a young woman in her twenties, had become a chapter officer not very long before the Simpson killings, and she wound up taking charge of the day-to-day operations. Talk about a baptism by fire! But Nicole delivered in an environment that would have caused most people to fold. She is not a big name in the outside world, but she is the kind of person who makes social activism truly successful and changes the quality of people's lives—perhaps your life.

No O.J.

One thing that was a constant worry for us, as for any not-for-profit, was money. The chapter's normal monthly phone bill was about $200; after the Simpson verdict, it soared to over $2,000. But something happened during this time that gave me one of my clearest insights into the differences between what I now know to be the Thought Police and genuine conservatives. Hundreds of our callers identified themselves as conservatives but said they wanted to help our efforts.

The conversations I had with these people were extraordinary. Never did they think they would be writing a check to NOW, they told me—nor had I ever expected to receive such unqualified support from those so commonly referred to within the feminist establishment as "the enemy." For those who did not support the whole range of NOW's activities, such as pro-choice work, I gave them my word that if they indicated "No O. J." on the memo line of their check, their money would be used exclusively in that effort.

I found, to my surprise—and I'm ashamed now to admit I was surprised—that my word was good enough for them. Strangers—conservatives—were willing to trust not only an avowed feminist but also an open lesbian. If the roles had been reversed and a conservative organization had launched an important project, I'm all too certain that you would not have seen the same kind of magnanimity from postmodern liberals. But these people, able to appreciate the work that was being done, stepped

> Never did they think they would be writing a check to NOW, they told me—nor had I ever expected to receive such unqualified support from those so commonly referred to within the feminist establishment as "the enemy."

over their political and ideological boundaries and joined in the fight, showing a true concern for the issues that transcended politics.

Religious, pro-life, and other conservatives who wrote a check to Los Angeles NOW because it was the right thing to do changed me. It was then that I realized, although we disagreed on many issues, there were fundamental questions about values that truly separated conservatives from postmodern liberals. For me, that finally exposed by counterpoint the soullessness of the Left.

Local Heroes

For an activist, one of the silver linings in a situation such as the aftermath of the Simpson trial is the people you meet. Most of the time, your members and supporters in the community participate by simply writing a check. You never get to meet them. Their lives are busy, and, well, that's what the activists are for—to go out there and get the job done.

Nicole Brown Simpson's murder changed all that for Los Angeles NOW. The tragedy brought forth some of the most remarkable people I have ever met, and from all walks of life, wanting to do something personally. Because I was on television virtually every night during that period, one could have gotten the impression that the anti-domestic-violence action in Los Angeles was the work of one person. Nothing could be further from the truth.

Besides Nicole Perlman, who shouldered so much of the burden, the volunteers who made the effort possible included Vanessa Coffey, an Emmy-winning television producer and writer, and Michelle Phillips, the singer/

songwriter, actor, and writer who is in the Rock and Roll Hall of Fame as a member of the Mamas and the Papas. Carol Ann Leif, one of Los Angeles's leading stand-up comedians and writers, also played a fundamental role, as did Lynn Wasserman, the daughter of Lew Wasserman, former president of MCA, the most powerful talent agency of its time. Unlike some leaders within the feminist establishment, Lynn plays an incredibly important role in the direction and success of feminist efforts in Los Angeles and nationally—but she does so quietly. Carol Ann, by the way, is Lynn's daughter. Yes, it is now the Wasserman *women* who are making a difference in the world! Then there was the attorney Joel Sachs and his wife, Dr. Joyce Sachs, a psychotherapist, who offered so much support and insight.

One volunteer, David Dismore, who has been a stalwart NOW activist since the early 1970s and its longtime archivist, screened and recorded every television newscast, every day, so we could stay in touch with how the news media were portraying domestic violence, its victims, and our work. Dave was instrumental in our being able to keep our finger on the pulse of the city, and ultimately the nation, while our work became increasingly focused and intense.

> Everyone left that project knowing that he or she did make a difference, that the power of one is the greatest power of all.

In our little office, people such as these rubbed shoulders with bartenders, housewives, cartoonists, and car salesmen. When volunteers arrived to work the phones or help prepare fliers, they never knew whom they would be sitting next to. We had more phone lines installed; stashed in a closet was our old answering machine, now transformed into the "No O. J. Hotline." Once again, the machine performed with valor and distinction. I've kept it as a memento.

Hundreds of people (in shifts, of course!) toiled in the L.A. NOW office day after day and night after night. Most of them I never got a chance to meet because everything was moving so quickly, but they are the real heroes—the people who came by during their lunch hours or took time off from work or brought their families on the weekends to raise money or to tell people about a candlelight vigil for victims of domestic violence. That experience exemplifies what makes me love this city and the people in it.

It also reminded me that although we Americans are ambitious and driven, we are also the most generous and compassionate of people. These volunteers were there not for the glory or the excitement, not to get noticed by the press, but because something simply had to be done. It reminded me how exquisite individualism can be and how it is the key to healthy activism. Everyone left that project knowing that he or she *did* make a difference, that the power of one is the greatest power of all.

Marching on Brentwood

Our first order of business was to organize something immediately that people frustrated by the verdict could participate in, and so I called for a candlelight vigil at the

Federal Building. Located in Westwood, the Federal Building has several features that make it every activist's favorite demonstration spot in Los Angeles. It's right off a freeway exit, it's on one of the busiest intersections in the city, it has tons of free parking, and at night you can just show up. It was perfect.

We announced the vigil through our phone banks, via a couple of live news interviews, and on our newly rechristened hotline. Newscasts also continually announced the event. With just a few hours' notice, 1,500 people arrived at the Federal Building. There, as at all of our demonstrations, we collected money for service organizations, distributed material to get people more involved, and generally educated about the issue. Donations to Los Angeles NOW went up, but so did donations to other organizations in the city that worked on the issue of violence against women.

Even after the vigil, frustration continued to build, as did media coverage. I started to realize that the vigil was not enough and that we needed to do something bigger—like a march. I had never planned a march before, but I knew it had to happen.

I think it was on a Tuesday that I announced to the volunteers that we were going to have a march in Brentwood on Friday. The room suddenly got quiet. Mouths dropped open, just for a second, and then Nicole Perlman, who by now was a seasoned veteran (but who also had never planned a march!), said, "Okay, let's go."

Normally, you have to have a permit to march down a street. We didn't. You also have to have a gathering site. We didn't. You also have to get the word out. That didn't seem to be a problem: the rule was that whoever was doing an interview would pitch the march, and we had live interviews scheduled on virtually every local newscast every day.

We were also doing interviews for outlets ranging from Japanese television to the *Washington Post* and *Nightline*. Our focus remained firmly on domestic violence. I was determined not to let the public forget the victims or the issue. We learned that battered women were calling domestic-violence hotlines in desperation. They felt that the verdict had sent a message to their batterers that not only will you not be punished for beating your wife, but you can also even get away with killing her. Our work had never been more important.

We finally decided on the route for the march; we would gather about a quarter mile from Nicole Brown Simpson's condominium, march down San Vicente to Bundy, and then march back. Despite the lack of time to organize, our march attracted more than 5,000 people. It was the largest march in Los Angeles since the organizing effort for the Equal Rights Amendment in the 1980s, and it ended up being one of the most moving experiences of my life.

When we reached the Bundy Avenue condo, something happened that was not planned at all—the crowd spontaneously began to sing "Amazing Grace." Imagine—5,000 people, of all colors and ages, men, women, and children, marchers, reporters, celebrities, deputy district attorneys, even the police, holding their candles, singing in unison, and crying at the same time. That's what the verdict did to Los Angeles. The march itself was the epitome of what activism should strive to do: turn tragedy into a personally and socially transforming experience. I've never been more proud.

The Rehabilitation That Never Was

After Simpson's acquittal, the attempts by Simpson's friends to rehabilitate his image began almost immediately. Don Ohlmeyer, then West Coast president of NBC and probably Simpson's most prominent supporter in the entertainment industry, announced that *Dateline* was going to do an interview with Simpson the following week.

Given Ohlmeyer's relationship with Simpson, my immediate worry was that this "interview" was going to be a fluff piece. I contacted Ohlmeyer's office, but he refused to take my call. We then put his office number on our trusty hotline. Ohlmeyer called me within an hour.

I told him that we were concerned about the interview. I explained that we would not request that it be canceled, but we expected NBC journalists at least to ask the important questions. Ohlmeyer was evasive. At one point I asked him how he felt about shaking Simpson's hand. Did he think about how many times that same hand had beaten Nicole, and how it had most likely held the knife that decapitated her? After a moment of silence, Ohlmeyer said, "I don't know what you mean." I suppose if you're O. J. Simpson's friend, it's easier not to know what such things mean.

As soon as the interview was announced, we started receiving information from various sources inside NBC, including actors on popular evening and daytime programs and executives who were disgusted by the idea of Simpson using their network to clean up his image after the damaging trial. Many of the people who contacted us wanted to know how they could help in getting the interview canceled. I encouraged them not to agitate for cancellation but to maintain the drumbeat for *Dateline* to ask serious questions.

As in the *American Psycho* campaign, we once again received inside telephone numbers, and we put those numbers on our hotline. It became increasingly difficult to get through NBC's main switchboard, and at one point NBC reported that its phone systems on both coasts had crashed because of the volume of calls. I liked the fact that individuals realized that they had every right to call and give NBC a piece of their mind.

The NOW chapter announced that a rally would take place outside NBC's studios on the day of the interview. We learned that people were planning to come in from as far away as Canada and Oklahoma to attend the rally. Once again, our message was to remember all the victims of domestic violence and to say that batterers should not think that the Simpson acquittal indicated a lack of concern about the issue in our society.

On the day of the interview, people began to gather early in front of the studios, and I went to the site to familiarize myself with the layout. It was then that a reporter told me that Simpson had canceled the interview. At a press conference, Johnnie Cochran complained that NBC had "changed the rules" about the format of the interview. He said that with the civil trial pending, Simpson had no intention of being grilled about the murders.

I'm convinced that it was the voices of the individuals who called NBC that made the difference. Living in their insular world, NBC executives had apparently thought a fluff interview with Simpson was a fine idea. Hearing from the marketplace seemed to have injected some decency into NBC's decision making.

Although the interview was canceled, the rally went ahead as scheduled, attracting more than 500 people. Actually, it would have been impossible to cancel the rally, with people coming from so far away.

No doubt Don Ohlmeyer finally figured out "what we meant" via a project that was geared to educate about domestic violence and to inject a populist involvement into fiefdoms like the entertainment industry. Television networks and executives help shape our culture, and yet they had to be *told* that it wasn't decent to pal up to a man who had repeatedly beaten his wife and finally killed her and another person. We really have a long way to go. Ohlmeyer, by the way, checked himself into the Betty Ford Clinic in December 1996 for alcohol dependency.[1] In 1999, his contract at NBC was not renewed.[2]

The Power of the Individual

What do the actions I've written about in this chapter have in common? They relied on individuals, classical liberals from both the left and the right sides of the political spectrum, coming together for a common purpose. They were projects that educated about a large issue that affected everyone. They improved our culture while respecting freedom of expression. None of the projects was geared to destroy an individual—not even O. J. Simpson. The Simpson campaign kept its focus on domestic violence, not on the Misery Merchants' favorite role model for young black men.

The defining difference between the New McCarthyism and legitimate activism is clear: *One seeks to destroy, the other to empower.* What we do as a community should empower everyone, regardless of whether they are on the same "side" or not.

Realizing that there is an alternative to the Thought Police is the first step to throwing off the chains of enforced guilt and silence. Yes, you can be a liberal and not accept as gospel the ramblings of the feminist or civil-rights establishment. You can admit that values and morals *are* important to you and not feel like a traitor. Or you can be a conservative and realize that you actually have things in common with true feminists. You can recognize that something *has* gone wrong and not betray your principles in that realization.

> Yes, you can be a liberal and not accept as gospel the ramblings of the feminist or civil-rights establishment.

Whatever our politics, we can reject the Thought Police, the Misery Merchants, and anyone else who tells us that we need to be sacrificed for the good of the "group." We know that is a lie. While remaining ourselves and not part of some homogenized mass, each one of us, *as* an individual, has a responsibility to the other individuals who make up our society to examine what we are told and speak up when we believe it is wrong. I say to each of you that if you can do that, then you, with your opinions in all their glory, will be heard above the din of the Thought Police as they shout for you to be quiet.

Notes

Introduction

1. George Orwell, *1984* (New York: Harcourt Brace, 1949).
2. Pat Buchanan, "A Lesson in Tyranny Too Soon Forgotten," *Chicago Tribune* (August 25, 1977), 3:3.

Chapter 1

1. "Text of Remarks by Joan M. Garry, GLAAD Executive Director, at Rally Against Laura Schlessinger at Paramount Pictures Entrance in Los Angeles, March 21, 2000," in GLAAD documents. Available at www.glaad.org/org/publications/documents/index.html?record=74
2. "Richard," interview by author, August 8, 2000.
3. Martha Deller, "School Counselor Assessed 20-Day Unpaid Suspension," *Fort Worth Star Telegram* (December 17, 1999), Metro.
4. James Brooke, "Rash Talk by Wascals Frowned On in Canada," *New York Times* (December 12, 1999), Foreign Desk.
5. George Orwell, "Letter to Francis A. Henson" (June 16, 1949), in Dennis Poupard and James E. Person, Jr., eds, *Twentieth Century Literary Criticism* (Farmington Hills, MI: Gale Group, 1985).
6. Available at: www.stanford.edu/group/King/index.htm
7. Federal Bureau of Investigation, Freedom of Information Act, "Stanley Levison." Available from: www.foia.fbi.gov/levinson .htm. Also see: FBI/FOIA, "Martin Luther King, Jr." Available from: www.foia.fbi.gov/mlkjrrep.htm and www.foia.fbi.gov/jehoover.htm. For a comprehensive analysis of King's associates' Communist Party affiliations also see: "Martin Luther King, Jr.-Congressional Record" available at: www.freerepublic .com/forum/a3a655d396f36.htm

8. Ibid.

9. Rita Dove, "The Torchbearer: Rosa Parks," *Time*. Available at: www.time.com/time/time100/heroes/profile/parks01.html

10. Julie Tamaki, "Bustamante Voices Regret for Racial Slur," *Los Angeles Times* (February 14, 2001).

11. Ibid.

12. George Skelton, "Not the Speech Cruz Bustamante Hoped to Deliver," *Los Angeles Times* (February 19, 2001).

13. See Tamaki.

14. Steve Chawkins, "Now a Word About Verbal Blunders," *Los Angeles Times* (February 21, 2001).

15. Steve Chawkins, "Mother to Fight School's Action Over Race Slur," *Los Angeles Times* (October 13, 2000), A.

16. Ibid.

17. Editorial, *Washington Times* (April 26, 1993).

18. Edward Moran, "He Liked Penn Diversity; Dream First Year Became Nightmare for Jacobowitz," *Philadelphia Daily News* (May 25, 1993).

19. Cover story, *Sports Illustrated* (December 27, 1999).

20. Available at: //sportsillustrated.cnn.com/features/cover/news/1999/12/22/Rocker/guilani.wav

21. See *Sports Illustrated*. Also available at //sportsillustrated.cnn.com/features/cover/news/1999/12/22/rocker

22. Eric Lichtblau, "Klansman to Apologize for Harassment." *Los Angeles Times* (July 21, 2000).

23. Ibid.

Chapter 2

1. Joann Wypijewski, "A Boy's Life," *Harper's Magazine* (September 1999).

2. Available under 'Archives,' 'September 1998,' at: www.uwyo.edu/comm/LNS.htm

3. Available at: www.fbi.gov/programs/civilrights/hatecrime.htm

4. Roberta Sulk, *Victim Impact Statement*, Albany County District Court, December 17, 1998. Also available at: www.geocities.com/daphismom

5. U.S. Department of Justice, *Uniform Crime Report 1999: Hate Crimes Statistics*. (Washington, DC: U.S. Department of Justice, 2000). Also available at: www.fbi.gov/ucr/99hate.pdf

6. Ibid.

7. Ibid.

8. U.S. Department of Justice, *Training Guide for Hate Crime Data Collection,* (Washington, DC: U.S. Department of Justice, 2000). Also available at: www.fbi.gov

9. Jodi Wilgoren, "Terror in Littleton: The Group; Society of Outcasts Began With a $99 Black Coat," The *New York Times* (April 25, 1999).

10. Ibid.

11. Irving Janis, *Groupthink: Psychological Studies of Policy Decisions and Fiascoes,* 2d ed. (Boston: Houghton Mifflin College, 1982).

12. Available at: www.csj.org/pub_csj/csj_home.htm

13. Ibid.

14. Available at: www.csj.org/rg/rgessays/rgessays_mindmanipulate .htm

Chapter 3

1. "Text of Remarks by Joan M. Garry, GLAAD Executive Director, at Rally Against Laura Schlessinger at Paramount Pictures Entrance in Los Angeles, March 21, 2000," in glaaddocuments. Available at: www.glaad.org/org/publications/documents/index.html?record=74

2. "History of GLAAD's Work Regarding Laura Schlessinger," in glaaddocuments. Available at: www.glaad.org/org/publications/documents/index.html?record=130

3. "Welcome..." available at: www.stopdrlaura.com/home.htm

4. Available at: www.glaad.org/org/publications/documents/index .html?record=2276

5. Available at: www.glaad.org/org/publications/documents/index .html?record=2286

6. Laura Schlessinger, interview by Jeanne McDowell, *Time* (July 3, 2000), 59.

7. Available at: www.stanford.edu/group/QR

8. Rabbi David Eliezrie, Letter to Elizabeth Coleman, ADL, May 31, 2000.

9. "Statement by GLAAD Regarding Eminem," in Media Releases: Available at: www.glaad.org/org/press/documents/index .html?record=2180

10. "Musical Gay Bashing Doesn't Sound So Good," in glaadalert. Available at: www.glaad.org/org/press/publications/alerts/index.html?record=952

11. The ACLU of Southern California. Available at: www.aclu-sc.org/news/releases/000925barbie.htm

12. Ibid.

13. Available at: www.stopdrlaura.com

14. Ibid.

15. "GLAAD Disturbed by Gainesville Times' Announcement to No Longer Print Gay and Lesbian Newspaper," in Media Releases. Available at: www/glaad.org/org/press/index.html?record=2259.

16. Ibid.

17. Ibid.

18. Ibid.

19. American Psychiatric Association. Available at: www.psych.org/public_info/teen.html Also see: United States Department of Health and Human Services, "Report on the Secretary's Task Force on Youth Suicides (Washington, DC: U.S. Department of Health and Human Services, 1989).

20. J. H. Lowinson, et al., *Substance Abuse: A Comprehensive Textbook,* 3d ed. (Baltimore, MD: Williams & Wilkins, 1997).

21. See United States Department of Health and Human Services.

22. Liz Smith, interview by Larry King, *Larry King Live*, Cable News Network, October 7, 2000.

Chapter 4

1. Max Boot, "O. J. Redux: Tawana Brawley Trial Spins Out of Control," *Wall Street Journal* (February 17, 1998).

2. Larry McShane, Associated Press, "After a Decade, the Tawana Brawley Case Goes to Court," *Los Angeles Times* (November 9, 1997), A-37.

3. See Boot.

4. See McShane.

5. George Will, "The Ultimate Emancipation," *Newsweek* (March 5, 2001).

6. David A. Bositis, *2000 National Opinion Poll: Politics* (Washington, DC: Joint Center for Political and Economic Studies, 2000).

7. Laurie Willis, "NAACP Leaders Accused of Racial McCarthyism," *Baltimore Sun* (February 25, 2001).

8. Greg Pierce, "Armey Counterattack," *Washington Times* (February 23, 2001).

9. See Willis.

10. U.S. Department of State, *Annual Report on International Religious Freedom for 1999: Afghanistan* (Washington, DC: U.S. Department of State, 1999). Also available at: www.state.gov/www/global/human_rights/irf/irf_rpt/1999/irf_afghanis99.html

11. Ben Stocking and Jack Fischer, "Jackson Group May Target Firm With Outspoken Boss." *San Jose Mercury News* (March 4, 1999), Local.

12. Ibid.

13. Steve Miller and Jerry Seper, "Jackson's Income Triggers Questions," *Washington Times* (February 26, 2001).

14. Gary Leonard, "Klan With a Tan: L.A.'s Reverend Jesse Lee Peterson Leads an MLK Day Protest Against That Other Reverend Jesse—As Told to Rick Barrs," *New Times* (January 20, 2000).

15. Ibid.

16. Monica Dewey, "Unions Finance Jackson Staffers," *Chicago Tribune* (March 26, 2001).

17. Ibid.

18. Troy Anderson, "L.A. County Supervisors Hold Out Against Mounting Labor Attacks," *Los Angeles Daily News* (October 16, 2000). Jill Stewart, *New Times* (October 19–25, 2000).

19. Jill Stewart, "Corrections," *New Times* (November 9, 2000).

20. See Anderson.

21. Douglas P. Shuit and Richard Winton, "Jackson Kept Hope Alive in Negotiations," *Los Angeles Times* (October 18, 2000).

22. See Dewey.

23. See Miller and Seper.

24. House Editorial, "The Jackson Money Trail," *Washington Times* (February 27, 2001).

25. John J. Miller and Ramesh Ponnuru, "On Jackson's Trail," *National Review* (February 27, 2001). The full complaint is available at: www.nlpc.org

26. Ibid.

27. "Stalemate in Decatur" on abcnews.com (cited November 10, 1999). Available at: //abcnews.go.com/sections/us/DailyNews/decatur991110.html

28. "Schools Close Amid Protest" on abcnews.com (cited November 8, 1999). Available at: //abcnews.go.com/sections/us/DailyNews/decatur991108.html

29. See "Stalemate in Decatur."
30. Paul Lieberman, "51% of Riot Arrests Were Latino, Study Says," *Los Angeles Times* (June 18, 1992), Metro. See also J. Petersilia and A. Abrahamse, "The Los Angeles Riot of Spring 1992: A Profile of those Arrested." *Police Forum* 3:4 (1993), 1–10; and J. Petersilia and A. Abrahamse, "The Los Angeles Riot of Spring 1992: A Profile of those Arrested," Document RP-418 (Santa Monica, CA: Rand Corporation, 1996).
31. Ibid.
32. Frank Clifford and David Ferrell, "*The Times* Poll: L.A. strongly Condemns King Verdicts, Riots," *Los Angeles Times* (May 6, 1992), A.
33. Jonathan Peterson, "Blame, Not Excuses, for Rioters," *Los Angeles Times* (August 6, 1992), A.
34. Available at: www.jointcenter.org/selpaper/poll_po.htm
35. See Peterson.
36. Pierre Thomas, "Study Suggests Black Male Prison Rate Impinges on Political Process," *Washington Post* (January 30, 1997): A03.
37. Available at: www.salon.com/news/col/horo/2000/09/05/profiling/index1.html
38. 966 F.2d 391, 394, n.4 (8th Cir. 1992), cert. den. 507 U.S. 1040 (1992).
39. State of New Jersey, *Interim Report of the State Police Review Team Regarding Allegations of Racial Profiling* (Trenton, NJ: State of New Jersey, 1999), 73. Also available at: www.state.nj.us/lps/intm_419.pdf
40. U.S. Department of Justice, "Youth Gang Drug Trafficking," *Juvenile Justice Bulletin,* December 1999 (Washington, DC: GPO, 1999).
41. Available at: //ojjdp.ncjrs.org/
42. Ibid.
43. Halford H. Fairchild, "Modern-Day Racism Masks Its Ugly Head," *Los Angeles Times* (September 11, 2000), Metro.
44. Ward Connerly, interview by Brian Lamb, *Booknotes*, C-SPAN (April 30, 2000). Transcript available at: www.booknotes.org/transcripts/50564.htm
45. Ethan Watters, "Ward Connerly Won the Battle, Now He's Facing the War," *Mother Jones* (November/December 1997). Also available at: www.mojones.com/mother_jones/ND97/watters.html

46. Ward Connerly, interview by author, November 2000.
47. Ward Connerly, Speech in accepting the Lincoln Leadership Award for Civic Virtue (February 12, 1997). Available at: www.acri.org

Chapter 5

1. Available at: www.dsausa.org/about/npc.html
2. *Ms.* (July/August 1996), 47.
3. Patricia Ireland, *What Women Want* (New York: Plume, 1996), 151–166.
4. Ibid., 155–156.
5. Brenda Feigen, *Not One of the Boys* (New York: Knopf, 2000), 295.
6. Callie Marie Rennison, Ph.D., and Sarah Welchans, U.S. Department of Justice, *Intimate Partner Violence* (Washington, DC: U.S. Department of Justice, 2000), 1.
7. Andrea Dworkin, *Scapegoat: The Jews, Israel, and Women's Liberation* (New York: Free Press, 2000), 14.
8. Available at: www.now.org/press/12-95/tbpi.html
9. Ken Noble, "Outspokenness on Simpson Case Has California Talk Show Host in a Cauldron," *New York Times* (December 1995).
10. Ibid.
11. Bettijane Levine, "Seizing the Day; NOW Leader has Done What O. J. Prosecutors Couldn't: Put Domestic Violence Up Front," *Los Angeles Times* (October 18, 1995), Life & Style.
12. Toni Carabillo, "NOW's Rush to Judgment: The American Psycho Connection," *On The Issues* (Summer 1996), 20.
13. Available at: www.now.org/board/tbwoc.html
14. Elizabeth Gleick, "Fighting Words," *Time* (January 8, 1996), 41.
15. See Feigen, 294.
16. James Barron, "Feminists Say Song Lyrics Are Degrading," *New York Times* (December 19, 1997), Metro Desk.
17. Department of Justice. Available at: www.ojp.usdoj.gov/bjs/pub/pdf/vi.pdf
18. Gloria Steinem, "Feminists and the Clinton Question," *New York Times* (March 22, 1998), Editorial Desk.
19. See Feigen, 299.
20. See Feigen, 284.

21. Alina Tugend, "For Patricia Ireland, a World of Feminism," *Los Angeles Times* (June 28, 2001), E-1.

Chapter 6

1. Ntozake Shange, interview by Rebecca Carroll, *Mother Jones* (January–February 1995).
2. Ann W. O'Neill, "2 Missionaries Guilty in Fatal Exorcism Case," *Los Angeles Times* (April 17, 1997), Metro. See also "Korean Missionaries Murder Case Pits Religion, Culture, Law," *Los Angeles Times* (April 6, 1997), Metro.
3. Ibid.
4. Ibid.
5. Patt Morrison, "When Cultures Collide," *Los Angeles Times* (August 27, 2000), A.
6. Yoshitomo Takahashi, M.D., and Douglas Berger, M.D., "Cultural Dynamics and the Unconscious in Suicide in Japan," in Antoon Leenaars and David Lester, eds., *Suicide and the Unconscious* (Northvale, NJ: Jason Aronson, 1996), 248–258.
7. Ibid.
8. Michael Walzer, *On Toleration* (New Haven, CT: Yale University Press, 1999), 103.
9. Kim Murphy, "U.S. Rules Skeleton Belongs to Indians," *Los Angeles Times* (September 26, 2000).
10. Andrew L. Slayman, "A Battle Over Bones," *Archaeology* 50:1 (1997).
11. Armand Minthorn, "Human Remains Should Be Reburied, Confederated Tribes of the Umatilla Indian Reservation" (September 1996). Available at: www.umatilla.nsn.us/kennman.html
12. U.S. Department of the Interior, "Memorandum: Determination that the Kennewick Human Skeletal Remains Are 'Native American' for the Purposes of the Native American Graves Protection and Repatriation Act (NAGPRA)." Available at: www.cr.nps.gov/aad/kennewick/c14memo.htm
13. Timothy Egan, "U.S. Takes Tribes' Side on Bones," *New York Times* (September 26, 2000).
14. Will Kymlicka, "Liberal Complacencies," in Susan Moller Okin, et al., eds., *Is Multiculturalism Bad for Women?* (Princeton, NJ: Princeton University Press, 1999), 31–34.
15. Available at: www.salon.com/news/col/horo/2000/05/30/reparations/index.html

16. Linda Chavez and John J. Miller, "The Immigration Myth," *Reader's Digest* (May 1996).
17. See Morrison.
18. Linda Chavez, "One Nation, One Common Language." Available at: www.ceousa.org/
19. See Chavez and Miller.
20. See Chavez.
21. Jim Boulet, "Schizophrenia in Los Angeles," *National Review Online*. Available at: www.nationalreview.com/convention .guest comment/guest commentprint081500a.html
22. Ibid.
23. Ibid.
24. Elaine Woo and Mary Curtius, "Oakland School District Recognizes Black English," *Los Angeles Times* (December 20, 1996).
25. Ibid.
26. Available at: //users.erols.com/jboulet/efnl497.htm
27. Available at: www.euroamerican.org/index.htm#Buttons
28. Available at: www.euroamerican.org/publicat/whitepap.htm# WP01
29. Ibid.
30. Available at: www.rainbowpush.org/commentary/031600.html
31. Louis Menand, "Mixed Paint," *Mother Jones* (May 1995).
32. Stanley Fish, "Reverse Racism," *Atlantic Monthly* (November 1993).
33. Ibid.
34. Václav Havel, "Faith in the World," *Civilization* (May 1998).

Chapter 7

1. Nina Burleigh, *New York Observer* (July 20, 1998). Available at: www.mrc.org/news/nq/dishonor1999/dishonor_videos.html#4
2. Evan Thomas, *Inside Washington*, WUSA Television (Washington, DC), May 7, 1994.
3. William Saletan, "Honest Bias," *Slate*. Available at: http://slate .msn.com/framegame/entries/00-12-19_95513.asp
4. Lisa Boone, "Morning Report," *Los Angeles Times* (July 5, 2000).
5. Center for Media and Public Affairs. Available at: www.cmpa .com/archive/medelite.htm
6. Available at: www.fair.org/reports/lichter-memo.html
7. FAIR. Available at: www.fair.org/extra/9601/grantsuc.html
8. FAIR. Available at: www.fair.org/extra/0508/jamal.html
9. Dan Rather, *CBS Evening News*, CBS, January 22, 2001.

10. Dan Rather, *CBS Evening News*, CBS, January 22, 1993.
11. Jim Rutenberg, "Why Dan Rather and CBS Limited Coverage of Levy Case," *New York Times* (July 23, 2001).
12. Ibid.
13. Media Research Center, *CyberAlert* (July 20, 2001). Available at: www.mediaresearch.org
14. Available at: www.mrc.org/about/welcome.html
15. Available at: www.mrc.org/news/reality/2000/Fax20001219.html
16. Margaret Carlson, *Capital Gang*, CNN, December 16, 2000.
17. Available at: www.mrc.org/news/reality/2000/Fax20001128.html
18. Ibid.
19. Ibid.
20. Faye Fiore and Geraldine Baum, "Livin' la Vida Dubya," *Los Angeles Times* (January 19, 2001), E-1.
21. Liz Smith, "In Hollywood, GOP Isn't Grand," *Los Angeles Times,* Calendar.
22. Ibid.
23. "Remarkable Pro-Life Women," *The American Feminist* (Winter 2000–2001). Available at: //sites.netscape.net/totallykate/articles/amerfem.html
24. S. F. Said, "Sous Les Bedsheets: The *Context* Interviews Charlotte Rampling," *Film In Context*. Also available at: www.thecontext.com/docs/3197.html
25. Gaby Wood, "The Eyes Still Have It," *Guardian* (January 21, 2001). Also available at: www.guardian.co.uk/Archive/Article/0,4273,4120504,00.html
26. Alan Riding, "The Joy of a Comeback That Leaves the Past Behind," *New York Times* (April 29, 2001).
27. Charlotte Rampling, interview by Christopher Cook, *Guardian Unlimited* (March 16, 2001). Also available at: guardian.co.uk

Chapter 8

1. Gregory Shepherd, "Letters to the Editor," *Chronicle of Higher Education* (July 14, 2000), B3.
2. Eric Langborgh, "Book-Burners Shut Down AIA Speaker at Berkeley," *Campus Report Online*. Available at: www.academia.org/CampusReport/2000November/censored.html

3. Ibid.
4. Dan Flynn, "A Dozen Affronts Against Free Speech," *Accuracy in Academia*. Available at: www.academia.org
5. Ibid.
6. Patrick Poole, "Book Burning 101." Available at: www.thefire.org/offsite/data/wnd bookburning.html and at: www.worldnetdaily.com/news/article.asp?ARTICLE_ID=20034
7. Ibid.
8. Andrew Brownstein, "Race, Reparations and Free Expression," *Chronicle of Higher Education* (March 30, 2001), A48.
9. See Poole.
10. See Brownstein.
11. Ibid.
12. Jonathan Alter, "Where PC Meets Free Speech," *Newsweek* (April 2, 2001), 31.
13. See Brownstein.
14. Ibid.
15. The full ad is available at: www.frontpagemag.com/horowitzs notepad/2001/hn01-03-01.htm
16. Christopher Gillot, Letter to the Editor, *Digital Collegian* (March 26, 1999).
17. Daryl Lang and Erica Zarra, "Feminist Festival Upsets Student, State Legislator," *Digital Collegian* (December 7, 2000). Available at: www.collegian.psu.edu/archive/2000/12/12-07-00tdc/12-07-00dnews-1.asp
18. Michael Janofsky, "Removal of Pupil's Project About Race Ignites Debate," *New York Times* (March 4, 2001), A12.
19. Ibid.
20. Ibid.
21. Ibid.
22. Scott Smallwood, "Professor Sues College Over Removal of Custer Poster," *Chronicle of Higher Education* (July 27, 2001). Also available at: www.chronicle.com/daily/2001/07/2001072705n.htm
23. Ibid.
24. Ibid.
25. U.S. Department of Education, Office of Civil Rights, *Revised Sexual Harassment Guidance: Harassment of Students by School Employees, Other Students or Third Parties*, (Washington, DC: U.S. Department of Education, January 2001). Also available at: www.ed.gov/offices/OCR/shguide

26. Agnes Diggs, "Instructor Not Guilty of Harassment, College Finds," *Los Angeles Times* (June 19, 1999).

27. Alex P. Kellogg, "Professor May be Sued for Calling Student 'Monica Lewinsky,' Judge Rules," *Chronicle of Higher Education* (February 5, 2001).

28. Ibid.

29. Alan Charles Kors and Harvey A. Silverglate, *The Shadow University: The Betrayal of Liberty on America's Campuses* (New York: Free Press, 1998). Also see John Leo, "Oh No, Canada," *U.S. News & World Report* (June 14, 1999).

30. Available at: www.umass.edu/wost/articles/vision2k/vision2k.htm

31. Available at: www.umass.edu/wost/articles/vision2k/recomm7.htm

32. Ibid.

33. Daphne Patai, "Speak Freely Professor—Within the Speech Code," *Chronicle of Higher Education* (June 9, 2000), B7.

34. Scott Street, "Promoting Order or Squelching Campus Dissent?" *Chronicle of Higher Education* (January 12, 2001), A37.

35. Ibid.

36. Ibid.

37. Ibid.

38. Leo Reisberg, "Student Press at Black Colleges Face 'A New Wave of Censorship,'" *Chronicle of Higher Education* (March 3, 2000), A47.

39. Ibid

40. Ibid.

41. Ibid.

42. Available at: //mojones.com/mother jones/ND95/gorney.html

43. Available at: www.browndailyherald.com/stories.cfm?S=0&ID =3545

44. Tom Hinckle, "Free Speech Under Attack," *Brown Daily Herald* (December 6, 2000).

45. Sarah Fick, "Censorship Hurts," Reader Comments, Heraldsphere Opinions, December 6, 2000. Available from: www .browndailyherald.com/stories.cfm?S=0&ID=3545

Chapter 9

1. Sallie Hofmeister, "Company Town: NBC Exec Admitted for Alcohol Abuse," *Los Angeles Times* (December 6, 1996).

2. Sallie Hofmeister, "New President Named at NBC Entertainment . . . ," *Los Angeles Times* (October 27, 1998).

Suggested Reading List

Hannah Arendt

The Origins of Totalitarianism
(Harvest Books, 1973)

The Human Condition
(University of Chicago Press, 1998)

Eichmann in Jerusalem: A Report on the Banality of Evil
(Penguin USA, 1994)

Daniel J. Boorstin

Cleopatra's Nose: Essays on the Unexpected
(Vintage Books, 1995)

The Discoverers
(Random House, 1983)

The Creators
(Vintage Books, 1993)

The Seekers
(Vintage Books, 1999)

Ray Bradbury

Fahrenheit 451
(Ballantine Books, 1995)

The Stories of Ray Bradbury
(Knopf, 1980)

(And everything else!)

Andrea Dworkin

Scapegoat: The Jews, Israel and Women's Liberation
(Free Press, 2000)

Intercourse
(Free Press, 1997)

Heartbreak: The Political Memoir of a Feminist Militant
(Basic Books, 2002)

Brenda Feigen

Not One of the Boys: Living Life as a Feminist
(Knopf, 2000)

David Horowitz

Radical Son: A Generational Odyssey
(Touchstone Books, 1998)

Hating Whitey and Other Progressive Causes
(Spence Publishing, 2000)

Aldous Huxley

Brave New World
(Harperperennial, 1998)

George Orwell

1984
(New American Library Classics, 1990)

Animal Farm
(Signet Classic, 1996)

A Collection of Essays
(Harvest Books, 1970)

(And everything else!)

Ayn Rand

For the New Intellectual
(New American Library, 1984)

Atlas Shrugged
(Signet, 1996)

The Fountainhead
(Signet, 1996)

Michael Walzer

On Toleration
(Yale University Press, 1997)

INDEX